# Making it Home

# Making it Home

## Place in Canadian Prairie Literature

**Deborah Keahey**

THE UNIVERSITY OF MANITOBA PRESS

© Deborah Keahey 1998
The University of Manitoba Press
Winnipeg, Manitoba R3T 5V6
www.umanitoba.ca/publications/uofmpress

Printed in Canada
Printed on acid-free paper ∞

Cover design: Kirk Warren
Text design: Karen Armstrong

---

Canadian Cataloguing-in-Publication Data

Keahey, Deborah Lou.

   Making it home

   Includes bibliographical references.
   ISBN 0-88755-656-6

1. Canadian literature (English) – Prairie Provinces –
History and criticism.★ 2. Canadian literature (English)
– 20th century – History and criticism.★ 3. Place
(Philosophy) in literature. 4. Home in literature.
5. Setting (Literature). I. Title.

PS8131.P7K43 1998          C810.9'32712          C98-920193-7
PR9198.2.P67K43 1998

---

The University of Manitoba Press gratefully acknowledges the support for its publishing program provided by the Canada Council for the Arts, the Manitoba Arts Council, the Department of Canadian Heritage, and the Manitoba Department of Culture, Heritage and Citizenship.

Le Conseil des Arts | The Canada Council
du Canada | for the Arts
depuis 1957 | since 1957

# Contents

# Acknowledgements

I would like to thank the following people and institutions for the various ways in which they helped to make this book happen.

Delores Keahey started the whole ball rolling many years ago, by teaching me how to read and write and love doing it. She and Herman Keahey, and more recently Laura and Bob Budde, have supplied much interesting raw data on issues of mobility and home, as well as welcoming home places to read, think, and write from at various times.

In Ann Arbor, the University of Michigan provided a Regents' Fellowship, which allowed me to begin the project. Richard W. Bailey encouraged me to let my mind follow my heart and then read the entire manuscript in draft, offering both his detailed, perceptive criticisms and his overall enthusiasm. Simon Gikandi provided an encouraging outside perspective in his view that the theories arising from the study have importance and interest beyond the field of Prairie literature.

In Winnipeg, the Department of English at the University of Winnipeg provided teaching employment, which both enabled me to complete work on the manuscript and provided the final incentive to do so. From my undergraduate days on, Dennis Cooley's passion for the politics of place and his interest in my work have been steady sources of inspiration and affirmation. Neil Besner read late drafts of my Prologue and Introduction, and his many "oy's" and exclamation marks lent some much-needed energy to the final revision process.

Clarise Foster, Sheri Austen, Deborah Schnitzer, and Jane Thomas all generously shared their wisdom about living and their expertise on the functions and dysfunctions of home, in many stimulating and sanity-saving conversations.

Markus Müller suggested the relevance of Freud's theory of the uncanny to my project, Marjorie Poor shared her knowledge of Aboriginal law and treaty rights, and Meíra Cook once insisted to me that sometimes a radish is just a radish, thus insuring that (in my usual perverse fashion) I would write otherwise.

The students in my fall 1996 course, Canadian Regional Literature, at the University of Winnipeg helped me to refine my sense of the problems and possibilities of studying literature from a regional perspective and reminded me of how important it is to engage with the literature that comes out of our own place and time.

My thinking on Fred Wah's poetics began when I sat in on a guest lecture given by Frank Davey in a graduate seminar conducted by Robert Kroetsch at the University of Manitoba in 1994 and has been refined since then with the help of Robert Budde, who introduced me to Olson's "proprioception" and also lent his eyes and ears to this project at many stages of its development.

As a reader for the University of Manitoba Press, Birk Sproxton made a spirited and eloquent attempt to goad me into making the book more personal and polemical, while, as Director of the Press, David Carr brought a refreshingly relaxed and reassuring touch to all his dealings with me. Carol Dahlstrom, Managing Editor, provided peace of mind with her thorough, efficient, and good-humoured copy-editing. Allison Campbell ably managed the marketing and promotion end of things, and Kirk Warren designed the perfect cover.

Finally, my deepest thanks go to Robert Budde and Robin Keahey, who remind me each day that English is endlessly delightful but delightfully disposable, and that home can be written in a variety of languages.

A portion of this book, in slightly different form, was presented as "Massive Attractions: Orbiting Home in Frederick Philip Grove's *Over Prairie Trails*" at the 1995 Free Exchange Conference at the University of Calgary.

# Prologue: Writing Home

### d word letter home

dear d. yes i've lost my mind such as it was nothing
seems real i was there & now here & why & what for & how
the hell am i gonna talk about home don't even know what
it is 'cept it's anything everything nothing you make it
find it leave it as you please & sittin' in the o'hare oasis
watching the endless lanes of lines of tri-state toll way
traffic lights speeding underneath & semi's rattling the
window panes you put your hand on to feel the possibilities
of indigestion or death you just know this isn't it though it
could be & trying to gauge the mood of the moment of the
movement to plot your on-ramp strategy how to make your
entrance how to reenter once you've gotten off track

(Debbie Keahey, *the d word*)

So I wrote at one time, wrote myself, wrote home, wrote myself home. Or
tried to. "Oasis" is the euphemistic title given to the overpass truck stop
facilities along the I-94 tollway around Chicago, a route I travelled more
times than I care to remember, back and forth between Winnipeg, Manitoba, and Ann Arbor, Michigan, driving to and from home, thinking about
home, moving homes here and there, there and here, driving and homing,
thinking myself home. But I'm ahead of myself. Here.

The state of being "at home" has several interconnected dimensions. To
be at home in a physical sense may involve feelings of safety, of being
comfortable and relaxed in your own body, and in the body's material
surroundings. Being at home psychologically may involve an acceptance of
who you are, and a sense of inner peace with yourself. The social dimension

of being at home may involve the feeling of being part of a larger community, of having a role to play within human networks of family, friends, lovers, and colleagues, while the spiritual dimension might involve a feeling of harmony with nature, or of having a belief and value system that gives order and meaning to your life. Finally, being at home in an intellectual sense may involve knowing and understanding the world around you, or some part of it, and being able to control, shape, and transmit ideas. In this sense, even academic writing has a performative homemaking function.

Like many writers – both scholarly and creative – before me, I began this project of writing about my home place only after having left it, during what I considered at the time a period of self-imposed exile from Winnipeg to Ann Arbor, where I was engaged in graduate studies. When I decided to go there, my sense of the place had been constructed primarily by glossy University promotional brochures showing elegant wood-panelled study halls and serene expanses of grass and trees, and also, oddly, by Donald Hall's wonderful pastoral and nostalgic poetry collection *Kicking the Leaves*, which I had reviewed for an undergraduate American poetry course a couple of years earlier. Although the poems are mostly set in the rural New Hampshire of Hall's childhood, for some reason I always associated the book with Ann Arbor, where Hall had recently given up a long-held teaching position, and such are the powers and quirks of literature and memory that Michigan has ever since been configured in my imaginative geography as a site of perpetual autumn.

### michigan falls

two men named this place ann
arbor in spring after their
wives & i wonder how

in fall they felt these
colours in the grey haze great
lakes river mist the maple's

red bright burning bushes
blush the poplar's yellow
exploding into orange &

how this fuchsia shock
& this bruise a palpable
purple blue felt & how

these others fallen
so green turned brown
in the overnight rain

To the rather idealized images I had of my destination, a contrary element was added shortly before my move when, presumably as a commer-
cially motivated advance in the technological process of shrinking the planet,
one Winnipeg cable TV company began acquiring the major U.S. networks through their affiliates in Detroit (an hour from Ann Arbor and over
1,760 kilometres from Winnipeg), rather than through the North Dakota
affiliates (right across the border) as they had in the past. One rather dubious result of this change was that Detroit news – most of it shockingly
sensationalistic and aggressively self-promotional compared to our (at the
time) staid Winnipeg counterpart – was now piped into thousands of Winnipeg homes several hours each day, irreversibly altering our collective sense
of space between the two places, and in turn, I think, altering our sense of
the places themselves.

Yet, it didn't take long on my arrival in Michigan to realize that information and influence do not flow equally in all directions in this "global
village." Ann Arbor, my "home away from home," was physically only about
an hour's drive from the Canadian border, but psychically it might as well
have been on another planet. To people there, Canada generally meant
Windsor (right at the border crossing), or the hunting and fishing grounds
north of the the Upper Penninsula of Michigan, or possibly something as
far-fetched as Toronto. When I mentioned Canadian literature to people,
they would eagerly offer the name Margaret Atwood, but their eyes would
glaze over if I suggested that there were a few other writers as well, and the
largest (and otherwise excellent) bookstore in town refused to believe that
there was a writer named Al Purdy whose books they could possibly order
for me. The word "prairie" there wasn't just a synonym for their own term
"plains," but a quaint-sounding anachronism, conjuring images of the T.V.
series *Little House On the Prairie*. The results of a Canadian national election
barely made the back pages of the *Ann Arbor News*. I was lucky enough to
find one professor, Richard Bailey, who had a genuine passion for all things
Canadian (I still haven't quite figured out why), but apart from him I couldn't

find a single person in all the humanities and social sciences departments at the University of Michigan who identified him- or herself as having even a minor interest in anything Canadian.

At any rate, in part due to the rigorous demands of my program and the single-minded passion typical of graduate students, and also in part due to my knowledge that my stay there was to be temporary, I neglected all but the intellectual side of the homemaking process, and what I discovered was that having only one dimension of home is woefully inadequate to a general sense of well-being. Homesickness set in. With a strong degree of nostalgia and naïve idealism, I longed to be back in the Prairie space where I had previously located myself, and where my primary filiative and affiliative ties remained. When I returned to Winnipeg to teach and write, however, reality quickly set in again. It is not *space* that matters, I realized, but what you do to make it *place*, and I returned to Ann Arbor and began this project.[1] If, as the cliché has it, you can't go home again, you can always create a new one. If you can't quite *make it home* in the sense of a physical journey, you can always *make it home* in the performative sense.

Of course, I probably should have known this all along, because for me the idea of "leaving home" in the first place is complicated by the fact that I grew up in a family that was always on the move. Up until my junior-high years, I had never lived in the same place for more than one or two years at a time, and I have paradoxically (perhaps schizophrenically) both rejected and replicated my parents' mobility pattern in my own life, alternately yearning for a deep-rooted sense of belonging, of firmly placed identity, and itching for the freedom to reinvent myself in the anonymity of a new, unknown space. It is no coincidence that in the twelve-month period before I conceived this study I moved myself and belongings an absurd *six* times. Nor is it coincidence that during this time I began writing an autofictional long poem that traces a variety of dislocations in psychic, social, and geographic space, and the persona's mostly futile and ironic attempts to place herself somewhere, anywhere – even, at one point (as in the epigraph for this prologue), in a busy tollway truck stop.

### arrival

unpacked & closeted my suitcase empty
to the basement down it's sent to misty
must & damp to gather dust a spider
spelling bee to catch an earwig jungle
gym i am

here now

the end of emotion this is it for
feeling for now the car lag drags
the senses numb mouth dumb
on the cold concrete feet that stumble
stomach grumbles nerves on auto
pilot i am

done, off

outta here

My decision to write about Canadian Prairie literature while in Michigan, then, may in part simply represent my perverse (Prairie?) tendency to do things in the most impractical way (one graduate chair told me I would never be hired if I did this project), but it might also be seen as another kind of intellectual homemaking process, an attempt to both literally and figuratively write my home place into alien space. Yet, if this kind of "writing home" has worked for others (as sometimes seems to be claimed), I must confess that I found it one-dimensional and ultimately unsatisfying. The project stalled several times and on more than one occasion threatened to be abandoned entirely. Perhaps my language was just not strong or magical enough, I thought, but increasingly I became frustrated with literature and language itself, craving some more direct reality to ground myself in (or some more direct ground to realize myself in, which amounts to the same thing). Only once I had returned to Winnipeg and recreated the physical, psychological, social, and spiritual dimensions of home there was I able to finally complete the study on its own terms. In other words, only once I freed the study from the burden of its impossibly large homemaking task could it accomplish its own more-modest intellectual one.

So I am both tempted by and sceptical of the complex links between literature and life. While I do believe that some of the homemaking activity of literary and other texts is bound to have "real world" effects on writers and readers, I also believe that we can't assume that that will always be the case or generalize about just what the effects are. We can't assume that an author's desire for home has been satisfied by writing about it any more than we can that a reader's desire has been by reading about it. If only it were that simple.

As I write this, I'm beginning to pack again for my second move in less than a year, this time into a (yes) mobile home. So now I'll have a literal one to match my figurative one. Or so the story goes. Write me sometime. There.

## life li(n)es

life lines lie, tickle the palm of your hand telling
futures clear as cereal boxes you believe yourself into.

do you believe?

life lines hold you, in place above the earth spinning so
fast you could fly right off without guy-wire arms to bob in
soft as old shoe laces tied in a dream of rabbit holes & big
ears.

do you listen at the thin edge
of sleep where stories crumble
themselves into others?

life lines write home, letters you look for each morning
to finger faint connections you lean to reach across the
vast space of a breakfast table.

do you read me?

# Making it Home

# Introduction: Homemaking the Prairies

(What does home mean?)
(Where is it?)

(Aritha van Herk, "Calgary, this growing graveyard" 330)

the home place: N.E. 17–42–16–W4th Meridian

the home place: 1 1/2 miles west of Heisler, Alberta,
                      on the correction line road
                    and 3 miles south.

(Robert Kroetsch, "Seed Catalogue," CFN 34)

*what do these letters and numbers mean kid?*
*where is this place?*
*is this all you have?*

(Andrew Suknaski, "Homestead, 1914: SEC. 32, TP4, RGE2, W3RD, SASK." 24)

"The home place" in Prairie usage is a synonym for "homestead." It suggests that home is singular and locatable – pinpointable – in space. Kroetsch gives us the precisely detailed legal address of his family homestead, but, like the police looking at Suknaski's ID, his birth certificate, we ask what all the letters and numbers mean. Kroetsch tries to help. A more casual description this time, a relative placing. All measurements of time and space, according to Einstein's theory of relativity, are relative to some arbitrarily chosen frame of reference – there is no "absolute position" or "absolute space": if a ping-pong ball bounces twice on the same spot on a ping-pong table on a moving train, it looks as if it happened in the same place for someone *on* the train, but for someone watching from *outside* the train the ball bounces at a very different place the second time, somewhere down the line (Hawking 17–18). You start from where you're at, from what you know, and work from there. Along the correction-line road, Kroetsch says, the line drawn on the land to correct for the effects of imposing a square grid on a round globe, dividing up the prairies into equal-sized parcels for settlement. The correction line and the physicist's relativity both function wonderfully as metaphors for the fundamental instability of our notions of place, of the way we impose various and changeable perceptual grids on space.

"Is this all you have?" the police ask Suknaski, and his long poem answers no, tells us his memory of the family history centred on his birth place, around the address given on his birth certificate. The meaning of the space itself is dependent on Suknaski's relationship to it, the time that has passed and the events that have taken place there. *Created* place there, rather, which is space inscribed by cultural, psychological, and social significance. Wallace Stegner says,

> I must believe that, at least to human perception, a place is not a place until people have been born in it, have grown up in it, lived in it, known it, died in it – have both experienced and shaped it, as individuals, families, neighborhoods, and communities, over more than one generation. Some people are born in their place, some find it, some realize after long searching that the place they left is the one they have been searching for. But whatever their relation to it, it is made a place only by slow accrual, like a coral reef. ("Sense of Place" 201)

Or, even more dramatically, "no place is a place until it has had a poet" (205).[1] Place and the home place are not absolute givens but are flexible constructions. Kroetsch and Suknaski "write home" in the way their long poems reflect and reflect on – address themselves to – remembered constructed places, and also in the way the poems *themselves* construct place and home. Literature takes on a performative homemaking function, and poets (and novelists, and dramatists) become literary homemakers.[2]

The notion of place has recently attracted much attention in postcolonial and cultural studies,[3] but it has long played a central role in discussions of Prairie literature, where place has overwhelmingly been defined in narrow, deterministic terms, as "the land" or the natural physical environment. This "environmentalism," as it has come to be known, almost a literary equivalent of historian Frederick Jackson Turner's "frontier hypothesis" of individuals in conflict with nature,[4] is nowhere better summed up than in Henry Kreisel's 1968 statement: "All discussion of the literature produced in the Canadian west must of necessity begin with the impact of the land-scape upon the mind" (6). In this conception it is the mind alone that is write-able or inscribe-able; the land itself is assumed to be a preexistent reality that we have immediate access to, unmediated by language or the structures of human perception.

As Howard Lamar points out, a further problem with the Turnerian per-spective is that the "emphasis on the struggle with nature and the praise of the pioneer spirit ignores central components in a life structure – occupa-tion, family, ethnicity, religion, peer relations and leisure – that have great-est significance for the self"(37). Home, as a central concern of self, is similarly preoccupied with these "other" components of being and iden-tity. But if, as Lamar suggests (48), the study of Canadian history has es-caped the environmentalist emphasis, until very recently the same could not be said for Canadian literary criticism.[5] A "realist" and deterministic approach to land and language has tended to permeate the major studies of Prairie literature to date – Edward McCourt's 1949 *The Canadian West in Fiction*, issued in a revised edition in 1970, Laurence Ricou's 1973 study *Vertical Man/Horizontal World: Man and Landscape in Canadian Prairie Fiction*, and Dick Harrison's 1977 *Unnamed Country: The Struggle for a Canadian Prairie Fiction* – and to influence the evaluation of individual texts.[6]

In its most extreme form, the environmentalist view leads to the direct equation of land with place, and place with home, as in Stegner's claim that it is not his "home town" of Whitemud, Saskatchewan, or the people in it that represent home for him, but rather the "tantalizing and ambiguous and wholly native smell" of the shrub wolf willow. Smelling this plant's leaves again after "forty alien years" collapses time and erases history, so that "the queer adult compulsion to return to one's beginnings is assuaged. A contact has been made, a mystery touched. For the moment, reality is made exactly equivalent with memory, and a hunger is satisfied" (*Wolf Willow* 18-19). Not only does Stegner firmly "place" home, he literally "plants" it.

The lure of this kind of elemental and nostalgic equation – of "rootedness" – is so strong that even Robert Kroetsch, Linda Hutcheon's "Mr. Canadian Postmodern," has succumbed to its appeal: "When I was a boy, living in the parklands and not on the true prairie at all, we children in spring used to strip the outer bark off a branch of silver willow and chew the sweet, stringy inner bark and believe that winter was over. The taste of the bark of the willow - silver willow, wolf willow – says to me what the smell of its leaves said to Stegner: this is the various place we call home" ("The Cow" 133).[7] Though perceived through the sense of taste rather than smell, "land" in Kroetsch's version of environmentalism, as in Stegner's, takes the place that logos has for Jacques Derrida when he identifies an ethic of presence and nostalgia for origins in Lévi-Strauss's anthropological work – it represents a centre, or originary point of presence, "a fundamental immobility and a reassuring certitude" beyond the play of language, and on the basis of which "anxiety can be mastered" (279). In some of its idealized forms, the notion of "home" similarly functions as just such a centre, not only "to orient, balance, and organize the structure [society, culture, the self] – one cannot in fact conceive of an unorganized structure – but above all to make sure that the organizing principle of the structure would limit what we might call the play of the structure" (Derrida 278).

In part to escape the limitations of equating home with place, critics interested in issues of immigration, exile, diaspora, and displacement have pried apart and problematized the concept of "the home place." For instance, Edward Said argues that the "idea of place does not cover the nuances, principally of reassurance, fitness, belonging, association, and community, entailed in the phrase *at home* or *in place*." Instead, he suggests, "[I]t is in culture that we can seek out the range of meanings and ideas conveyed by the phrases *belonging to* or in a place, being *at home in a place*" (8). Said's theorizing is intended to construct a more flexible notion of "home" than is sometimes admitted; that is, he wants to allow for the creation of "home" in different "places," and in a similar way John Berger has argued: "To the underprivileged, home is represented, not by a house, but by a practice or set of practices. Everyone has his own. These practices, chosen and not imposed, offer in their repetition, transient as they may be in themselves, more permanence, more shelter than any lodging. Home is no longer a dwelling but the untold story of a life being lived" (64). While the equation of such "placeless" homes with "underprivilege" is questionable, Berger's "repeated practices" are Said's "culture," and both achieve a more dynamic conception of home, but only at the expense of making place static.

What is needed for the Canadian Prairies, where the majority of the people (including "native" inhabitants) have experienced some sort of radical unsettling and/or been "settled" within the last 100 years, is a more flexible concept of the *relationship between* home and place, one that accommodates George Melnyk's point that "[i]f culture comes out of a different landscape, which it did for me, then the new landscape will transform that culture, modify it, revise it to some degree. It never eliminates it and puts something completely different in its place" ("On the Roots of Identity" 13). The comparison with environmentalism is instructive, for while *individuals'* readings of the land or "place" may be overdetermined by their own history or cognitive structures, to the point that their readings appear transparent or "natural," the significance of the *land* or *place itself* is relatively unrestricted, open to multiple and various readings. The concept of culture is just as susceptible to reification and ossification as are those of place and land, so there is no intrinsic merit in privileging it.[8] Rather than discard the notion of place entirely and replace it with the notion of culture, then, place must instead be reimagined as a creation of the social, psychological, and cultural relationships that people have to particular landscapes or physical spaces.

Re-reading Prairie literature with this more flexible concept of place in mind yields quite different results from those that we are used to, as can be seen by looking at Sinclair Ross's short-story collection *The Lamp at Noon and Other Stories*. Ross is one of the writers whose texts are frequently called upon to support environmentalist theories of prairie literature, and in the title story a troubled young couple, Paul and Ellen, quarrel bitterly in the "impenetrable fog" (13) of a dust storm on the 1930s Saskatchewan prairies. The wind, personified as "demented" (13), has eroded their farm land into a desert, and Paul feels that the earth "betrayed alike his labour and his faith" (15). Focussing on this personification of the environment, Laurence Ricou agrees with Margaret Laurence that the land in Ross's work is the "chief protagonist," and he argues that in this story, as in others, "the struggle of man with land results in isolated, lonely men and women. The neglect of human intercourse is a result not of conscious neglect, nor of boredom, but seemingly of gradual necessity. . . . The brutal prairie erodes all human sensitivity and sympathy, leaving man exhausted and beaten" (92-93).

This insistence on the agency and destructiveness of nature is, however, countered in the story by Ellen's knowledge that Paul has brought about his own ruin: "'You've plowed and harrowed it until there's not a root or fibre left to hold it down. That's why the soil drifts – that's why in a year or two there'll be nothing left but the bare clay. If in the first place you farmers had taken care of your land – if you hadn't been so greedy for wheat every year—'" (17). The disastrous consequences of Paul's attempt to make a home on the prairies – the loss of his land, the disintegration of his marriage, and the death of his child – are, in fact, not the result of "gradual necessity" at all, but of his own stubborn refusal to work for Ellen's father (16), to offer her the same "comforting and assuring" presence that he gives his horse (19), or to accept her past advice "to grow fibrous crops" (21). Opposing himself to everything that his wife advocates and all that she stands for, he does not so much internalize the landscape, as Ricou argues, as he turns the land into an image of himself, and of his own misplaced and desperate pride. Indeed, environmentalist readings of Prairie texts often involve a gender bias that validates the male characters' futile struggles as necessary and heroic, while discounting the female characters' homemaking knowledge as trivial or culturally inappropriate.

Canadian Prairie literature creates and represents a wide variety of relationships to the shared space that it is written out of and about, but even the notion of there being a "common space" is a constructed illusion, one that often privileges a particular type of landscape – rural, flat, un-treed – as being the norm or standard, the "true prairie." This standardizing tendency can be seen in E.F. Dyck's comment: "The prairie of Saskatchewan is unlike the prairie of the other two Prairie provinces: Manitoba's trees are found south as well as north, Alberta has its mountains, and the southern half of Saskatchewan has neither. I offer Turnhill as the quintessential prairie place: its name derives from a hill whose elevation is barely discernible to the naked eye; it has no trees over which nevertheless the wind blows unceasingly; it rolls endlessly under a relentless sky" (Introduction ix).[9] The impetus to identify a "quintessential" landscape is reflected in, or perhaps even caused by, the problematic doubleness of "prairie" as a synonym for this type of landscape and its broader usage, conventionally signalled by capitalization, for a politically defined territory, the Prairie provinces. Even the precisely same physical space, however, can be written in a variety of ways, and it is this variety that gives the lie to environmentalist arguments.

Given the problematics of landscape as a unifying factor for considering Prairie literature, it is tempting to locate the region's coherence in the realm of political and cultural affiliation, arguing that the Prairie provinces more closely identify with each other against eastern Canadian domination (economic and cultural) and West Coast decadence (economic and environmental). For example, Edward McCourt suggests that "there is a remarkable unity of spirit prevailing among prairie dwellers," which seems mainly to consist of the people being "young, aggressive, and united in their hostility to Ontario," and also their feeling that "Alberta is the far West; British Columbia the near East" (Preface, n.p.).

Whatever are the shared cultural or aesthetic concerns of the area, however, this sort of argument runs into trouble because many writers from Alberta, especially from areas in the foothills of the Rocky Mountains, the western "edge" of the Prairies, seem to affiliate westward rather than eastward. Or, at least this is suggested by their attraction to the B.C. landscape as a setting for their works, rather than the flat Alberta and Saskatchewan landscape to their eastern side.[10] On the political side, an obvious and highly significant difference is that the present NDP stronghold in Saskatchewan is polar opposite to the Conservative and Reform stronghold in neighbouring Alberta. Still other differences could be located in historical migration patterns both between and within provinces.[11]

Yet, as Fred Wah has suggested, regional classifications of writers and writing are both more difficult and easier than they might first appear ("Contemporary Saskatchewan Poetry"). For instance, in addition to such obvious affiliative signs as participation in the activities of local writers' guilds, it may be observed that a large number of writers who have some connection to the Prairies exhibit mobility and settlement patterns that suggest, for whatever reasons, a kind of comfort "home" zone, or a connection across and within a well-defined regional area.

Robert Kroetsch, for instance, is from Alberta, spent several years in the United States, but then returned for many years to Manitoba. Dennis Cooley is from Saskatchewan, after a stay in the United States returned to Saskatchewan, and now has similarly settled for some time in Manitoba. Birk Sproxton was born in Manitoba and teaches in Alberta. Marie Annharte Baker has lived in Manitoba and Saskatchewan. Rudy Wiebe has lived in Saskatchewan and Alberta. David Arnason is from Gimli, Manitoba, studied in New Brunswick, and now lives in Winnipeg. Aritha van Herk was born in central Alberta, studied in Edmonton, and now teaches in Calgary. Such continuities and cross-fertilizations argue, it seems to me, for the possibility of treating a group of "Prairie" authors or texts together.

Many of the "identifying" factors I have mentioned – writers' activities and settlement patterns, political party affiliation – are in some sense "extraliterary," suggesting that the concept of "the Prairies" as a region is not so much inherent *in* the texts of "Prairie literature" as it is constructed and imposed *on* the literature. Individual texts tend to construct individual, particular places, and only at some very high level of abstraction can these then be seen to be parts of a whole. To say that the Prairie region, like other regions or even nations, is not "natural" but invented, is not to say, however, that it does not exist. As a popular, political, economic, and critical category, it is widely used and accepted and thus takes on a life of its own, with its own performative function in continuing to actually *create* that which it supposedly only *names*. For instance, in addition to the three major studies of Prairie literature that I have mentioned, there are also a number of literary anthologies and collections of essays that create and solidify the identity of Prairie literature as a literary "field."[12]

A few words about the structure and contents of this book are in order. The body of work that could be considered Prairie literature is very large indeed, and it is expanding at a rapid pace with the growth of local book and chapbook presses. To get a sense of the variety of ways in which home and place are configured in this literature, my first step was to read, with as open a mind as possible, well over 100 primary texts. From that reading a constellation of recurring issues emerged, which after much juggling and refinement became the chapter structure of this book.[13] Once that structure was in place, I chose individual texts to represent a diverse and interesting range of approaches to the topics in question. The form of the book thus arose organically from the body of work it studies (or at least as organically as is perhaps possible), rather than representing the imposition of externally conceived categories or the application of imported theories. In reversing the usual flow of ideas from "centre" to "periphery," the study thus demonstrates that regional literatures can be the source of theories that then have international significance.

All the texts I chose had to satisfy three main criteria. The first and most obvious was that they must be able to be classified as "Prairie," either on the basis of author affiliation or the "pointing" characteristic noted by Eli Mandel in his much-quoted analysis of Milton Wilson's comments on regionalism: "[I]t is not place alone that matters but a direction, an attraction – something like the movement of a compass needle; not where it is, but where it points matters. My image for the prairie writer then, . . . is not necessarily the one who is in the west, or who stays there, but the one who returns, who moves, who points in this direction" (146). So, for instance, Kelly Rebar might have been excluded on the grounds that, though she is from the Prairies, she has moved eastward, at least for the time being; however, her play takes place in Alberta, the "home ground" where she was born and raised, even though she has since lived in many other locations outside the Prairies. A similar case could be made for Emma Lee Warrior, who now lives in Washington state but whose short story "Compatriots" also takes place in Alberta, where she grew up.

The second criterion, also fairly obvious, was that the texts must provide an interesting and unique perspective on the issues they are used to represent, and the third was that the various issues I address must be implicated quite centrally in the texts chosen (as opposed to being minor or peripheral concerns), so that my reading of the particular issue at hand should also function to provide a relevant and reasonably coherent reading of the text as a whole.

Beyond these specific criteria, in deciding which texts to include, I have also considered the range and balance of the study as a whole. So I have attempted where feasible to include early or mid-twentieth-century texts to compare with later twentieth-century ones, and I have also been conscious of ensuring that a range (though by no means an exhaustive or systematic or "representative" one) of cultures is present, as well as a range (again, not exhaustive) of genres. Similarly, in the name of balance, some very well-established prairie writers – Margaret Laurence, Sinclair Ross, Dorothy Livesay, and Eli Mandel, for example – have been passed over so that I could present a selection of newer and less-established (or less-studied) writers.

Some of my choices of individual texts may no doubt appear idiosyncratic. For example, David Arnason is primarily known as a short-story (and more recently novel) writer, but his long poem *Marsh Burning* illustrates one aspect of my topic very well, and it is also a very finely crafted, moving, and engaging piece of writing – one of his very best works. Similarly, Frederick Philip Grove is primarily known and studied as a novelist, despite the fact that many critics find his best writing in the autobiographical sketches in *Over Prairie Trails*.[14]

Because Grove's sketches are ostensibly "non-literary," in the past they have not seemed an appropriate object for literary analysis, but such restrictions are outmoded because the literary field is now broadening to include such writing as "subliterary" journals and hybrid fictocriticism. In a similar vein, I have chosen to write about Maria Campbell's and Laura Goodman Salverson's autobiographical texts because of their historical significance and their intrinsic interest – formal and thematic – for my topic, despite the fact that they do not score highly if judged according to *traditional* literary standards.[15]

Defining terms is usually a tricky business, and "home" is no exception. It is not, for instance, simply a domestic residence but instead can be placed in or around a larger community, or even the entire earth. It can be a physical location or a psychological sensation. It can be individual, social, or communal. Similarly, "place" can be a geographical location, but it can also be a symbolic, social, cultural, or psychic one. To know "your place" can mean to know who you are, or how you are defined by others, and your relationship to the world around you.

The complexity of the concept of home, both as noun and as verb, is also revealed in the fact that it is entirely possible (and often actualized) to be "not 'at home' at home." That is, there is often a strong disjunction between an actual experienced home and the abstract idealized home. Such a disjunction between reality and ideal is not unusual or unique to the idea of home, of course, but it does create difficulties for writing about it. If a character is "at home," does that refer to the actual or the abstract? I have tried to clarify the matter through context, for the most part, with the additional use of quotation marks to indicate a problematic, often because ideal, use of "home." I have not excluded one or the other sense of the word from my study but instead have, where necessary, made the discrepancy the object of my attention.

In chapters 1 and 2 of this study I look at various ways in which space has been inscribed with significance in Prairie literature. In the first I consider the ways in which empire (British first, and later American and Canadian) has overdetermined Prairie homemaking strategies, and I view empire as an absent cause in order to account for Prairie literature's ambivalent relationship to postcoloniality. In the second I look at texts in which the homemaking strategies appear to be more flexible but in which alternate personal or familial versions of the past, or history, continue to have wide-ranging influence.

In the last three chapters I turn my attention to the various "places" of place in literary concepts of home; that is, I examine the various ways that place functions in relation to notions of home. In the third I examine texts in which home is firmly placed, as a stable centre that can be left and returned to on a literal level. In the fourth I look at cases where a radical displacement leads to an attempt to "re-place" home, and at the different forms that this re-placing can take. In the fifth and final chapter I look outward to explore the possibilities of the entirely "placeless" home.

Through these various discussions, three salient points emerge. First, whatever are the other concerns of the seventeen texts I have looked at, an overriding concern with the concept of home can be seen to permeate them all. Home appears to be such a fundamental human concern that all manner of other activities are absorbed or co-opted into its large construction project. Second, home takes many conceptual and metaphorical forms and is constructed through various and complex networks of social, psychological, and cultural factors. Any attempt to generalize a model for achieving it is problematic at best, since the specific material and historical circumstances of each individual will alter the effects of any given strategy. Third, of all the factors influencing the creation of home and its success or failure, land and landscape in themselves have relatively little effect or importance.

# Imperial Inscriptions

*1*

Neither the Western past nor the Western present will make sense until attachment to property and attraction to profit find their proper category as a variety of strong emotion.

(Patricia Nelson Limerick, The Legacy of Conquest 76)

homesteaders came with plows
tore the earth
lay a gingham patch
on a floral apron
fastened it with road allowances and fences

(Thelma Poirier, "squatters and homesteaders" 46)

What Althusser's own insistence on history as an absent cause makes clear, but what is missing from the formula as it is canonically worded, is that he does not at all draw the fashionable conclusion that because history is a text, the "referent" does not exist. We would therefore propose the following revised formulation: that history is not a text, not a narrative, master or otherwise, but that, as an absent cause, it is inaccessible to us except in textual form, and that our approach to it and to the Real itself necessarily passes through its prior textualization, its narrativization in the political unconscious.

(Fredric Jameson, The Political Unconscious 35)

Published within a year of each other in the mid-1920s, Martha Ostenso's *Wild Geese* and Robert J.C. Stead's *Grain* both feature a central male character who is intimately bound to the prairie land, and whose relationship to the land is mirrored in his other relationships, familial and social. The meaning they have attached to the land, the significance they have inscribed on the

prairie space, determines not only their failure or success in making themselves "at home" in "their place," but also their very conceptions of home
and place. The epistemological structures and value systems that underlie
their approaches, their inscriptions, are locatable in empire, which functions as a version of Jameson's "absent cause," never spoken directly, but
speaking itself through the two texts.

In both cases the home that is written is overdetermined by imperial
history and imperialist ideologies, though in very different ways and with
different results. Ostenso's Caleb Gare erases history and internalizes empire, embodying and enacting its principles as an individual in the present
tense. Stead's Gander Stake, on the other hand, is placed within the external history of empire, positioned as a worker in and for Canada, the new
dominion. Passion for property and profit take two very different forms:
Caleb's individualist greed is Gander's production of "common wealth";
Caleb's essential isolation is Gander's membership in both his immediate
communities and the "imagined community" of British empire.[1]

Gander's world is not only inscribed and controlled by an overseas imperial base, however, for the Prairies also exist for him in a colonial relationship to the Canadian economic and political power base in southern Ontario.
Economist Paul Phillips has written on the way in which the Prairies were
conceived as a "western frontier" for the economic elite of "Central Canada"
and as a means for them to fend off the imperialist designs of Americans.
He argues that Confederation

> was founded on regionalism, a concept which did not consider the re-
> gions to be equal. The Prairies were to provide a frontier for central
> Canadian investment, a market for eastern manufacturers and consumers
> for the commercial trades of the St. Lawrence merchants. It is clear that
> the original intent of the framers of the British North America Act was
> to give the federal government the important economic development
> powers and leave to the provinces the powers that were considered of
> merely local interest. (57-60)[2]

The idea that Prairie matters (including literature) are "of merely local
interest," reflecting only "regional" concerns and values, while central
Canadian matters (again, including literature) are, if not "universal," then at
least are of "national" interest, is one that persists into the present.

Further, while physical occupation of the Prairies may have prevented
overt colonization by the United States, American economic control of
Canada – present in the 1920s and increasing dramatically in the latter part

of this century – amounts to a third layer of colonial overdetermination. Frederick Philip Grove said (somewhat melodramatically) in 1929:

> South of our borders lives a mighty nation which is reaching out with its tentacles over the globe – with a view towards the Americanization, as it is commonly called, of that globe. . . . The very word Americanisation is a challenge to us; for though we are Canadians, we also live in America. . . . The fight is on between the ancient ideals of Europe and those of this new America which is asserting itself from day to day. There are those who have found a name for the process: The Drift of the Nations. The centre of gravity, they assert, of the white world is shifting. . . . No better ground can be found to study that drift than the broad west of this Dominion of ours. (*Needs* 142-43)

The long-term effects of all these three levels of empire, and of the conflicts between them, on Prairie homemaking possibilities are dramatized in Kelly Rebar's play *Bordertown Café*, first performed and published in the late 1980s, some sixty years after *Wild Geese* and *Grain*. Produced nearly a decade later, in the 1990s, Ian Ross's play *fareWel* adds a fourth level of colonial overdetermination to the picture, by presenting a First Nations' perspective that exposes the inherent imperial function of status-quo Canadian nationalism.

## Martha Ostenso's *Wild Geese*

Among the most interesting silences in *Wild Geese* are those involving its geographic setting and the national or "ethnic" background of its main characters. While we know from biographical information that Ostenso based the setting on the area near the narrows in the Interlake district where she had taught school briefly, place names have been fictionalized, Winnipeg, where she lived while writing the novel, is referred to simply as "the city," and there is no reference to Manitoba or Canada. For a novel in which "place" plays such a central role, Ostenso seems not to have wanted to "place" it. The desire to have the setting unmarked by explicit regional or national location may be linked to Ostenso's childhood years in Minnesota and North Dakota, and her residence in New York just before writing the novel, or to the fact that she was writing it specifically for the purpose of submission to the best North American novel contest of American publishers Dodd, Mead, and Company, which it won. In other words, an explicit rural Manitoba setting may have been regarded as too "regional," in the "merely local" sense, for Ostenso's "international" aspirations.

Beyond possible motivations, however, the disaffiliation of the setting from the specific geographic space that generated it has interesting effects. One of these is that it mirrors the erasure of history that is characteristic of Ostenso's description of the Gares, which itself mirrors the Gares's desire to escape their own past, embodied in the ill-kept secret of Amelia Gare's illegitimate child, Mark Jordan, which Caleb uses to blackmail Amelia into silence and submission. Apart from the suggestion that Mark Jordan believes that his mother was an "English gentlewoman" (76, 191), Caleb and Amelia Gare are represented as being vaguely suspended in space and time. There is little indication that they came to the Prairies from anywhere, or that they are going anywhere. In contrast, virtually every minor character in the novel is given background: the Gares and Lind Archer, the school-teacher who might function as a figure of the author, are surrounded not by unmarked "Canadians" but by Icelanders, Swedes, Norwegians, Hungarians, "mixed bloods," half-breeds, and Indians.[3]

As a model of "multiculturalism," Ostenso's novel is telling. We might assume that if the central characters' backgrounds are unmarked they should be associated with the author's, but Ostenso was born in Norway to Norwegian parents, and Gare, Archer, and Jordon hardly work as Norwegian names. Ostenso does not inscribe her own history in the novel, just as she is silent on that of her main characters. If they are to be taken as "North Americans," then that identity, by default, becomes British. Even though ethnically they comprise a clear minority among the characters in the novel, their unmarked status suggests the way in which empire succeeded, at least from the perspective of some people, in imposing British identity as the "norm" over the diverse immigrant groups who settled the Prairies. Ostenso's suppression of her Norwegianness and her apparent desire to affiliate herself and her novel with the "dominant" culture suggest an element of identity anxiety and immigrant "cultural cringe."

Caleb Gare is obsessed with the idea of "knowing your place," but his own place is only vaguely located in time and space – "place" for him refers to a person's position within the strictly defined social structure that he imposes. The erasure of history and geography in his representation dovetails nicely with his internalization of the principles of empire. He has the "timeless" quality of nations, which Benedict Anderson suggests "always loom out of an immemorial past, and, still more important, glide into a limitless future" (11-12). Caleb says that the homestead cabin he built will "stand forever" and that "[t]he Gares are farmers, from way back. No Gare ever did good at anything else. No – [the children will] not leave – they'll not leave" (192). When he says this, his voice is "soft, intent, as if he were repeating to himself the words of a charm" (192), suggesting the performative function of language. Caleb's language has the power to create his place, his empire, reality: "'What I want to be, I *am*'" (241), he says, and *is*.

Further, just as Anderson argues that nationalism must be understood in relation to "the large cultural systems [such as empire] that preceded it, out of which – as well as against which – it came into being" (12), Caleb must be understood in terms of the circumstances that generated him, and that he then swallowed up into himself. There is no need to identify his circumstances in the novel because in a sense he has *become* his circumstances. His "place" is a process: imperialist expansionism, feeding off – swallowing up – and forming his own identity through the digestion of all that is Other, the past, the land, cultural difference, the bodies and spirits of his wife and children. His "home ground" is acquiring as much of it as possible. He is "at home" only within himself, and to make a home in the prairie space he must possess it, expand himself to contain it.

This is just the opposite of what the novel often seems to suggest. Caleb is described as a servant to the "god" of land (216) and his children as "sacrifices" to it (105), through their enforced labour and devotion: "There was a transcendent power in this blue field of flax that lifted a man above the petty artifices of birth, life, and death. It was more exacting, even, than an invisible God. It demanded not only the good in him, but the evil, and the indifference" (147). The displacement of his sexuality onto his relationship with the land, the flax that he gives a "stealthy caress – more intimate than any he had ever given to woman" (147), and his eventual erotic death, sucked down into the "irresistible" and "insidious" muskeg (298), suggest his possession *by* the "mistress" land that he has tried to control.[4] But this perspective displaces agency and blames the "victim," a position that perhaps becomes more obviously problematic if we consider the long history of rape as a conventional metaphor for both colonization and plowing.

Caleb is victim not of the land, but of his self-created and self-imposed relationship to it. He runs into the muskeg because he is trying to save his flax field from an encroaching bush fire, and the sensual relationship he has to his flax is due to the esteem it brings him, as a "slow growing, deliberate, delicate" crop (264), and its high market value. Just before the fire he had learned that the price of flax had gone up, and

> the news was sufficient cause for him to go out to the flax field that evening with his lantern to look out on the broad wealth of it. A short time now, and it would be taken off. And there would not be a farmer in all the country around so rich as Caleb Gare. It was well that even Amelia

did not know the extent of his fortune. It might make her avaricious, or turn her head.

    Caleb thought of the Bjarnassons. They were well supplied with this world's goods, too. But they could not raise flax like this. They did not go much beyond cattle and horses, that bred in the flesh. There was a spirit in the flax – the growing of it was a challenge to a man's will in this gaunt land. It took Caleb Gare to raise flax. (272)

His true passion is not "the land" but the profit and property that enlarge his identity. When he looks at his growing hay stacks he sees the "product of *his* land, result of *his* industry. As undeniably his as his right hand, testifying to the outer world that Caleb Gare was a successful owner and user of the soil" (213). Similarly, the novel frequently appears to present a deterministic, "environmentalist," view of the relationship between the land and the human psyche, diverting attention away from Caleb's imperial attitude toward both the land and his family. Lind describes Caleb as "a spiritual counterpart of the land, as harsh, as demanding, as tyrannical as the very soil from which he drew his existence" (35), indeed "nothing but a symbol of the land" (92), and Mark says that humans are "only the mirror of our environment" (93). If Caleb is a servant of the land and his family are servants to him, then it may appear that the land is only acting *through* him, that the mode of production *requires* him to bind his family together to meet the farm's labour needs, to suppress their spirits in order to reduce them to beings with only brute physical strength. But we have reason to suspect that he could actually afford the "hired man" he says he can't afford, and the main instrument that he uses to "break" his family is blackmail, a social contract that relies on cultural notions of morality and "honour": "[H]e firmly believed that knowledge of Amelia's shame would keep the children indefinitely to the land" (184). And he also uses blackmail to acquire more land from his neighbours, to expand his holdings. His relationship to the land and to its other inhabitants is anything *but* "natural."

    The environmentalist argument suggests that there may be only a single "authentic" response to a landscape, that there is a single appropriate "home" in each "place." Not only is this an extremely limiting view, but in this case it also functions to "naturalize" imperialist ideologies and conceals a possible male bias. Wallace Stegner has noted that "frontiers provide not only the rawest forms of deculturation but the most slavish respect for borrowed elegances" (*Wolf Willow* 23). His terms make neither option appear attractive, perhaps, but the latter especially so; at least the former has some potential "masculine" appeal. Historically, what men saw as the adventure and opportunity of frontier settlement was often experienced as an "unsettling" move for women, who were often the first to try to transplant or recreate the social and cultural contexts they left behind (Lamar 38-39).

Amelia Gare's past, with its vague suggestions of what Caleb considers "fineness" and "high ideas," is the element of her that he attempts to suppress in order to maintain his authority over her, and this is only one part of his larger attempt to erase history, which is symptomatic of his internalization of empire. It is not enough for him to control time in the present tense, as "the clock by which the family slept, woke, ate and moved" (64). He must also *restrict* time to the present tense. Not only does he attempt to control the knowledge of Amelia's illegitimate child in order to freeze her and the future of their children in the eternal present moment of his expansionism, mimicking the Jeffersonian hope of a society developing through space rather than time (Limerick 94), but he is also made uncomfortable by her use of cloth napkins, one of Stegner's "borrowed elegances": "[A]t each plate she laid a carefully ironed, worn napkin. It was one of the little observances she had carried over from a somewhat gentler life. Caleb had always ignored the napkin beside his plate because it symbolized something in his wife's life that he had tried to obliterate – a certain fineness that was uneconomical and pretentious. Amelia had known better in the last five years than ever to ask for money for new napkins" (175). To convert her into one of his "territories," he must wipe out her pre-history, the experiences that have formed her identity, and furnish her with a new identity that has no existence outside him.

Their daughter Judith, who has never been far off the farm, finds the culture imported from the city by Mark Jordan and Lind Archer, dancing and music, foreign yet familiar – as if it is in her blood, inherited through her mother's memory: "It was all so new to her, and yet it seemed part of the thing to which she belonged" (115). This "ancestral" memory threatens Caleb's power to keep Judith within the labour pool, as it draws her toward the "other world" that it represents for her, and Caleb attempts to reinscribe the city as a threatening site of law, courts, and prison in her imaginative geography, blackmailing her for her attempted murder of him. Caleb's complete intolerance of difference, his need to absorb all forms of otherness and transform them into the "sameness" that constitutes his identity, prevents the mingling of cultures that Amelia and Judith might have used to create successful hybridized homes for themselves. In his attempt to impose his particular cultural relationship on the prairie space, he writes an "anti-home," a "home place" in which his family is radically "out of place," and it is one that ultimately destroys him.

## Robert J.C. Stead's *Grain*

Whereas Caleb's empire is internal and he has the authorial agency and power to write his own home place, to inscribe his environment, Stead's Gander Stake in *Grain* is presented as being more subject to the inscriptions and narratives of others, in particular of an empire that is external to himself. And, appropriately, whereas history and geography are erased in Caleb's representation, Gander is represented as being fully "placed" in space and time. The fictional farm community setting of Willow Green is clearly identified as being in southwestern Manitoba, between Brandon and Winnipeg, we are given the year of Gander's birth (1896), and his parents are identified as being of British heritage and having moved fairly recently to the Prairies from "the East," which in Prairie usage usually means Ontario.[5] Further, the events of World War I serve to anchor the novel in a larger historical context, contextualizing and "textualizing" the prairie space. Athough it ostensibly takes place "elsewhere," the war largely determines the significance of the space that Gander inhabits and the meaning of his activities there.

Unlike Ostenso's "multicultural" Prairie community, Stead's is decidedly monocultural and British. Whether this reflects his own experience or assumptions absorbed from his work in the colonization department of the CPR and the federal government's Department of Immigration and Colonization, his representation agrees with the official imperial goal of replicating British culture and social structures on Canadian soil, through assimilation if not through actual British settlement.[6] The first and only mention of the British background of the novel's main characters comes halfway through the novel, when we are told of Gander's father, Jackson Stake, and his neighbour Mr. Fyfe, that "[i]t was typical of their British outlook that it did not occur to either of them to so much as wonder what the outcome [of the war] would be" (88). The lateness and obliqueness of the reference suggests that the characters would have been assumed British by Stead's audience unless otherwise marked.

The novel's only indications of ethnic diversity on the Prairies are the suggestion in a drill sergeant's use of the phrase "It's discipline, me lad, discipline" (126) that he might be of Scottish background, Mrs. Stake's comment "There was a German family lived near us when I was a little girl. Nice folks, too, but he drank too much beer, although I'm not sayin' only Germans do that" (89), which distances Germans not only in space but also in time, and the presence of a "Chinese restaurant" in town. The latter is striking in the way it relates to deculturation and market forces, two of the determinants in Gander's homemaking process:

> The "Chink's place" was a comparatively new establishment in Plainville. It rejoiced in a painted signboard, "No Sing – Wun Lung," which occasioned much local merriment. If the owner knew the reason for the amusement he gave no hint, but it is a good thing to have men come into your place of business smiling. Gander patronized the slant-eyed gentleman with the vocal disadvantages not on account of the wit in his signboard but in order to escape the tyranny of tablecloths and napkins with which the Palace Hotel insisted on encumbering its guests. Besides, the meals were ten cents cheaper. (122)

The phrase "vocal disadvantages" plays, of course, on the signboard's unintended message, but it also suggests anxiety over language differences and the way language can be a barrier to having one's identity understood or recognized, for "no one seemed to know whether the [signboard] name was singular or plural" (123).

Even though the term "Chinese restaurant" may not have implied for Stead, as it would now, a restaurant that serves only or even mainly Chinese *food* (Gander eats pork and potatoes there), it is somewhat odd that Gander feels more culturally at home there than among the "borrowed elegances" of the royally named "mainstream" establishment. Ironically, despite the novel's overwhelmingly British perspective, for Gander the Chinese transplant appears more "local" or "at home" in the prairie space than the imperial one. But of course even the Chinese restaurant is a sign and legacy of empire, its presence a result of the workers brought in to construct the railway that built the nation.[7] And it is further overwritten with imperial notations when two local girls enter the establishment to attract the attention of and flirt with the uniformed soldiers eating lunch there, prompting Gander to feel so insecure about his own comparatively unkempt appearance that he leaves and gets a haircut. This even though he associates such pretenses in others with "a reprehensible kind of pride, which concerned itself with appearances, and with what people might think" (167).

Like Caleb Gare, Gander is in general opposed to all pretenses and borrowed elegances, but, whereas Caleb's opposition was linked to his desire to suppress history, Gander's is linked, at least initially, to his rather rigid notions of gender. White tablecloths, scrubbings, dinner graces, all are linked with a "domestic" space that is internal and "female," so that even at school the boys eat their lunches outside the building, while "the girls, always more fastidious, ate theirs from their desks inside" (35). The prairie space is gendered along traditional division-of-labour lines, so that work in the open fields is "a man's place" (57, 59), and the smaller spaces – the garden where Gander's mother, Susie Stake, works "bent over" (150) and the house interior where she "had to move about in a very stooped position" (57) – are controlled by women.

Not surprisingly, Gander "regarded domestic service as beneath the dignity of a man" (47), and Jackson uses his power to expand *his* holdings for many years before "giving" Susie the new house she has wanted, despite the fact that the woman's labour is more "productive" than his:

> [H]e saw no further than the need of bringing more land under cultivation, to grow more wheat; and even while he pursued this policy he would have told you that he lost money on every bushel of wheat he grew, and that it was the cows, the hogs, and the hens that held the farm together. And Mrs. Stake, had she been standing by, would have reminded him who it was that milked the cows, and fed the hens, and mothered the young chickens, and, perhaps, threw the chopped barley to the hogs. (41)

Similarly, Jo Burge says that the cows and hens she cares for are her household's "mainstay" (190), yet Gander feels rather heroic helping her with the "many spots where a man's muscle and management were needed" (191), stubbling-in the fields that her ill husband hasn't been able to attend to, and thus giving them not much more than the *appearance* of things being better.

As Stead challenges the notion that "domestic work" and "bringing home the bacon" are not sometimes the same thing, he also challenges Gander's rigid gendering of domestic space and activities, primarily through the character Cal, a hired man who eventually marries Gander's sister, Minnie. When Cal is hired, his first act is to scrub the granary, his temporary lodging, to a condition that Gander describes as "effeminately clean. That sort of thing was all right in a house, where there was a woman to keep the dust on the jump, but a he-man never troubled about such matters" (157). Gander jokes, "He'll be puttin' lace curtains on the grainery, next" (159), and he is annoyed that Cal turns the cream separator for Minnie, calling it "no job for a man" (161).[8] But since Gander has also had to admit that "Cal, in spite of his eccentricities, was measuring up to his standards of a he-man" (157), he also has to admit the possibility that Cal is not merely breaking, but *redefining*, gender roles, so that he "had, at least by inference, suggested that turning the cream separator was a masculine occupation" (162). Gander's objection to this is thoroughly practical – he doesn't want his mother to get ideas that he should similarly help her.

While Gander's rigid gender notions and definition of "he-men" are being challenged by Cal's presence, the presence of World War I simultaneously imposes a rigid gender role on Gander. The war functions as a novelistic device to explore affiliative ties between the new nation and the "home country," and, just as cultural borrowings that Gander sees as pretentious were primarily associated with women, so it is primarily women who demonstrate the strongest "home ties," and who push the resulting narrowly defined "heroic" roles on the community's men. Gander's would-be girlfriend, Jo, hopes that he will "play the hero as other young men of the district were doing" (93): "Like any honest girl, she was not satisfied that she alone should be proud of Gander; she wanted other people to be proud of him. She wanted to see the stoop taken out of this back, the hitch out of his gait, the drag out of his legs. Then, when the papers began to glare with reports of atrocities in Belgium, she wanted the heroic in Gander to well up and send him rushing to arms, to the defence of womankind, to the defence of Josephine Burge!" (106). Jo sees the war as something extremely personal and "close to home"; she fully identifies with the European allies, to the extent that to fight for them is to fight for her. Sending troops over from Plainville "'makes us feel that we're in it,'" she says, "'and doing our share'" (92).

Similarly, when Gander's sister, Minnie, rides the fields one day with him, she has a fantasy that Gander is "part of it": "I was just thinking as I rode up on the back of the binder that the wheat was Germans and the knives were the Allies. It was great fun watching them topple over, in whole regiments" (95). She acknowledges that she is "too big a girl now for make-belief," but still would like to feel "that—that—*some* of us—is—is cutting 'em down" (96). Even Gander's parents have the feeling that "in some way the Stakes should be represented not only in the wheatfield, but on the fighting-line" (134), and Minnie's and Jo's collapsing of space, their "identification" of places, is also a strategy used by a recruiter: "'Believe me, men,' he was saying, 'this is as much our fight as it is England's. The Germans have got to be stopped somewhere. You all agree to that. Now I say, stop them in Belgium. Better fight them in Belgium than Plainville. Eh? . . . What's that? Over in three months? Yes—it'll be over here in three months, if everyone stays at home'" (91). Gander, however, wants to think of the war as "something distant and impersonal" (90), and Stead offers geography as a defense of Gander's "patriotism": "[A]fter all, the war was away in Belgium or some such place, which was in Europe or Asia or some such place. Gander was not very sure of his geography, but of this much he was sure, that the Atlantic ocean lay between, and the British Navy ruled the Atlantic Ocean, so what was there to worry about?" (106).

The relationship between the Prairies and Europe is not, however, strictly defined by geography but by historical, social, and cultural structures. Gander is able to redefine the relationship for his own purposes only by redefining his social role, his "function" within his home place, in such a way that it is still compatible with the expectations of others. In a world where children are thought of as women's "contribution to the state" (16), it is not surprising that from the beginning Stead gives Gander a strong sense of the social significance of his farm work. A great deal of his excitement over the new steam engine comes from its capacty to "thresh in a dozen hours the wheat to feed a hundred families for a year" (54). So it is good news for Gander when, in the second year of the war,

> the world – the Allies' world, at any rate – had awakened to the quite obvious fact that the war must be won by wheat. Growing wheat became a patriotic duty into which Gander fitted like a cylinder nut into a socket wrench. He could grow wheat, and none of that "form fours" nonsense about it. True, there were still some who refused to see in the growing of wheat the highest expression of service, some even who were frank enough to suggest that the prospect of a high price had more to do with the sudden increase in acreage than had any patriotic motive. (127)

Although Jackson Stake is initially excited at the prospect of the war raising the price of wheat (88, 90), he is later represented as having expansionist desires that are solely because of the desire to help produce more much-needed grain for the war effort, and he even worries that the high price of grain is "blood money" (138). And, though Gander's grain may well be "mightier than siege guns and battleships" (120) in controlling the outcome of the war, he has little control over it, for "whenever he bought he had to pay the seller's price, but whenever he sold, the buyer dictated the figure" (121), and he has no choice but to accept the official grading standards imposed on his produce.[9] Stead thus minimizes the importance of the market forces at work in Gander's actions, depicting him rather as a community-minded, essentially social, being, motivated by non-market forces. Profit and property for Gander are means to an end, not ends in themselves. As Caleb Gare uses them to *construct* his isolationist, contained self, so Gander's contingent, social self is *constructed by* them.

In contrast to this fully social representation, Stead presents a rather environmentalist view of Gander's early sense of being fully at home in his space: "[N]ever in all his days on the farm and the prairie did Gander know the pang of loneliness. This was his natural environment; he was no more lonely on these prairies than is the coyote or the badger" (56). But Gander is at home more because he is comfortable with his social role than because of anything inherent in the natural landscape, and with the arrival of new social pressures, especially those related to empire's imagined community as promoted by the women of his immediate community, he begins to isolate himself, so that "[f]rom even his mother and father he [withdraws] as into a shell" (134). Eventually, so much pain has been written over his space, localized in his place, that he leaves it, for, as Jo has advised him, "'If you get out you may forget – at least, you will get away from the edge of the precipice. If you stay here you will always be in danger of slipping over'" (202).

The novel's ending appears contrived or flawed *if* it is viewed as Gander leaving for another woman, Jerry, who can get him a job in the city, and leaving what may seem to be, in environmentalist terms, his first love – the land.[10] Gander's love has never been the land itself, though, but rather the machinery that he uses to control it and the "manly pride" (44) and esteem that operating it brings him. Jackson Stake may have an "elemental fascination of the soil" (45), but what stirs Gander is "the romance of machinery, of steam, which at the pull of a lever turned loose the power of giants!" (54). Gander once gets very excited over a possible rain, prompting the authorial comment, "Gander was a farmer. All his instincts were rooted deeply in the soil" (79). But we soon learn that his reaction "had been a sort of reflex of his father, rather than a cry from his own heart" (80). Developing his own identity includes coming to terms with his own desires, and the steam engine is several times referred to as a rival to his love for Jo, while the "half-caressing touch" (99) he gives it recalls Caleb Gare's caress of his flax. Gander has already realized that Jerry was a poor substitute for Jo, and in the note he leaves for Jo he says, "I've got a good job in a garage. I like working with machines" (207). In moving to the city, he has an opportunity to transfer his great love to a new environment, and the ending is thus consistent with his character.

But Gander is not so much leaving *for* something as leaving *something*, trying to escape the past and move through space into the future. Gander believes that hope is the "most wonderful of all medicines" (199), and when he decides to leave for the city he refers to it as "taking his medicine" (207). While his move parallels the larger historical movement that Stead documents of population migration from rural to urban areas, he does not go for education as Minnie does (135), nor because he believes, as his father does, that Winnipeg is a "compassionate city" (55) "where there's lots o' money" (58). Unable to control the inscriptions of others on his country space, he heads off to what he hopes will be a blank space on which he can inscribe his own significances. He places the possibility of improvement firmly in the future, equated with a change in space, despite Stead's clear suggestion that the past cannot be erased or denied. Imperial history overdetermined Gander's homemaking possibilities on the prairie, and, like Stead's critique of the "march of progress" (48), we are left suspecting that Gander's move will create at least as many new difficulties as it will solve old ones: "[T]he seasons had worn away, each bringing its new need, and each new need, when supplied, creating other needs in its wake, as is the way with a civilization which grows more complex with each accomplishment" (87).

## Kelly Rebar's *Bordertown Café*

Things can indeed get more complex, and Rebar's play *Bordertown Café*, which takes place in a café adjoining a farm on the Canadian side of the Alberta-Montana Border – or as one character, the seventeen-year-old Jimmy, says, on "the Canadian side of nowhere" (19) – dramatizes a rural Prairie identity crisis of an even-greater magnitude than that represented by Ostenso and Stead. The plot revolves around Jimmy's decision either to stay on the farm/café with his mother and her parents or to move south to join his father and his new wife, and the three generations of characters are obsessed with the forty-ninth parallel – a dividing line that Wallace Stegner has aptly described as being "as disturbing as a hair in butter" (*Wolf Willow* 84).

Rebar demonstrates the interconnection of public and private interests regarding this border by using a set that shows in the first act the supposedly private side of the café (the kitchen, bedrooms, and bath) and in the second act the public side of the café (the customer-seating area). The kitchen itself "bridges public and private use" (11), while "Jimmy's bedroom either introduces the back suite and one must pass through his room to get to the back, or it is in some way shown to be a room without privacy" (11). Similarly, the customer side of the café is the site of all the personal family conflicts in Act 2, so the apparent binary is shown to be quite illusory. This depiction of the public and private sides of the individual characters' lives as two sides of the same coin also functions to suggest that we can extrapolate from the "private" experiences of individual characters to larger, general, "public" patterns of behaviour and attitude.

The characters of the play define the rural prairie itself primarily in terms of its bleak economic prospects and its "emptiness," both in landscape and culture. The presence of the café indicates that it is no longer possible to make a living solely from farming, and, largely because of this, rural to urban migration has taken its toll. Most of the local population has left and, as Jimmy says, "[h]ouses 'it were here're long gone" (19). Jimmy likes going to the States with his father to see that "there's somethin' besides nothin' out some people's windows," and he suggests, referring to the family café: "We should get one of those big tractor-trailers and haul this unit outa here, straight into town. Where we can at least be part of life. This – *this* is the last thing a Canadian sees when he leaves home and the first thing an American sees when he arrives" (19). Similarly, his grandmother, Maxine, says that when Jimmy ran off the road into a telephone pole he "hit the only vertical object in a hundred mile radius" (27), and she remembers rather bitterly her postnuptial trip to Alberta from Minnesota, when two days "were spent on the train waiting for Saskatchewan to end" (89).

Rebar indicates the effects of American imperialism on Prairie economics by the use of off-stage sound effects. At the very beginning of the play, the sound of a combine approaching and then fading away is used, and shortly after that an oil tanker gears by and fades away too. Significantly, Jimmy sleeps through the combine sound, jerking awake only when the sound stops (12), indicating that it is a soothing and familiar sound, while his mother, Marlene, stops all activity, as if distracted, while the tanker passes (13). These sound effects alternate throughout the play, symbolizing the declining farm economy in Alberta and the rapidly developing oil business, which consists mostly of American companies using Canadian resources.

This "foreign" ownership and a misplaced nostalgia for old times are also shown in the following exchange regarding the old, out-of-use gas pump and "ole Texaco star" out in front of the café:

MARLENE: I used to watch those little coloured balls hop around when the gas was pourin' – and if I had my way we'd still have that pop machine out front, that Orange Crush.

JIMMY: It wasn't good for anything but slappin' shots against, and you got no right to put a claim on the pump, or the star. They aren't even ours. We never owned that gradge.

MARLENE: You see anyone around here care a darn? You see anyone wantin' to buy us out and put up a big Voyajer? It's never gonna be a big draw in here.

JIMMY: You wanna turn a profit, you gotta go one way or the other. Which no one in this family can ever do.

MARLENE: What're you talkin' about.

JIMMY: Turn it back into a truck stop. Or upgrade into a resternt. Who ever heard of a café on the bald-headed prairie with no place to gas up? (74-75)

Further, who would want to gas-up there even if they *did* have a working pump, what with cheaper American gas just across the border? Ironies abound, and every plan for economic action and agency appears inevitably doomed to failure.

Lacking an adequate regional identity with "positive" content, the characters struggle to define themselves and their lives against and between rural and urban attractions, regional and national identities, and British traditions and anachronisms and American commercialism and rootlessness. The play's "resolution" comes only when the son, Jimmy, realizes that being tied by bonds of family and culture to the Prairies does not require insularity or limited experience or awareness of the larger world. Only when he strengthens his identity by adding a national awareness to his regional experience is he able to reject the allure of America.

The four characters who act in the play – Jimmy, his mother, his maternal grandmother and grandfather – as well as his absent father and off-stage paternal great-grandmother, all represent various kinds and degrees of national and regional identities, and their relationships to empire. While the characters struggle to resolve the conflicts in their own lives, then, the play also operates on the level of allegory. The struggle is a representative one, meant to suggest the larger struggle of the Prairie population in general.

Jimmy, the youngest character, experiences the deepest anxieties caused by American imperialism, while his paternal great-grandmother, the eldest, is the most influenced by British imperialism, and so they each appear to embody a particular phase of Canadian history. Jimmy's maternal grandfather, Jim, a quiet, laconic man, is the fullest representation of "at home" Canadian Prairie character. He is intensely tied to the land through his farming, knows exactly what he has to do, does it, and never doubts the value of his work. Jimmy's mother, Marlene, on the other hand, is restless and indecisive, feeling she should change her name to Marlene Didn't for all her inaction and missed opportunities. She represents Canadian identity with substantial experience of the United States – much of it inherited through her mother, Maxine, who is from Minnesota and moved to Canada when she married at a young age. Maxine still holds America as the standard, or norm, against which Canada is judged, and Marlene tells her, "[T]hings would be a whole lot smoother around here if you'd quit callin' anything out the ordinary Canadian" (33).

Jimmy's father, the truck driver Don, represents the United States most completely, being from there and making only brief business trips through Canada. He embodies irresponsibility (never showing up when he says he will) and also mobility and rootlessness. Jimmy complains, with little exaggeration, "If I wanna see the guy, it's in his rig" (18), and Maxine says that Jimmy is the "only boy in the world hasn't seen the left hand side of his father, just the right – steering" (27). Don's remarriage, to an American woman, after leaving Jimmy and Marlene in Canada, symbolizes American self-interest and the lack of concern for or interest in their northern neighbours. That he tries to lure Jimmy away with visions of material well-being and adventure is indicative more of a superficial sense of culture and home than of any "deep" family feeling.

The café's having both Canadian and American flags in the seating area (67) indicates the need to appeal to customers from either side, and it also symbolizes the very divided nature of the family unit itself. Despite such mixing of blood and experience across family lines, however, stereotypes about the different nations appear relatively intact. Rebar's play is interesting not so much for what it tells us about Canadians and Americans and the English as for what it tells us about what Canadians like to believe about Canadians and Americans and the English. The play is rampant in its use of popular stereotypes and for the most part tends to reify national myths and norms rather than question them. It is even tempting to link the play's widespread success with its reflection and endorsement of these stereotypes, which function to build a sense of audience identification and community.[11]

For instance, Maxine refers to her otherwise nameless mother-in-law as "her royal highness" and "her majesty" (38), equating her in a negative way with the Queen. She also always refers to her and Jim's sister Thelma as living in an unreal world, drinking tea and being judgemental, "[s]ittin' on their royal haunches all their narrow lives – critisizin'" (72-73) – which is a popular stereotyped view of British culture and character. Similarly, the play invokes stereotypes of Americans as active, progressive, expansionist, wandering, irresponsible, unfaithful, wild, exciting, loud, sassy, violent, well-off, and materialistic, and of Canadians as passive, backward, traditional, steadfast, responsible, faithful, calm, bland, quiet, prissy, peace-loving, poor, and "civilized."

National culture is also defined according to concrete differences that take on heightened symbolic significance. Maxine, for instance, has an exaggerated preference for American cigarettes, asking Jimmy, "Run across the line and get your Max a package o' Lucky's before I affixicate myself on these of your mother's" (68). And she shows her American side when she equates the existence in Canada of the New Democratic Party with communism, saying, "Trust Russia to drop 'em down through Edmonton" (64). She jokes about Jim having "[t]he CBC on in the barn. Most educated cows in the country" (42), and while she is a regular viewer of American television, watching the primetime soap opera *Dallas* (71) and commenting on an Oklahoma woman who "got herself on Good Mornin' America for winnin' too many toaster ovens" (23), she pokes fun at both American and Canadian television: "Now you take television. The stuff they put on down there? Trash. You wanna know the name of a good program on TV? [A]nd it's been on for twenty, thirty years and it's Canadian, it's not American, it's on the CBC and it's—the—the—it's bin on the years—it's—oh, what the hell's the name o' that show?" (69).

When Rebar doesn't ironize Maxine's clichés in some way, as she does here, she generally has her put her own humorous twist on things, turning the identity issue into a more-or-less playful or serious joke. For instance, Maxine warns a customer from Texas: "Buddy you better get ready to not know how fast you're driving, how hot it is aside, how hard the wind's blowin' or how much gas you're gettin' for your so-called dollar. As for readin' directions on any box or carton—it's all in the wrist action—you'll see alot a mode da emploi's—means flip it over to English—wrist action—Canadians got real strong wrists, prepares 'em for hockey careers" (49). Here she plays off climate and currency differences, bilingualism, and the Canadian hockey obsession all in one fell swoop.

Jimmy is the play's representative hockey enthusiast. He gets upset when harvest conflicts with hockey conditioning, wishing he could start his last year of high school "like a normal human hockey player" (17), praying "just please God, let me score a hat trick" (82), and saying his American father "wouldna known luck from skill, he's never even been to a hockey game" (82). On the other side, Marlene tells him, "Your dad could throw a ball," to which Maxine replies, "All Americans can, they're the best baseball players in the United States, 'er the world" (31–32).

The play also uses language differences between characters to point up national difference. For instance, the following exchange relies for effect on pronunciation differences:

> MAXINE: [I]t's a cryin' shame these kids don't know their American history. Sittin' on the most powerful nation in the world and all they wanna do is play hockey.
>
> JIMMY: We know more about you than you know about us.
>
> MAXINE: We?—us?—hey!—*you're* more American than you are Canadian!—and I know my Canadian history!—what there is of it. But I don't forget my American ruts, and you don't neither.
>
> MARLENE: (*Entering from the front.*) A daily over.
>
> MAXINE: If it wasn't for me you'd know zip about your ruts—capital Zee-I-P.

JIMMY: My what?

MAXINE: Ruts, ruts, where ya come from.

JIMMY: I think she means roots, doesn't she Granddad.

MAXINE: I said ruts.

JIMMY: Spell that zip again, Max—was that Zed-I-P? (41)

For the "ruts" case, as for the later "ruf" (roof, 81), "prat'ly" (practically, 49) and "dawg" (dog, 49), Rebar uses non-standard spelling to demonstrate Maxine's "nonstandard" pronunciation. Since English spelling is relatively standardized across North America and elsewhere, despite the wide range of pronunciations that the written language corresponds to, the attempt to represent dialect through spelling inevitably marks difference, or otherness, from an assumed norm.[12] In the same way, Rebar marks a vague kind of uneducated "hick" status through unusual contractions, as in Jimmy's "gradge" (garage) and "resternt" (restaurant) (75).

Vocabulary differences are also played up, as when Jimmy corrects Maxine's "county" with "district" (42). Another example involves familiar names for "mother." Jimmy calls Marlene "Mum," and Jim calls her "your Mum" (associated with British English), while Marlene calls Maxine "Mom" (associated with American English). This usage pattern ties in with the popular myth that Canadian English has no "positive" content, being constructed only through difference from British and American norms. This myth runs very deep, allied as it is with what Ronald Wardhaugh identifies as the Canadian tendency to be only against things, rather than for anything. So, despite the linguistic "fact" that Canadian English "is not a composite of archaic or rustic features or a potpourri of British and American speechways but a true national language" (Bailey, "English" 152), the Canadian lexicographer T.K. Pratt argues that a true Canadian national dictionary ought to supply usage notes "to guide Canadians between competing American and British practices" (63).

While, for the most part, Rebar reifies such identity myths and stereotypes, there are occasions when her irony and humour go further, to begin to deconstruct the binary constructions she works with. For example, American "largeness" and commercialism are countered by a reference to the West Edmonton Mall, and the kind of "nonsense" and frivolity associated with the United States is also linked with Calgary, which has restaurants with salad bars, where you can "get served parsley with a bran muffin by a waitress named Tom" (75). Maxine's chief gripe about her mother-in-law's supposed British uppitiness is also shown to be more a matter of perception than reality. On her first meeting, she walked in "expectin' I don't know what and *what* does the woman do but warm the teapot. Hands me her best English china just *hopin'* I'd break it, which I did" (89). Jim counters, "It wasn't her best, it was just some cup I got at the show" (89), but the fact that Maxine assumed that it was fine china shows that she *did* have expectations and that they are largely responsible for her continuing hostility toward her in-law.

Similarly, the hockey/baseball split isn't as complete as it first appears, because Marlene reminds Jimmy of the time he "fired the hardball through the window" (81), and in the following exchange Jimmy challenges the absolute nature of the division:

> MAXINE: Hockey isn't nothin' down there, it's not even played.
>
> JIMMY: They play hockey down there.
>
> MAXINE: Well they shouldn't! They're gonna be beatin' yas at your own
> game before much longer, and then sellin' it back to you, that's
> the way these people operate, I was raised down there, I know
> how they think—me, us, we're first, we're best, gimmie that—
> you wanna buy it? (69)

To defend and reconstruct her desired perception of national difference, despite its obvious flaws, Maxine shifts the ground of the argument to appeal to yet another stereotype.

That she relies on both positive and negative stereotypes of each country suggests that her way of thinking may be linked more to a need to "identify," to know and place things that resist easy categorization, than to a patriotic impulse. She also has prejudices about regions within the United States, believing, for instance, that "people from, say, Kansas south, are nine out of ten of 'em that come in here full-fledged porkers" (26), and when she learns that Jimmy is thinking of moving to the United States she changes her tune dramatically from the predominantly positive stereotypes in Act 1 to such claims as that "nine a-outa ten Americans . . . carry guns" (original ellipsis), that "America had no business even goin' to Vietnam. Or to any of these other trouble spot countries. . . . Not to mention the moon," and that "violence in America is somethin' the Russians don't have" (68).

In a nostalgic moment, she tells Jimmy, "America is just not the place you think it is. It's not the place it used to be," to which he responds, noting the shift in her stance from their earlier conversations, "Yeah, it seems to've changed an awful lot since this morning even" (69). Yet, despite her equivocation, she insists that she will be "buried in American soil" (38), suggesting the lure of the birth place as site for significant life events. Similarly, Marlene, born on Canadian soil, insists, "[I]t was my choice to come back up here, to have my baby north o' that border" (33). Jimmy shows the same desire for consistent "home ground" when he says, "I'm marrying someone same side o' the border," but when Maxine asks him "What side would this be?" he can only answer "No side" (70).

Yet another way in which Rebar both uses and challenges stereotypes is in the gendering of nation and home, as when Maxine says, "Everybody needs someone to look after 'em – or I mean, women don't, they got it built-in, but men, they do" (69). Given that many of the stereotypes invoked of America and Canada also feed into traditional gender stereotypes, with male as loud, aggressive, and active, and female as quiet, submissive, and passive, and given that Jimmy's father is American and his mother Canadian, it would be tempting to suggest that Rebar is gendering America and Canada male and female respectively. However, this is at least partially countered by the larger family history, in which the previous generation, Jim and Maxine's, consists of a Canadian man and an American female, reversing the nation-gender identification.

Whatever the gender of nation, however, and whatever effects Rebar achieves to challenge the totality of national identity, national boundaries are still a – or perhaps *the* – issue in the play, and Jimmy is caught smack dab in the middle, straddling the line. He wishes the issue would disappear, saying, "American, Canadian – back, forth – like it *mattered* what a guy was – why couldn't I've bin born in Australia? nowhere *near* the American border?" (60), but the decision to stay with his mother or to move to the States with his father compels him to choose between the two.

Throughout the play, Jimmy struggles with his divided identity and his conflicting desires, but a turning point comes for him when his grandfather lets slip that he was once in Halifax:

JIMMY: Halifax? You were in Halifax?

JIM: I was there when the war ended.

JIMMY: Wait a sec, wait a sec—you mean to say—this is just hittin' me—
 you bin off the prairies? (99)

Jimmy's incredulous tone and exaggerated surprise at this information suggests that he has had a vision of his grandfather – and by extension the Prairie identity – as being insular in outlook and experience. With this negative image shattered, Jimmy then finds the courage to assert himself against his father's pull, and to fully affiliate himself with his mother and the Canadian side of his identity.

He rejects his father's invitation to share his "twelve hunderd square feet" of snazzy new house, telling him, "[M]aybe I'll take a pass on movin' down there actually" (100), and then lets his pent-up anger and frustration loose, chewing him out for all his missed visits and phone calls, and concluding, "[Y]ou're eighteen years too late, Dad" (101). But his final decision to go instead to Hawaii with his mother for Christmas is also ironic, for, as Maxine had earlier pointed out, "Hawaii's part o' the United States" (92). In somewhat paradoxical fashion, then, his Prairie home is made fully secure only when he has accepted a national outlook and is able to rebuff the American imperial threats to his identity while at the same time shamelessly accepting whatever American opportunities will benefit him.[13]

## Ian Ross's *fareWel*

National imperialistic threats to identity are also the central subject of Ian Ross's play *fareWel*, but here the destructive colonial power is not America but Canada itself. Set in the fictional Partridge Crop Reserve, which represents the government-controlled system of segregated "Native" homelands, the play deconstructs Canadian national identity by asserting First Nations' presence, centrality, and current movement toward self-government and self-determination. Some of the key issues in the play, then, are who has the power to inscribe space, how they get the power, how they use it, and what kinds of responsibilities follow (or should follow) from having it. Ultimately the play offers an alternate nationalism based not on homogeneity but on pluralism, not on exclusion but on inclusion, not on conquering outside territory but on developing an internally cohesive and immediate (vs. "imagined") sense of community.[14]

The title term "fareWel" is an inversion and colloquial usage of "welfare" and operates as a doubly ironic synecdoche for continuing economic control and oppression of Native people. The play is structured around the Reserve inhabitants waiting for their late welfare cheques, and it becomes clear that these government "handouts" are not generous provisions for independent living, but rather are disabling inducements to dependence and loss of self-esteem. By the time the cheques arrive at the end of the play, the character Phyllis says, "[N]ow that it's back I kind of don't want it anymore" (95), to which her friend Rachel replies, "You always think goodbyes are bad. But sometimes they're good" (96). Being "on welfare" (note the syntax of addiction) means quite the opposite of "faring well," then, and the possibility of saying "farewell" ("goodbye") to welfare is seen as a positive step toward self-determination, pride, and well-being.

As with the cheques, the band's chief is absent in Vegas during the play and arrives at the end anticlimactically, since the people have elected a new chief in his absence: Teddy, who is going to try to bring gambling to the Reserve to build the economy. The two patterns merge, then, to indicate the people's spiritual (if not technically "legal") shift of loyalty from the old system of status-quo welfare dependence to the hope of future self-determination.

In his handling of these and other matters, Ross structures the play in what might almost be thought of as a different kind of "healing circle," with the ending offering both tight formal closure and a more open-ended indication of social change through the repetition-with-difference of symbols, actions, words, and ideas from the beginning. As another example, the play begins and ends at the community church, both times with a wake taking place (a wake itself being appropriately a time of both ending and beginning). At the first wake, salmon sandwiches are served, and the comic but wise character Sheldon (Nigger[15]) gets a toothache from eating a fish bone (27), while at the end of the wake sardine sandwiches are served and Sheldon says, "It kind of stinks, but it's pretty good. . . . Since my tooth got fixed I eat fish again" (90).

Similarly, a shift to self-acceptance and a more secure identity is shown in the words of the young gas-sniffer Melvin, who opens the play by saying, "You kids go home. . . . You're not supposed to play around the church. Go home" (13), and who reverses this near the end of the play when he says, "Hey you kids. Come here [to the church]" (95). Children also carry the dramatic weight of change when Phyllis notes that her children aren't playing at the dump anymore (where she was earlier telling them to go to get them away from throwing the ball against the house) and instead are picking saskatoons and thus being economically productive rather than a resource-drain (95).

The church itself functions as a primary symbol of home, both in Melvin's reclaiming it as a community centre and in its being renamed to indicate the uncertain course of self-determination that is under way. Act 1 opens with the sound of a drum beating, which is gradually overpowered by music from the church, whose sign reads The Partridge Crop Pentecostal Church (13). Act 2 opens with the reverse, the church hymn being slowly overpowered by a drum beating, and the sign has been changed to Creator's Church (61), indicating the desire to return to an originary, or "pure," tradition. Finally, the move toward a pluralistic view of community is represented when the church is renamed Partridge Crop Pentecostal Church of the Creator and the church music's rhythm "is a cross between the country feel of earlier and the drum" (90). Yet, despite the play's rhetoric of "co-existence," Melvin reminds us that all these definitional difficulties are a result of the introduction of English language and culture, saying, "They keep changing this place's name. They should just call it Ahnamay igamik" (94), which would simply be "church" in Saulteaux.

Language issues such as this one are used throughout the play to mirror the larger questions of identity, culture, and power that the characters struggle with. Teddy notes that Bazooka Joe bubblegum comics are printed in French and English because "this is Canada" (40), while Sheldon asks the store owner, Walter, "[Y]ou got any Bazooka Joe with Saulteaux on them?" (86), thus exposing the fictionality of the two-founding-nations history of Canada. Melvin wants Sheldon to teach him Saulteaux as part of his desire for secure "Indian" identity, and when the character Teddy gives a speech designed to get him elected as the new band chief with the primary agenda to advance the cause of self-determination, he addresses the people in Saulteaux (56-57). An English translation for this long section is given in the printed text but was not in the 1996 Winnipeg premiere performance, offering a disorienting shift in perspective for the mostly white theatre audience.[16]

Another linguistic strategy for disrupting the audience's potentially complacent trust in the English language is the extensive use of punning and word play. Many of these cases function as both entertainment and education, as when the slippery term "native" comes up for some good-humoured scrutiny:

> NIGGER: We're supposed to sing *O Canada* before our meeting or *God Safe the Queen*. (*Singing.*) "O Canada. Our home and native land . . ." – (*He punches up "native" for added effect.*) A Native person wrote that song.
>
> MELVIN: That's not what it means.
>
> NIGGER: Sure it does. Native. That's us right.
>
> MELVIN: Yeah, but not like that. (51)

A second exchange also draws on this double meaning, offering a playful explanation of the principles of polyvalence:

> MELVIN: See Nigger. What is that?
>
> NIGGER: What?
>
> MELVIN: That thing in Teddy's hand.

NIGGER: A smoke.

MELVIN: Right? What do you do to a fish?

NIGGER: Eat it.

MELVIN: Or?

NIGGER: Catch it.

MELVIN: Or you can smoke it. Right?

NIGGER: Yeah.

MELVIN: OK. So you can smoke a fish. What's that coming out of that cigrette?

NIGGER: Smoke.

MELVIN: Right. Smoke coming out of a smoke. Or you can smoke a fish. Or smoke a cigrette or a cigrette's a smoke.

NIGGER: Oooooooohhhhhhh. I see. So. You can smoke a fish or a cigrette, or you can call a cigrette a smoke.

MELVIN: Yeah. It's just like "our home and native land." Native means two things. (74-75)

Melvin's claim here that the two cases are "just like" each other is indeed true at some high level of generalization, but the comparison is of dubious specific usefulness, and it also appears to depoliticize the contentious issues of identity and place involved in the term "native." This is perhaps odd, given that elsewhere in the play Melvin is keenly concerned with the politics of naming reality. When Teddy tells him, "You're Bill C-31. Only real Indians can work for the band," he responds simply, "I'm a real Indian" (39-40), demonstrating his cynical distance from official language and his rejection of the government's divisive attempt to label and regulate identity.

Bill C-31 is not explained within the play but functions as convenient shorthand for the ultimate absurdity of national attempts to legislate identity. The 1985 amendment to the Indian Act granted Indian status and treaty rights to women and their first-generation descendants who had unfairly lost their status under the old system. Prior to the amendment, a Native woman who married a white man automatically lost her status and rights, while a white woman who married a Native man automatically gained status and rights. This system attempted to impose a simplistic binary system of knowing onto a complex reality, and codified male power and privilege by acknowledging identity only through patrilineal descent. Bill C-31, then, recognizes not only the highly abstract, arbitrary, and discriminatory manner in which identity had been fixed, but also the very real, concrete, and detrimental political, economic, and social effects that followed.

One of the great ironies of the play is that Teddy, the person most aggressively pursuing Native self-government for the band, is also the character who has most fully bought into the rigid official discourse about identity and difference, even though it cannot account for his own personal reality:

> TEDDY: I got you that gravel. You wouldn't even have got any if it wasn't for me. You're a Bill C-31er.
>
> MELVIN: I got that gravel. You didn't . . . I even asked before you and yet they gave everyone gravel except for me. That's how you can tell who's Bill C-31 on this reserve. They're the ones with dirt on their roads.
>
> TEDDY: That's 'cause you're not pure.
>
> MELVIN: I'm more Indian than you. (*TEDDY laughs.*) In my heart. In my heart.
>
> TEDDY: All you got is a card and some bullshit treaty number.
>
> RACHEL: Teddy you're not even pure yourself. Your granny was part white.
>
> TEDDY: Woo nab in, pisahnabin. (Sit down and shut up.) (58)

In his reference to dirt roads, Melvin alludes to Reserve discrimination against those who recently had had their rights restored by those who perceive them as encroaching on the Reserve's already inadequate resources. As Teddy later says, "You're just a bunch of mooches. Taking away from us real Indians" (77). Viewed in this context, Teddy's argument here about racial "purity" may actually represent a displacement or projection of economic anxieties, as indeed "race" is often a naturalized code for economic, social, or political privilege and power.

Yet his hostile and defensive Saulteaux response to Rachel's reminder of his own mixed heritage also suggests that it may be anxiety about his own identity that causes him to cling to the government's hierarchical system of naming and privilege. Rather than reject the system that would shame and deny him power, then, as Melvin has, Teddy appears instead to have fully bought into it, with the result that in order to feel good about himself he must label and judge others negatively.

There also appears to be a strong gender component to Teddy's obsession with Bill C-31. His violent dismissal of Rachel, telling her to "sit down and shut up," is part of his general attempt to exclude the women from the discussions about self-government, as he tells them, "No women allowed here, at this meeting" (47), and he tells the other men, "We'll also have to keep an eye on those stupid women" (76). His misogyny is also apparent in his hypocrisy of both condemning prostitutes and using their services. In one breath he admits, "One time in Winnipeg, I phone the hooker escort service and tell them to send me over a real pretty one," and in the next he takes the self-righteous stance, "What kind of reserve would I be running here if I let hookers live here?" (59).[17]

In fact, Teddy's attitude toward women mirrors that of pre-Bill C-31 legislation, so it appears that his antagonism toward Melvin arises at least in part not simply because Melvin regained his status but because he regained it through his *mother* regaining hers. Ironically, there are indications that Teddy doesn't even accept the responsibilities that might adhere to his own paternity, as Rachel once says, "So Teddy's gonna have another kid. What's that make . . . four? ten?" (20), and she later needles him, "Why don't you go look after Margret and your baby, instead of making things worse for us" (59).

In his perpetuation of divisive government rhetoric about race and gender, then, Teddy serves to foreground and problematize the "self" in "self-government." His vision of a self-governed reserve has been overdetermined by past imperial practice and is thus a restrictive and exclusionary one in which, he says, "[W]e'll decide who's an Indian. No more of this blonde-haired, blue-eyed Bill C-31ers, coming on our reserve and taking our money. And the Indian religion. The true religion will be what we practise. No more of this whiteman's church" (57). Clearly, Teddy wants to reserve the right to determine who the "we" is in all of this, and ultimately his vision serves an individualistic rather than a collective or communal ideology. In fact, the "we" changes to an "I" soon enough, when he says, "[N]obody will stop me when I get rid of every fuckin' Christian on this reserve" (63).

This view that power should be used egotistically to control the construction of place is ironized and critiqued by the overall context of the play, and the character Robert tells Teddy, "This is why self-government will never work. Because there'll always be people like you" (85). Rachel, on the other hand, voices the view that what the reserve needs first and foremost are the community values of the past. "It used to be different," she says. "We took care of each other, and our children" (55). And she links this caring attitude with tolerance and respect for all people and says: "[I]t's time to make things right. To say goodbye to the things that keep us down. Our people's future comes from the past. Not male or female. Pure or mixed. Christian or Traditional. It's all these things. Together. Respected" (88).

The end of the play suggests that this pluralist approach is indeed the future of the Reserve. Sitting on the steps of the newly renamed Partridge Crop Pentecostal Church of the Creator, Sheldon says, "I've never seen nothing like that before. Half this place Christians. Half Traditional. And nobody fighting. That's good eh?" (90). Even gender distinctions are blurred with a touch of comic cross-dressing when Rachel asks Sheldon, "How come you got a woman's shoe on?" and he replies, "Me and Melvin couldn't find my other one, so we went to the dump. I liked this one" (91). Ironically, the problem of poverty actually becomes part of the solution here, as it creates the conditions that enable the creative and healing blend.

The final move, which enables Melvin to feel secure in his own blended identity, is when he turns his anger outward onto the government that has marked him and made him dependent, as opposed to the other options of internalizing the anger (where it could contribute to a cycle of shame, depression, and alcoholism) or wrongfully projecting it onto innocent people (as Teddy does by hating Native Christians and Bill C-31ers). Melvin's final stance is one in which the complexity of reality is, in fact, not a stumbling block to secure identity and self-respect but the very means to them:

> I figured out I'm an Indian from these two parts of my Treaty card. See. My face is on one half and my number is on the other half. That picture is what people see. The number is what the government sees. And the card's like me. In two parts. Part white. Part Indian. And you put them together. And you get an Indian. Me. But not 'cause the government says so. 'Cause I said so. I had to get mad to find that out. That's good eh? (94)

The separation of "people" and "the government" in this passage is one key prerequisite to recognizing, distancing, critiquing, and casting off the national-imperial overdetermination of past reserve life.

A second prerequisite is reversing the normative hierarchical conception of national space and the unidirectional flow of influence and power that this configuration is based on. Reserves and Native culture are typically "placed" in the most devalued position in the top-bottom and centre-margin models of spatial relations, but Sheldon, with his usual comic wisdom, recognizes a different arrangement:

> NIGGER: [W]e're teachers. That's what Indians are. When white peoples came here a long time ago it was us who taught them. We showed them what to eat and we brought them turkey. And stuffing. And cranberries. That's what white people have Thanksgiving for. Except they don't share our turkey with us anymore.

MELVIN: Where'd you learn that?

NIGGER: In that book about Indians. That's where I know an Indian
      guy wrote *O Canada*. And you know what?

MELVIN: What?

NIGGER: We're gonna teach the white people again how to live.

MELVIN: How?

NIGGER: Lots more white people are gonna be poor. And they're gonna
      be on welfare. And because we already know how to live on
      welfare. We're gonna teach them how to live again.  (74)

Note that, while Sheldon places his people firmly in the "centre" of Canadian culture, he does so not to assume authority or superior status over
others but to promote a sharing, helpful, mutual relationship.

Taken as a whole, then, the play suggests that the means to a productive,
vital, inclusive form of First Nations' self-determination is neither to simply follow nor wholly reject the dominant model of Canadian nationalism,
but rather to borrow and redefine the concept of nation while rejecting
the destructive and restrictive elements, such as simplistic binary, hierarchical, racist, and sexist thinking, inherited as the country's legacy of empire. A
daunting task, no doubt, but one that Ross presents as both possible and
necessary.

# Relative Geographies

*2*

I have thought myself home,
run through immeasurable space
ahead of time, could not wait for it.

(Stephan G. Stephansson, "Thinking Home" 41)

The marsh up north was afire – as it had been off and on for a matter of twenty-odd years. The fire consumes on the surface everything that will burn; the ground cools down, a new vegetation springs up, and nobody would suspect – as there is nothing to indicate – that only a few feet below the heat lingers, ready to leap up again if given the opportunity.

(Frederick Philip Grove, *Over Prairie Trails* 34)

The population of Winnipeg is six hundred thousand, a fairly large city, with people who tend to stay put. Families overlap with families, neighborhoods with neighborhoods. You can't escape it. Generations interweave so that your mother's friends (Onion Boyle, Muriel Brewmaster, and dozens more) formed a sort of squadron of secondary aunts. You were always running into someone you'd gone to school with or someone whose uncle worked with someone's else's father. The tentacles of connection were long, complex, and full of the bitter or amusing ironies that characterize blood families. . . . These surprises used to drive Peter crazy, the oppressive clannishness they implied and the embarrassments, but Fay again and again is reassured and comforted to be part of a knowable network.

(Carol Shields, *The Republic of Love* 67)

Relationships between time and space are central to constructions of home places. In one model, space may gain significance from what has happened in it through time, as in the overdetermination of home by empire in Ostenso, Stead, Rebar, and Ross. Post-Einsteinian space is immeasurable, unmeasurable – thus "unknowable" – outside of time. There is no knowable space, no place, without time; we can't even recognize one without the other. But if we can't escape the interdependance of space-time, Stephansson raises an alternate homemaking possibility: the creation of home in the mind, the imagination, in mental rather than physical landscapes, and not *through* time but *ahead* of it. Anticipatory, hopeful, preemptive or projective, the performative function of thought – of language, of literature – *creates* home, independent of material conditions and history, or at least aspiring to such independence. Place becomes a function of its symbolic significance, individual or collective, psychic or mythological; geography becomes a tracing of relative and variable significances. As with Grove's burnt marsh, though, the past, or the "real," may linger just below the written surface, ready to reemerge and interfere with writerly intentions, for history, as Jameson says, "is what hurts, it is what refuses desire and sets inexorable limits to individual as well as collective praxis, which its 'ruses' turn into grisly and ironic reversals of their overt intention" (102).

The potential variety of symbolic geographies for a given space, the diversity and limits of intentions, can be seen in the writing of the area in and around Winnipeg and beyond by Kristjana Gunnars's *Zero Hour*, David Arnason's *Marsh Burning* and Laura Goodman Salverson's *Confessions of an Immigrant's Daughter*. The geographies written in these texts are all "relative" in three equally important senses: first, their differences from each other demonstrate the ways in which the significance of place is dependent on ("relative to") individual human perception; second, the histories or pasts they draw on in their inscriptions are primarily the personal ones of family and ancestors (or "relatives"); third, they each map the significance of place largely through comparison and contrast with ("in relation to") that of a variety of other places.

The three texts are also connected in that all three writers have Icelandic backgrounds: Gunnars was born in 1948 in Reykjavík, Iceland, and lived there until age sixteen, immigrating first to the United States and later to the Canadian Prairies; Arnason was born in 1940 in Gimli, Manitoba, the main settlement in the Icelandic reserve New Iceland, which was established in the 1870s on the west shore of Lake Winnipeg about sixty-five kilometres north of Winnipeg; Salverson was born in 1890 into the transplanted Icelandic community in Winnipeg. The texts also share an autobiographical element, more or less problematized: Gunnars's text is cata-logued under "biography" but can be read as a poetic, deliberately "artful" novella; Arnason's text self-consciously mixes myth and reality, putting into question the distinction between them; Salverson's text, with its mixture of romanticism and realism, presents itself as autobiography but has larger-scale epic aspirations because the ostensible "hero," Salverson, presents her-self as representative of her people's struggle to adapt to their new Canadian home.

## Kristjana Gunnars's *Zero Hour*

Like Gander Stake leaving for the city at the end of *Grain*, the narrator of Gunnars's *Zero Hour* travels to Winnipeg hoping to find a blank, uninscribed space. "To write you this," she begins her text, "I have come to the Gateway to the West. Not because the West is intriguing. But because it is there: open, dry, with little culture and much politics" (9).[1] She tries to control the meaning of the space according to her purpose in travelling there, which, since no other motive is supplied, appears to be to come to terms with her father's death, to make herself at home with it. At the opposite extreme from Shields's writing of Winnipeg as a large extended family, a "knowable network," Winnipeg for Gunnars is to be a place of no culture, no possessions, no history, no personal past; ironically, it is also the place of remembrance and, perhaps, of writing. It is a place where there is no "fixed" connection between the physical space and its symbolic significance, so Gunnars can construct Winnipeg as an appropriate setting for a physical homemaking process that in turn she constructs as an appropriate setting for her mental homemaking process.

Her text, Gunnars says, "is about the ability to start a new life" (76). While tending her father in his last days at his home in a small town in Oregon, she had often had the urge to buy a house there, thinking, *"I want to start a different life. To forget about all that has passed up to this day. I want to move here and live here forever as if nothing else existed"* (87). The desire to erase time mimics her father's journey. In the room of his deathbed, "time did not pass. All times of the day and night were the same for him" (21), and when he had earlier been hospitalized she says, "It was not the beginning of the end. It was the end. It was the countdown: five weeks to death. To zero" (29), collapsing time and erasing, if not duration itself, then at least its hu-man significance. Gunnars describes death as "the abyss of timelessness" (98) and her father's last hours as "a match of wits between him and the clock," observing, *"There is no zero on the clock.* To get to zero, you have to step outside of time" (122).

To step outside of time with her father, she must leave the place where the past is localized, and the destination she chooses is one with conventional and long-lived associations, promoted by the imperial vision, with both spatial and temporal "emptiness." Mirroring this emptiness, Gunnars leaves "Regina city,"[2] where she was writer in residence, with only a very small red car, one red dress, and a typewriter. Even the dress is stripped of history, for she says, "It was a dress I had never worn" (13), and on the drive to Winnipeg she has a comic battle with the car's odometer, which can be read as a vain attempt to erase space and time from her perception: "Suddenly the odometer was showing an incredible distance covered in a remarkably short time. The numbers rolled around on the meter at breakneck speed. I punched it back to zero and it rolled forward again equally fast. I punched it back to zero again and again" (18). Yet even in her minimalist approach to travel we see, ironically, the way in which history creeps in, cannot be avoided, for the colour of her car and dress – red – is overwhelmingly associated with her father in the rest of the book: he has a red typewriter, red table, red cabinet, red cap, red letters on his clock radio, red azaleas in his garden, and at his burial place "the sunrise spreads its red wings over the waiting land" (124). Like the scientists' hypothetical temperature "absolute zero" (Asimov 304), absolute degree zero *living* is unattainable, try as Gunnars might to achieve it.

There is an element of environmentalism in Gunnars's description of her parents' home place: "I had forgotten what a luscious, mild, damp, gentle climate does to wake up the sleeping soul and give rise to human affection and generosity. I had forgotten how such openness takes away all fear and makes you able to trust again" (87). But when she projects her desire for absence onto the prairie space she is aware that her projection is just that: "It seems quiet, but that is an illusion. The quiet is in the soul" (9). Similarly, of the desert-like "high prairie" southwest of Regina she says she had the frequent thought

> that a place could not be more empty than this and still be a place. Yet I knew it was not true. There was plenty there if one cared to analyze the minutiae of the prairie soil and plains scrub. Plenty of insects, wild plants, particles in the air. But it was a mental emptiness of a kind: as if no one had ever walked here before.
>
> It is an unnamed place, I thought. A landscape without language. Before language.
>
> Then one day I discovered how wrong I was. (22-23)

Encountering a Cree powwow in progress, she must admit the presence of culture, tradition and history, which she (like the earlier colonists) wanted to deny, but even this she tries to "reduce" in some way: the grieving dancers, she realizes, *"were not talking.* It was pure loss. Loss without commentary" (25).

Feeling that she has "come to that place in life where there is nothing below" (9), the narrator muses on the possibility of a language to mirror her psychic state, which she refers to as "ground zero" writing, a reference to Roland Barthes's "degree zero" writing. By analogy to the linguistic concept of neutral or zero elements between polarities, such as the "amodal" indicative between the subjunctive and imperative moods, consisting in their absence, Barthes posits a neutral, colourless language, a non-style or oral-style, a "style of absence which is almost an ideal absence of style" (77), which finds its purity in the absence of signs. This transparent form, he argues, conjures an "Orphean dream" of "a writer without literature" (5), and what he calls art with "the very structure of suicide" (75). He concedes, however, that you *can't* escape the past and "ancestral and all-powerful signs" (86), and he sees this as the tragic element in writing: degree zero writing is an impossibility, except as silence.[3]

Tongue-in-cheek, Gunnars suggests the same, when she says that she imagines degree-zero writing to be "a writing in which the author does not know what to do" (10), and she packs the first few pages of her text with intertextual references to other authors and theorists, as if to make clear, perhaps ironically, that *she does* know what to do. But she also speaks of the need for language without meaningless "intellectual decoration" (27-28), which she associates with "a laundering of emotions" (17), and in general her language is stripped-down, clear and direct, using relatively simple vocabulary and syntactical structures. She says that her father's "final story is no longer possible to write. It cannot be sentimentalized. It cannot keep its emotive qualities. It cannot be told as a story," so we "are left with a story that is not a story. A novel that is not a novel, a poem no longer a poem" (29). She also gives us doctors' language, "without decoration" (39), which reduces life and death issues to "a matter of numbers" (42), and which is also the language of science and math that her geophysicist father spoke. The "reduction" of language is thus also a kind of homecoming, a homage, and also, perhaps, a making up for her childhood failure on a math exam (52-53).

Births and deaths, Gunnars says, are events that change you "from one person into another, . . . like moving into a new home. The old one was familiar. You were comfortable, you had a routine, you recognized the neighborhood. The new home is an empty shell. The street is unfamiliar, the neighbors are strangers, the smells, sounds, colors are jarring. There is no furniture, no rug, no lamp" (12). Her Winnipeg apartment is bare and white, a "blessedly empty and private place," and she thinks, "I want to put nothing in here. To let it stay empty. I want to be free" (27). The absence of material possessions mimics the erasure of history that she seeks, but she has not, like her father, escaped time itself. As she had observed that "life does not pass; it accumulates" (26), so she cannot maintain the zero condition of her living space: First "I bought a mug to drink coffee from. Soon I had a huge house with many rooms, lots of light, and one ceramic mug. It was a relief to have nothing, but I suspected it would not last" (34), and then,

> [a]s I suspected, items began to float into the second floor window of the mansion I had acquired as my own for a while in the Gateway city. A kettle, fashioned in Holland out of black steel. A white plate, a black saucer, a white cup. A pad to sleep on, two pillows. Two deep blue towels. A garden chair and table, white, began to stand in the sunroom. Here I put my typewriter.
>
> I sometimes think it is not possible to keep an empty life. Life itself is material. It was a comfort of a kind to know that all the items around me were things I had never seen before. (49)

Denying her own agency in the accumulation, she also wishes to view the new items as historyless, but as with her red dress earlier there are ironic suggestions that even here the past is not being escaped. While the "deep blue towels" and her "navy blue sheet" (64) suggest a local adaptation, displacing the past as they mirror the "deep blue, navy" water of the Red River (75), the garden furniture in her sunroom where she does her writing replicates her father's patio furniture in his garden where he did his writing.

As her apartment functions as an image of her symbolic death and rebirth, so Winnipeg, with its coding as the "Gateway city," functions as a transformative site. Gunnars writes it as a temporary home, a transitional place, not only in her personal geography but also in its larger socioeconomic function:

> This is where the grain that grows in the vast fields between the Shield Country and the Rockies is gathered and stored. From here it is distributed to the East. This is also where the goods manufactured in the East are collected, sometimes assembled, and sent onto the dispersed farm

hamlets and colonies, the tiny country communities with one church at
the center of town. This is the city of the warehouses. (19)

Winnipeg acts as the collection, assembly and distribution point for Gunnars's
memorial act, as well as the place where her journey literally and figuratively "turns around." That she refers to it as the "Gateway to the West"
seems odd, given that that suggests an approach from the east, when she
approached from the west, from Oregon via Regina. Winnipeg, then, should
function as the gateway to the East, or at least as the back door of the West.

The physical trip eastward, however, functions rather differently in
Gunnars's symbolic geography, for she has said that "beyond the West there
is the ocean. The jungle. The rains. That is a place to long for. To think
towards. I think towards the western coastline of this continent, where mist
is in the air" (9). Like Stephansson "thinking home," Gunnars thinks toward the West Coast in the sense that the trip eastward was one into the
memories that are localized on the Coast. Oregon is the site of the past that
she recreates in the present on the Prairies. And Oregon may also function
as the thought-toward *future* in the sense that only through coming to
terms with the past and its pain can she be at home, and "move on" with
her life. Thus, when the "novelty of being alone" (101) begins to fade, she
sees that her days in Winnipeg are "drawing to a close" (102), and she is
reminded that it is "moving season" by a condominium developer's tempt-
ingly simplistic billboard slogan, *"[I]f you lived here you would be home now"*
(121).

When Gunnars has finished telling the story of her father's death, his
"going home" (123) to his "final resting place" (124), her son appears in the
text in Winnipeg, without explanation – like magic, as if because the story
is ready for him. He functions as a representation of the future, of the
continuity of generations, and with his violin playing she knows that "soon
all the empty rooms would fill with music" (127). On the literal level of the
narrative the ending is massively confusing. Why is the son suddenly in
Winnipeg? Where has he been before this, when Gunnars was presumably
alone? Is she or is she not getting ready to move from Winnipeg? If she is,
then how will the left-behind rooms be filled with music? Will the son stay
behind? These questions become less important, however, if the ending is
read for what it contributes to the text's symbolic geography and performative homemaking function. It adds a future tense to Winnipeg's inscription as an empty present in which to recollect the past, and it is at this
moment of association with "whole time" that the city appears most homelike. The literal move becomes unnecessary once Gunnars is ready to move

on, metaphorically, because this means that her internal, psychological "home place," so long under construction in the text, is ready for occupancy.

Gunnars's early attempt to achieve degree zero, then, to escape time, is replaced by an acceptance of continuity, of the past and future being like Winnipeg mosquitos: *"They were here before we arrived and they will be here after we go"* (38). And like the city's mosquito spraying, the attempt to destroy time may have been both dangerous and necessary: "Every summer Gateway people raise the issue in City Council: how do we know for sure, they ask, that this chemical will not also kill us? There is a long debate until everyone is overcome by insect bites and a tacit agreement to spray is reached" (65). Degree-zero writing is possible only as silence, and degree zero living only as death; both are, in a sense, self-contradictions. Gunnars can follow her father's journey only so far in those directions, but doing so may offer a respite from pain, however temporary and partial, a clearing of the material to ease the memorial.

Continuity of another sort is suggested when Gunnars visits the Icelandic Festival in Gimli. Among the amusement rides, boat races, barrel dunkings, selling of sweaters and ceramics, performance of music and poems, and official pomp and ceremony,

> David Arnason, the writer, stood up in his black suit and imposing grey beard. During the course of his speech, he said: Iceland has produced world class artists and achievements out of all proportion to its small size. This is because they know that talent is everywhere. *If a country wishes to survive with its culture and integrity intact, it must nurture the creative talents of its own citizens. It must protect its own culture.* (93)

*Zero Hour* rejects the folklorama version of culture, with its emphasis on easily reproducible representations (of costume, cuisine, and crafts, for example), in favour of a culture of "character." Gunnars's father tells his doctors that he comes *"from a culture where to die in bed is the worst calamity that can befall a man"* (62), and we are told that in his academic work "it was what he brought from his Nordic culture that set him apart" (83) — his kindness to his graduate students, standing by them and opening his home to them (84).

Like her earlier reference to Cree culture on the Prairies, Gunnars's invocation of Gimli and Arnason ironically undercuts (or intertextually deconstructs, if you will) the innocence that her text pretends to have about previous inscriptions, literary and otherwise, of the space around Winnipeg. The Gimli that Gunnars encounters is one written over, for instance, with the history of Icelandic settlers, some of which Gunnars herself gave poetic voice to in her earlier books *Settlement Poems 1* and *Settlement Poems 2*. Like the space the earlier immigrants travelled over and settled, "the place is bottomless with stories" (*SP1* 9), and filled with "settlement runes" (45) for deciphering, for making *into* story, as Gunnars's books do, writing significance into space, space into place.

## David Arnason's *Marsh Burning*

David Arnason has also been at work with such story-making and literary mythologizing, as in his story "The Sunfish," which provides a founding myth for Gimli and neighbouring towns involving a talking fish, fertility rituals, love potions, and family scandal. In his long poem *Marsh Burning* he is similarly concerned with writing a "domestic" Icelandic place. Like *Zero Hour*, Arnason's poem can be read as a "homeward" journey through space and time, and like Gunnars's persona, Arnason's finds himself at one point in an empty apartment in Winnipeg. Both journeys are prompted by family crises, in Gunnars's case the death of a father and in Arnason's the death of a marriage, and both texts are concerned with and enact the construction of places and selves, of place through self and self through place.

Arnason's five-part long poem[4] moves from a present story time in New Brunswick westward and forward in time to Winnipeg, and then north and backwards in time to Gimli. At the same time, it moves from a world known through received Norse mythology to one known through the discourses of modern science, to one in which myths are made out of individual experience, first those that *could be* the narrator's and then those of early Icelandic settlers. Home and the self are constructed through the movement from collective ancestral to impersonal, to personal, and then to individualized ancestral systems of language and knowing. Arnason's persona finds at one point that the mirrors in his house are beginning to warp, so "their frames twist / and the reflections they give / are crazy and askew" (269), and the poem suggests that in the absence of any unmediated access to reality we must similarly learn to perform perceptual tricks, juggling space and time and perspective:

> . . . the clock in my kitchen
>
> is reflected in the mirror in the hall
>
> so that time is backward
>
> and I must look into my eye
>
> to see the reflection
>
> reflected true (270)

The text opens in New Brunswick,[5] a landscape already far removed from that of the Prairies, here made even "stranger" by its being perceived and written as the world of Norse mythology. Thor speaks through the thunder, "rumbling and threatening in the distance / there beyond the Naashwaak / over Oman's creek" (257), Odin, the god of poetry, who gave up one eye in exchange for wisdom and knowledge of the past and future, appears in parodic form as a man who "had one good eye only / and said he was a Jehovah's Witness" (259), and Thor's warning that "the world ash is rotting / eaten from without and within" (257) – one of many signs that Ragnarök, the end of the world, is approaching – is "brought home" by a young man's warning about a tree in the persona's yard: *"you should call a tree surgeon / that ash you have is rotting from within"* (268). While this world likely appears strange and fabulous to most readers, the mythology under- lying it has been sufficiently localized and naturalized for the persona that he is not surprised by his experiences and does not question his "reading" of them. He presents his narrative as objective, neutral description; the landscape appears inscribed at all only from the reader's ironic point of view.

Elsewhere, in *The Icelanders*, a kind of "poem about ancestors" (7),[6] Arnason has written about his childhood in Gimli and the process involved in such localizing of myth and naturalizing of perceptual and cognitive structures:

> It's hard for a child, and not much easier for an adult, to separate the myths from the reality, one kind of story from another, and that's why the landscape of the Interlake is forever charged for me with the unseen presence of heroes. My grandfather used to tell me stories from the Ice- landic sagas but he didn't tell me that those stories were literature. What was the point? It would make no difference to a child. And so, when he told me the story of Grettir Asmundson, Grettir the strong, who swam the half mile from the mainland to the island carrying fire and the fire didn't go out, I assumed that Grettir lived on Hekla Island, and that he had swum from Riverton. When he told me the sad story of the burning of Njal, I assumed that Njal was a couple of miles west, probably between Sigurdson's farm and Narfarson's. I'd seen the charred remains of some old shack or granary, and assumed that was likely the place.
>
> That's the way stories get rooted in a new land. (110)

The persona of *Marsh Burning* has transplanted the imaginative geography of the Interlake region onto the New Brunswick space, but if this is one type of "homemaking" strategy, it is shown to have limitations. For one thing, the "immediacy" of the mythological dimension of the landscape takes place within a general failure of all other communication systems: the nearby power station is three times struck by lightning (260, 263), a bridge is damaged by flooding (265), telephone and mail and television systems go haywire (266), and "radio signals are strong / stations from as far away as Texas / crowd and jostle so / that nothing can be heard (267).

A second limitation to the homemaking potential of transplanting myth is that while the ability to read the signs of place is an important part of feeling at home or secure in a space, the signs from Norse mythology that the persona reads here are all about impending disaster. He says, "there are things I must know / if I am to protect my family" (259), and the knowledge he does gain prompts the urgent refrain, "I must make plans" (270, 271), and the closing imperative, "I must go" (273). The journey he first imaginatively projects and later undertakes is the homeward one along the "route to Gimli":

> past Thunder Bay  Kenora  bursting free
>
> at last into the open prairie
>
> right at Winnipeg  then north
>
> and I am
>
> home (262)

There is comfort in the "knownness" of this route, the sense that it is well-travelled and familiar, as well as in the anticipated physical and psychic release that following it offers. There is comfort too in the ease with which the destination is described, the one-word line "home," and in the easy grammatical, spatial and psychological identification of the subject *with* that destination. "I *am* home," the persona says, anticipating the text's construction of self and place simultaneously and through each other.

Section 2 of the poem opens with the actual move back to the former and remembered home place. The "pull" of this place is so powerful that it acts as its own energy source, creating and sustaining movement:

> past the elevator at Dufresne
>
> we slid faster and faster
>
> the road becoming flatter as we moved
>
> as if the car no longer needed power
>
> but could glide
>
> did glide
>
> into the heart of that prairie

> into Winnipeg
>
> into home (274)

In the earlier projected journey, "home" was Gimli, and Winnipeg was on the route there; the last two lines of *this* passage *could* indicate a spatial progression of the same sort – first into Winnipeg, then into home – but the parallelism of the lines also suggests an alternate symbolic geography, one in which Winnipeg and home have grammatical and semantic equivalence, meaning either that Winnipeg simply *is* home or that Winnipeg and Gimli are now considered parts of the same place.

Such a collapsing or identification of spaces involves an expansion of the notion of place from referring to a single point on a map to something approaching a region. In this particular case the manoeuvre draws on the popular dual-home "cottage culture" that connects Winnipeggers, especially in the summertime, to various spots along the shores of Lake Winnipeg, and we can see this connection in the swift locative shift across a later stanza break:

> intricate patterns on the wing of a moth
>
> stunning itself against the light bulb
>
> above my cottage door
>
> leaning against the balcony
>
> on the fourteenth floor of the Regency Towers
>
> Winnipeg spread out before us this night (275)

The idea of the "dual-home" is complicated in Arnason's case by the traditional "second home," the cottage, being placed at the site of his first, or originary, home, Gimli, and this slippage enables an ironic reading of the persona's attempted homecoming, for while the two home spaces first appear to have equivalence, it soon becomes clear that Winnipeg does not in fact share the "homely" significance of its northerly neighbour.

The persona's homecoming is also ironic in that its intended effect, the "protection" of his family, does not occur. Instead, the text presents us with his "circumambulations of desire," a motel-room affair with a woman met at a blood-donor clinic and picked up at a church, the slow, uneven disintegration of the marital relationship, his wife's voice "across the table in the bar, . . . flat and hard," saying "this is the way it ends," and "my daughter's letter in my pocket / *Daddy please come home* / like acid working on the hardest stone" (280). The fundamental fatalism of Norse mythology, the underlying knowledge that the eventual destruction of all creation is inevitable and inescapable (Crossley-Holland xix), is in this second section given a modern twist. All sense of agency and responsibility for the disintegration of the family unit is displaced onto the scientific principle of entropy, the idea that systems, when left on their own, will tend toward disorder. The "dying of desire" is measured by "one tick / of the entropy clock," and is depicted as a "natural" part of

> the neutral distillations of decay
>
> slow fire in the heart of rocks
>
> wet burning in the trunks of dying trees
>
> each to its elements
>
> phosphorous nitrogen carbon from clay
>
> split/shattered (279)

Agency is further suppressed or denied through the larger pattern of failed intentions and expectations that the text has established prior to this point. For instance, the dwarves on the persona's front lawn in New Brunswick "could not expect a ride / but a half-ton Ford stopped near them / they leaped into the box and it was gone" (260), his neighbour has a glass eye, "a jewelled eye / with a clock in the centre" on which the numbers and hand movement are backwards so that "he can read it in a mirror," but "the clock is always wrong" (261), Canadians rush wheat to the people of "Bangla Desh" [sic], which "they will not touch / preferring famine" (264), and after moving back to Winnipeg the persona finds that "again that year the world failed to end" (274). Yet, while the text insists upon the "randomness of order" (274), there is also a hint of the order in randomness when the persona and his soon-to-be lover part at the blood-donor clinic, "having given just enough clues / that [they] might accidentally meet again" (276).

An uneasy combination of fate and free will, action and inaction, then, leads the persona to a personal wasteland of sorts, an apartment of "polar emptiness" with a "blank waste of rugs" and "barren sweep of wall" (280) in a "frozen city" (281). Continuing the entropy metaphor and also suggesting the idea of "midlife crisis," the second section of the poem ends on a pivotal note:

> my life half over
>
> poised on the fulcrum of descent
>
> I lie on my mattress

> on the floor
>
> in a room without furniture
>
> paintings haphazard
>
> on the hooks of former tenants
>
> my books in boxes
>
> filled with lies
>
> about beginnings and endings. (281)

The empty apartment, as in Gunnars's *Zero Hour*, functions as a site for recollecting the past, and the "descent" that begins in Section 3 of the poem is into memory; the forward-moving narrative line is abruptly broken, and we are placed back in time, into a past that is, significantly, located not in Winnipeg but in Gimli. This structural movement in time and space can, then, be read as yet another homecoming attempt.

*Marsh Burning* itself resists "lies" about beginnings and endings, the apparently deceptive ease of coherent, linear narrative, in favour of a structure that spirals back on itself, mimicking the persona's desire to return home at a point of crisis, to "reground" himself before moving on. And again, this spiral movement is part of a larger pattern of circle imagery and metaphor that the text has already established. While the lure of the linear is suggested in the persona's wondering if he is perhaps experiencing "the final spring" (271) and his noticing, just before leaving his New Brunswick home, "that pattern in the tiles" of "broken circles" (273), the overriding textual pattern is one in which circles only appear to be broken. A neighbour who attempts suicide is "found and saved" (272), the persona on his way to Winnipeg passes "the burned out forest deadfall / now greening again" (273), and even Ragnarök, the apparent end of the world, is deceptively unfinal, for after it a new cycle of time and life will begin, the few survivors repeopling the world, so that "[t]he end will contain a beginning" (Crossley-Holland xxxviii). Even the entropy metaphor takes an ironic and circular twist if we consider that it is only in closed systems of equilibrium that entropy results in disorganization and disintegration – in non-equilibrium conditions, the randomness associated with entropy can actually lead to higher levels of organization, order, and life.[7]

This pattern of subverted finality is continued in Section 3 of the poem, where a hawk circles overhead (283, 288) as a predatorial reminder that life comes from death, and this suggestion is also implicit in the idea of marsh burning, which operates as both title and metaphor for the whole poem.

The end of Section 3 describes the persona's grandfather's yearly spring burning of the dead marsh growth: "With a can of gasoline and his torch / he walks the edge of the lagoon / touching the dried reeds and rushes *into life*" (290, my emphasis). No motive is given within the text for this activity, but it is sometimes done to clear out the edges of the marshes so that birds can nest there,[8] so it is simultaneously a destructive and creative act, akin to the poet's need to clear space within the existing discursive systems for new articulation and, perhaps, to the need to break apart a family unit to make way for new growth, to destroy one home in order to create a new one.

There is both potential and danger in this wiping out of the old, for

> One year the fire did not stop
>
> but circled our house
>
> so we had to go out with wet sacks
>
> beating at the flames.
>
> We saved the house
>
> then looked to Old Arni's shack
>
> a half a mile away
>
> where flames still leaped and danced.
>
> We tried to help him
>
> the old man blind and crying
>
> but it was much too late. (290-91)

Once again, intentions do not correspond to realities, apparently innocent actions can have devastating consequences, especially for those who are involved only peripherally or by circumstance, an old blind neighbour or the daughter whose letter pleads with her father to return. There is further irony in the marsh-burning metaphor too, in that while on the surface it appears that the old is done away with in order to make way for the new, the new growth actually comes from the same old roots – there is no escaping the past; circles, when broken, reappear as spirals, and the persona can begin a new life only by returning to his "roots" and building from them.

Section 3 of the poem operates structurally to suggest just such a building process and presents itself as a dramatization of the way in which place is inscribed with significance. It begins with a collection of minimal images and statements that in themselves carry little meaning for the reader, and then it expands on each of them, so that when at the end of the section the first portion is repeated it has taken on a very different and much fuller meaning. For instance, the story of the marsh burning first appears merely as "a fire when it's / much too late" (282), which could refer to just about anything or absolutely nothing, depending on the experiences and knowledge that the reader brings to the text. In each case Arnason's poem works to create meaning by moving toward specificity, concreteness, the familial, familiar, and personal, so "strawberries on a bed of clay" (282) become "strawberries yellowing into red / against a bed of clay / in my grandmother's garden / between the spruces and the lilac bush" (283), and then are moved into a present tense memory narrative:

> Strawberries are yellowing into red
>
> in a bed of clay in my grandmother's garden
>
> between the spruces by the railway fence
>
> and the row of lilacs
>
> at the edge of the lawn.
>
> My grandmother is watering her peonies.
>
> I want a strawberry
>
> but they are not ripe. (284)

The poem insists again and again that it isn't things themselves that are important, but "the hold the mind takes / on these things" (282, 284), and the same could be said of physical landscapes or spaces. Spaces are like signifiers that can potentially be attached to any signified, but if the connection between them is in theory arbitrary, the poem suggests that once connections are made through and by personal experience they are not easily altered or broken. The layers of the persona's personal memories are what enable the gradual inscription of significance on "Gimli," which construct it as "place," as "home."

Section 4 of the poem continues this gradual accrual of meaning through the listing of objects and narration of story fragments that appear to be personal memories centred around Gimli, and the fifth section adds further layers of significance by moving further back in time, presenting found and fabricated textual fragments in the voices of the nineteenth-century Icelandic settlers who began the process of inscription that Arnason's poem now continues. The first-person narrative "I," which up to this point has been identifiable as referring to basically the same "self" (a pseudo-autobiographical or autofictional representative of "Arnason" at various points in time), is here radically displaced and dispersed. We no longer have any clear sense of who is speaking, or how many different people are speaking, and the chief effect of this is to suggest that the previous "I" has been or is now creating itself through these others, through their pasts, which once were as personal as his own but which now appear public, as "history," and many of the stories share common themes across the generations: home, family, children, heart-ache, death, decay, fire, failed intentions, and the break-down of communication systems. As the poem says, "this has happened before / it will happen again" (313).

This final section of the poem is also structured as a circle, or spiral, which turns back both on itself and on the poem as a whole. While we might have expected Gimli to be the "source" of the Norse mythology found in the first section, when we actually get there with Arnason's ances-tors we find instead "thunder without a godhead, lightning that strikes although it isn't thrown" (302). This suggests the persona's "progression" through successive discursive systems, abandoning each in search of some-thing more personal, meaningful or adequate, but at the end of this last section all the previous systems are picked up again, juxtaposed, and offered collectively in a ritual invocation of

> all the miraculous molecules
>
> knitting and un-
>
> ravelling  electricity
>
> bathed in a sea of amino acids
>
> nucleotides  bending with the moon
>
> blood and sap mingled on a cross
>
> Fenrir
>
> > with the sun and the moon
>
> in his belly
>
> > > Odin and Thor
>
> jostled by the random vectors of entropy
>
> > > > (a hard journey over snow
>
> > > > smallpox
>
> > > > > scarring the moon
>
> > > > death by drowning
>
> > > > death by fire). (314)

We are given no "happy ending" as in Gunnars's text, no sense of a fully constructed or "recovered" and coherent self moving forward, securely, in time. We are left instead with "fragments / of a vision / fragments of a life" (314), but there is a final irony in the text's aspiration for this to be "the end / the final tie / the line broken / the circle closed" (313), for a closed circle is also, necessarily, a continuous line that can have no end. There can be no "final tie" because generations follow generations. Life follows and grows from death, the text has insisted, and if there is no escape from the past there is also no escape from the present and the future; the empty apartment in Winnipeg, the site of recollection, is no longer as empty as it was when we left it. Memories have accumulated in it, just as objects did in Gunnars's apartment, and memories, this text suggests, are what make a space a place, a place a home, a home place.

## Laura Goodman Salverson's
## *Confessions of an Immigrant's Daughter*

While Winnipeg functions chiefly as the *site of home recollection* in Gunnars's and Arnason's texts, it appears primarily as the *recollected home site* in Salverson's text. The turn-of-the-century "muddy village" (19), far from being a place of empty apartments, no memory, and little culture, is for Salverson a place of full houses, many significant memories, and much culture. The full reasons for her choice of Winnipeg as prime home site, however, emerge from her account only obliquely, through its comparison with the many other locations in the text's complex physical, symbolic, and economic geography. In other words, home, for her, is a relative concept.

The intricate interconnection between history and geography in Salverson's imagination is demonstrated early on in her text through her lengthy historico-geographical account of the Winnipeg Hospital, where her father undergoes an operation for an "abscess in the lower brain" (9), and that "the old-timers saw as a symbol of the height of humanitarian progress in the west" (90). In addition to such obsessive historical accuracy of detail as naming all fifteen of the men on the hospital's founding board of directors, she presents an extensive locative summary, running to nearly two pages, and beginning thus:

> The first building occupied by the hospital was owned by Mr William Harvey, and was situated on the north-west corner of McDermot and Albert Streets, where the once-famed Marriaggi Hotel afterwards stood. This became the Winnipeg General Hospital. The accommodation here was, however, quickly exhausted, and the hospital was moved to other

quarters, somewhere in the rear of the present Bank of Montreal, and shortly thereafter to yet another house on Notre Dame Avenue, owned by Dr Shultz. From there the hospital was transferred to premises owned by Mr John McTavish, situated on the Red River, south of Broadway Bridge. (89)

And so on and so on, Salverson records a seemingly improbable number of moves, one after another. Since the history of the hospital is tangential, at best, to Salverson's "life story," it is tempting to speculate that she includes it here because it captured her geographical imagination by mirroring, in a sense, her own family's history of nearly constant movement.

Salverson's epic autobiography begins *in medias res* with her family's move back to her birthplace, Winnipeg, after brief stints living in Minnesota and North Dakota. The first of many such "retreats," the book's opening thus establishes the pattern of departure and return that it will follow throughout. From Winnipeg, her family moves to the small community of Selkirk, Manitoba, and then back to Winnipeg. This is followed by a move to Duluth, Minnesota, then south to Buckatunna, Mississippi, back north to Duluth and, completing the backtracking trail, to Winnipeg in 1912, when she was twenty-two years old. Salverson then moves briefly on her own to Duluth and back to Winnipeg in 1913, and then, with her new husband and son, she moves in succession to Regina, Winnipeg, Prince Albert, Regina, Edmonton (with short trips back to Gimli and Winnipeg to do research for her first novel), and Calgary, where the narrative ends with the publication of *The Viking Heart* in 1923.

Each of the locations along this complex itinerary has its own range of associations. North Dakota, for instance, is presented as a fabulous, isolated and rather scary place, populated with witches and gnomes, haunted by imaginary wolves, "the savage tongues of this dark land, itself the voice of the wilderness" (11), and warmed only by distant farmhouse lights "in the midst of an ocean of darkness" (12). Selkirk is open and wild, "untamed," inhabited by Métis people whose culture Salverson's family doesn't understand, and thus tends to fear. The deep south, Mississippi, is also presented in fantastic, unreal terms, as a primitive backwoods, "what seemed empty wilderness" (296) with a "primeval" village, "old as time" (298), and marked by extreme social divisions and restrictions based on both gender and race. Saskatchewan in general is presented as isolated, poor, and labour conscious, while Alberta is prosperous and spacious, with plenty of time and leisure for writing.

The symbolic value of the family's various destinations is also determined in part by frequency. When transience is the rule, as it is here, rather
than the exception, frequency can take on a weight normally assigned to
duration. The Salverson family's numerous moves contain one major and
two minor looping patterns, which are more easily seen when diagrammed
in outline form:[9]

|      | Iceland (parents immigrate) → |
|------|-------------------------------|
| 1887 | Winnipeg (Laura's birth 1890) → Minnesota → North Dakota → |
|      | Winnipeg → Selkirk → |
|      | Winnipeg → Duluth → Mississippi → Duluth → |
| 1912 | Winnipeg → Duluth → |
| 1913 | Winnipeg (Laura marries) → Regina → |
|      | Winnipeg → Prince Albert → Regina → Edmonton |
|      | [Winnipeg visits] → |
| 1923 | Calgary (Laura publishes first book) |

The minor loops are around Regina and Duluth, which are returned to
once and two times respectively, while the major loop is around Winnipeg,
which is returned to at least six times, five of these after aborted attempts to
settle comfortably elsewhere.

Numbers alone can tell us that there *is* significance, and asking why the
returns took place provides several possible answers to *what* the significance
is. Duluth, for instance, is attractive as a site of extended family relations and
childhood friends. It is the home of Salverson's aunt, her father's sister, with
whom they can stay during economic hard times, who runs a home for
unwed mothers, and who provides Salverson with a more active, robust,
and worldly view of womanhood than her mother does. It thus paradoxically represents both security (the known and familiar) and excitement
(the unknown and possibility).

Regina, on the other hand, appears as a kind of literary centre in Salverson's
geography. She reports the existence there of a "literary society which met
every week in the public library," and her attendance at "the outstanding
event of the winter, . . . a little party given in honour of Mrs McClung, who
had just returned from England, and was lecturing in Regina. Just an intimate, friendly gathering, at the home of Mr and Mrs McLeod, but, for me,
it was a memorable occasion – my first introduction to a Canadian author"
(399). By providing evidence of both local and national interest in and
production of literature, Regina offers an attractive and nurturing sense of
community for Salverson as a beginning writer.[10] Yet here, as with so many
of her other moves, there is also an underlying economic motive – both of

her moves to Regina are to follow her husband, whose job with the railway takes him there.

Like Duluth, Winnipeg is a site of family significance, but it is so more in terms of major life events, being her parents' original destination from Iceland and also her own birthplace. In addition, it provides an alternate kind of extended family through its strong and supportive Icelandic community, which, despite the very harsh living conditions, is keeping Norse spirit and culture alive. It is a place not near "centres of civilization" (29), but where in times of crisis the Icelandic community can be counted on to band together for aid and comfort. Like Regina, however, Winnipeg has a key economic association, in this case with readily available, if less-than-attractive, jobs. Time and again Salverson's father leaves Winnipeg in search of a "better life," usually in the form of self-employment or land ownership, and time and again he is forced back into "The Saddlery" sweatshop system he both despises and depends on for sustenance.

The desire to move or to "stay put" is highly gendered in Salverson's text, with her father representing the spirit of wanderlust and her mother representing the opposite, the desire to stay rooted in one place. Her mother romanticizes Iceland, her old home, as a place "where life moved with dignity" (33), and she opposes every single move the family makes away from Winnipeg, which she views as the next best thing to her ideal home. Salverson describes this difference in outlook as "a conflict which was never to end, and precluded any solid, satisfying home life, in the conventional sense" (17). As might be expected, this gendering of home also extends to her mother's role within the domestic realm, which Salverson describes as that of "a commanding executive" (107).

Salverson, a practical feminist, rejects the domestic role her mother tries to train her into, affiliating herself more closely with her father's spirit of adventure, and she blames her mother for alienating her from her father: "[I]t was papa who came nearer to understanding me. That this incipient understanding was not permitted to grow and outlast childhood was, I think, my mother's fault. In the end, she weaned me completely away, made an alien of the parent whose vagaries I share, and, as I now know, diverted my normal instincts into channels of activity for which I had no natural talent" (108). Yet on other occasions she has a certain critical distance from her father's footloose philosophy, as when he engineers the family's departure for Mississippi: "[A]gainst every one's counsel, and to mamma's heartbreak, he sold the house and everything else that mamma's economy had made possible, and off we went on the mad adventure" (205). Salverson actually embodies a mix of both her parents' temperaments, and she once even admits that she "longed, as never before, for the warmth of the kitchen, the reassuring hum of the old copper kettle" (204–05).

Ironically, on several occasions Salverson's father forces the family to move but then isn't able to follow them himself. For instance, he sends his wife and children ahead to set up house on "a piece of land on the outskirts of Selkirk" (152) with the intent of joining them as soon as he has the finances in order. Salverson says, "I at least hoped his dream would come true . . . Oh well, he did join us for the occasional weekend – which is perhaps all that dreamers deserve in a world such as this" (154, original ellipsis), and the family ends up moving back to Winnipeg before he has a chance to join them. Similarly, on the first move to Duluth the mother and children are on their own at first: "Father was still in Winnipeg, you see, working off our fares and saving for his own" (180), and on their second stay in Duluth he is forced to leave early: "In the fall papa's job played out, and he went to Winnipeg" (346). Then: "In the late spring papa wrote to us from Winnipeg that he had a permanent job with my uncle, and had taken a small house" (353), and so the family moves back up to join him.

In a further ironic twist, this pattern is later replicated in Salverson's relationship with her husband, an American railway man named George. When they are first married she insists that they must live in Winnipeg, despite its lower economic prospects:

> We set up house in prophetic fashion, with a few sticks of furniture bought on the instalment plan, on a salary of eighty dollars, less than half of what he had been getting in the United States, where the cost of living was a great deal lower than in Canada. But I had the fixed notion that here I must live. I supposed I wanted to feel rooted somewhere, to feel that, other things failing, I had at least some sort of spiritual home. (375)

Yet in the very next paragraph economics wins out: George loses his Winnipeg job, finds a position in Regina, and Salverson moves without a word of complaint.

The pattern continues: "[George], who had never been free of an office in his life, caught the sort of fever every living creature suffers at least once in a lifetime. He wanted to go on the land, to revel in the marvels of the wide open spaces" (379). But his desire is as much economic as anything else: "[N]ow George had the grand vision of the independent life of a landowner! Shades of dear papa's dream!" (381). He returns to Winnipeg, alone, to work in Winnipeg and save the money to file a claim on a piece of land forty kilometres north of Prince Albert, eventually moves Salverson in to set up residence, and then returns, alone again, to Winnipeg to continue working to finance the new venture. Like her father with his Selkirk dream, Salverson's husband is never able to settle himself on his land, and the couple soon ends up back in southern Saskatchewan.

When Salverson and her husband move to Edmonton, she says, "[I] used up my flagging energy getting settled" yet again, and says, "It was the first real home I had ever had. And I had it exactly thirty days!" (410) before the next move is under way. Her description here of Edmonton as her first "real home" is odd, since, despite the nearly constant moving she has experienced throughout her life, Winnipeg does acquire a status something like a "primary home place" in her text. It is the geographical centre and the primary point of return in both her life and her text, and it eventually acquires a magical magnetic quality beyond the economic and familial attractions it offers.

When she returns there from Duluth, for instance, she says she experiences what she always does on returning to "the golden west": "a quite irrational thrill, as though something in the air itself is a missing part of me, and that now I am complete. A queer sense of coming home that has nothing to do with houses or people, or any tangible thing acceptable to reason" (356). This "queer sense" of intimate belonging – of belonging at the very level of being and identity – is nothing if not what we normally think of as one quality of a "real home," in the ideal sense of that term. We should not, though, expect literal consistency in this, of all texts. Ironically, for a text that is so much about memory, Salverson's seems to lack any memory of itself, erasing itself as it goes along so that the narrative is unaware of itself from one moment to the next, engendering numerous ironies and contradictions. From Salverson's point of view, this isn't a problem, though, but a natural extension of the subjective nature of all knowledge. For, if space and home are relative for her, as her symbolic geography suggests, then so is "reality: . . . bound as we are within the individual consciousness," she says, "truth is a purely relative term" (95).

# Centres of Gravity

*3*

Until two weeks ago this place had been home – a place to come to from the field, from the bush, from school.

(Martha Ostenso, Wild Geese 72)

One of those places you leave
but want to come back to.

(Lorna Crozier, "Home Town," Angels 109)

Originally home meant the center of the world – not in a geographical, but in an ontological sense. Mircea Eliade has demonstrated how home was the place from which the world could be founded. A home was established, as he says, "at the heart of the real." In traditional societies, everything that made sense of the world was real; the surrounding chaos existed and was threatening, but it was threatening because it was unreal. Without a home at the center of the real, one was not only shelterless, but also lost in non-being, in unreality. Without a home everything was fragmentation.

(John Berger, And Our Faces, My Heart, Brief as Photos 55-56)

the horses   pawing the empty fall
the hot breath on the zero day   the man
seeing the new man so vainly   alone

we say with your waiting wife   (but she
was the world  before you invented it
old liar)   "You had a hard trip?"

(Robert Kroetsch, "F.P. Grove: The Finding," SHP 47)

Just as the sense of place itself can be variously constructed, so the *place* of place in relation to home is multiple. In one version, itself multiple, the home place appears as a powerful centre – physical, imaginary, psychological, or emotional – around which the individual self can orbit and, occasionally, land. The "pull" of home reveals itself in the tensions between arrivals and departures, presences and absences, desires and fulfillments, attractions and repulsions. Like gravity, this sense of home is often visible only through its effects. It is a force, a form of energy, as much as a substantial entity, but this force is generated by two "massive," attracted, even massively attracted, objects, and in this case the subject-object, the object that is granted subjectivity within the literary work, usually calls the other object "home." Though home also "calls" the subject, it rarely, perhaps can never, in a paradoxical sense, itself become subject, can never speak itself, for if it does it is transformed into something else, with an elsewhere and other home of its own. The subject becomes unstable object for its other; we enter the slippery territory of human relationships, the pushes and pulls of the grammars of love.

What constitutes the home place, then, Berger's "center of the real," may be thought of as something with great metaphorical weight or mass *vis-à-vis* the literary subject, and these "centres of gravity" are variously written of and around in Frederick Philip Grove's *Over Prairie Trails*, Lorna Crozier's *Inventing the Hawk* and Dennis Cooley's *this only home*. In Grove's and Cooley's texts, central male protagonists circle a home that telescopes from the microscopic to the macroscopic, from the tiny world of the single domestic unit in the former to the planet earth, a cosmic view, in the latter. Crozier's poetry works with home on a scale closer to Grove's, and approaches it somewhat oppositely from the other two texts, from the inside rather than the outside, as it were. Yet, despite their differences, the three texts display, at their cores, a remarkably similar sense of the home place as a grounding that somehow enables, and sometimes provokes, various forms of flight.

## Frederick Philip Grove's *Over Prairie Trails*

Grove's autobiographical sketches in *Over Prairie Trails* document his weekly travels by horse-and-buggy and cutter between the town in southern Manitoba where he lived during the week teaching school and the place where he spent his weekends, some fifty-four kilometres to the north in the bush where his wife lived, taught school, and took care of their young daughter. This domestic space, or family residence, he once refers to as his "wife's cottage" (81), but he also repeatedly refers to it as "home." Oddly, in half these references, an apparently random selection, he uses quotation marks around the word in his text, suggesting some anxiety about the instability of its meaning.[1] In contrast, he also refers several times to his house in town as "home," but never in quotation marks. The doubleness of his home cannot in itself account for Grove's anxiety, then, for only one "half" of it is, through punctuation, placed in doubt.

Like Josephine Burge's melancholy reference in *Grain* to "the place that [she calls] home" (180), Grove's use of quotation marks points to a disjunction between language and reality, between ideal and material, in his conception of home. When he uses the term "homelike" to describe two sets of farm buildings along his route, the defining feature is their being sheltered in bluffs, one "of planted cottonwoods" (16) and the other natural, "of tall, dark-green poplars" (17), giving it what he later calls "that friendly, old-country expression" (23), which seems to consist for him in the human landscape being well fitted to the natural one. His immigrant history[2] shows itself in his association of the old country, Europe, with *gemütlichkeit*, comfort, hominess, hospitality, familiarity, and safety, when speaking of a dinner visit to the home of friends in town: "How sheltered, homelike and protected everything looked inside. The hostess, as usual, was radiantly amiable. The host settled back after supper to talk old country. The Channel Islands, the French Coast, Kent and London – those were from common knowledge our most frequently recurring topics" (77).

In contrast, he describes another group of farm buildings as being rather "unhomelike," though he does not use the term:

> The door in front, one window beside it, two windows above, geometrically correct, and stiff and cold. The house was the only green thing around, however. Not a tree, not a shrub, not even a kitchen garden that I could see. I looked the place over critically, while I drove by. Somehow I was convinced that a bachelor owned it – a man who made this house – which was much too large for him – his "bunk." There it stood, slick and cold, unhospitable as ever a house was. (16)

Grove guesses that this is a bachelor's house because it does not display what he calls in his wife "a woman's instinct for shelter and home" (109). But, besides its lack of shelter, this house suffers from what Grove describes in another context as "overrigidity of the lines: . . . It is unfortunate that our farmers, when they plant at all, will nearly always plant in straight lines. The straight line is a flaw where we try to blend the work of our hands with Nature" (23). In other words, the "unhomely" home is the one that appears "out of place," the one that does not disguise its newness in a new country.

Grove's family residence is set in a clearing in a shrubby thicket, rather than, as in his ideal, being nestled in a bluff, and, though it looks "as peaceful in the evening sun as any house can look," when he drives up to it he is "overwhelmed by the pitifully lonesome looks of the place" (139). It seems, however, that this sad demeanour is created not, as in the last case, by an inharmonious relationship with nature, but by its isolation from social networks: "I was still nearly four miles from my 'home' when I first beheld it. And how pitiably lonesome it looked! Not another house was to be seen in its neighbourhood" (69). On one occasion Grove describes driving his wife and daughter over to a neighbour's for a visit (106), but in the main he represents their imagined loneliness as being due to *his* absence, not a generalized social vacuum. He continually pictures them waiting, worrying, and longing for his return, and here he projects that loneliness onto the house in which they live.

Grove's house in town, on the other hand, is grounded both in a strong social community and in his *presence*. If this house represents a relatively unproblematic (if ultimately unsatisfying) home for him because he lives there the majority of the time, then it may be his relative absence from his "wife's cottage" that problematizes it as a home site. This sense of nonresidency, of nonparticipation, and thus of being something of an outsider in what he perhaps feels *should* be his "true" home, is captured when he thinks of his wife and child and is filled with "gratitude for the belated home they gave an aging man" (45). This is home as gift, as object of exchange, external to the self, created and controlled by others, something he can share only through their generosity rather than *living* it as they do. His wife and child are not only *at* home, they *are* home, for him.

Yet, despite this home's problematic status, which lies precisely in its stasis, its objectification, Grove needs it to function as he does. This is so not only because it is thanks to his "wife's co-operation in earning money" that he is able to buy the horses and "driving outfit" that he needs (57-58), but also because six of the seven sketches in his book describe "homeward" journeys north. In the binary scheme of horse and house that Robert Kroetsch has plotted in Prairie fiction,[3] Grove is very much a "horse" figure in that he is always on the move, but he gets the money for the horse *from* the house, and his reason for getting the horse is to get *to* the house: "I wanted to get home," he says. "I had to have a horse that could stand the trip" (15).

This tension between horse and house, between journey and home, permeates Grove's text and is typical of his always wanting – and, it seems, usually *getting* – things both ways. He constructs himself both as rootless wanderer and responsible homebody, saying in one breath that he loves "Nature more than Man" (11), and in the next that he "lives and breathes" for his family (12). He loves the feeling of being "detached and free" (16), is full of vague "wander instincts" (63) and an occasional "desire to go on and on, for ever, and to see what might be beyond" (67), but there is also "sadness in [this] mood, such sadness as enters − strange to say − into a great and very definitely expected disappointment" (64), and it is often thoughts of home that keep him in motion when he would otherwise prefer to rest: "Not for a moment did it occur to me to turn back. Way up north there was a young woman preparing supper for me. The fog might not be there − she would expect me − I could not disappoint her. And then there was the little girl, who usually would wake up and in her 'nightie' come out of bed and sleepily smile at me and climb on to my knee and nod off again" (44-45). The doubleness of his desire is encoded in his comment, "Fridays, at four o'clock, a real holiday started for me: two days ahead with wife and child, and going and coming − the drive" (12). Through the journey homeward Grove is able to resolve and satisfy his multiple, seemingly contradictory, impulses.

Only one sketch describes a journey back to town and work, which Grove accounts for with the explanation "[S]ince I was coming from 'home,' from the company of those for whom I lived and breathed, it might just be that all my thoughts flew back with such an intensity that there was no vitality left for the perception of the things immediately around me" (12). Perhaps so, but it also seems that home as centre of gravity generates story more when it is acting on his whole person rather than only on his thoughts − that is, when he is approaching rather than leaving it. Of course, his whole person is of greater mass than his thoughts alone, and the greater the mass the stronger the attraction, gravitationally speaking, so family home as "goal" becomes central to his construction both of himself and his text.

The ending of the sketch describing a return trip to town offers a stark contrast to the endings of the other sketches with their warm, joyful senses of reunion, of great accomplishment and worthwhile effort. Grove arrives in town to no greeting, no audience, and the trip takes on a tone of drudgery rather than adventure: "The livery stable was deserted. I had to open the doors, to drive in, to unhitch, to unharness, and to feed the horses myself. And then I went home to my cold and lonesome house. It was a cheerless night" (127). The short, simple sentences announce his arrival at what might almost be called the absence of home, as compared to the complex, even convoluted, syntax he writes in, rhapsodic, on rejoining his wife: "[W]hile we were walking up to the yard − had my drive been anything brave – anything at all deserving of the slightest reward – had it not in itself been a thing of beauty, not to be missed by selfish me – surely, the touch of that arm, as we went, would have been more than enough to reward even the most chivalrous deeds of yore" (55). Resorting to uncharacteristically archaic diction, the language of medieval romance, Grove here tries to semantically downplay the "heroism" of his journey even as he stylistically elevates it.

Similarly, just before this passage, when he first meets his wife in the yard and she expresses her concern for his safety, he tells us, "There was something of a catch in [her] voice. I did not reply" (55). He lets her worry stand, and thus lets his heroism stand, at least in her eyes. And it is, after all, her gaze and that of her daughter that matter, for it is their fear, their anxiety, their waiting and longing for his arrival and distress at his leaving again that enable and create his risk-taking, his valour, his courage, his adventure. Paradoxically, and here we see Grove having things both ways again, he can also use their fear to excuse his failures of nerve. Thus on one occasion he postpones his departure from town on the grounds that he "might get lost and not reach home at all," which "would not be fair to wife and child" (76), and on another occasion he rationalizes his caution with the argument "I knew that my wife would be sitting up and waiting till midnight or two o'clock, and I wanted to make it. So I avoided all risks and gave my attention to the road for a while" (150).

Grove's wife and daughter, then, are not only home as enabling audience and goal of journey, but they are also home as audience for the self's performance of its own construction. They are also home as audience for the text's reperformance of the construction. The original edition of Grove's book contained the dedication "These pages were written for my wife and my little daughter to read by the evening fireside," and at one point he says, "Surely, surely, I owe it to them, staunch, faithful hearts that they were, to set down this record so it may gladden the lonesome twilight hours that are sure to come" (70). This is text as alibi, as substitute for the author's presence, authorizing his absence, but it is also text as offering, as recompense for the anxiety he caused his waiting family while he was out "fighting storm and night to my heart's content!" (70). Text as confession, text as guilt.

This is also text as instructional medium, in at least three different senses. After a particularly perilous journey through snow, Grove says he feels as he had felt "coming home from [his] first big trip overseas. It seemed a lifetime since I had started out. I seemed to be a different man." And he registers his disappointment that his wife "would not surmise what [he] had gone through" (101).[4] Her lack of knowledge about his experience, her lack of understanding, prompts his need to write it so that she can, in a sense, experience it for herself. The telling of the story under her gaze thus reconstructs and certifies – reinvents and guarantees – his experience and the identity developed through that experience. His text makes him real through its being "learned" by others.[5]

We find the second sense in which the text offers itself as instructional medium when, at one point, in the middle of a lengthy description of the effects of wind on snow, Grove says, "[I am] aware of the fact that nobody – nobody whom I know, at least – takes the slightest interest in such things," and he comments, "Our school work in this respect seems to me to be most ridiculously and palpably superficial. Worst of all, most of it is dry as dust, and it leads nowhere" (112-13). Grove positions his text against this general trend, presenting knowledge always "in action," and this desire to teach, to educate, takes on a third and very personal dimension when he relates it to his daughter, and through her to ideas of immortality and the "meaning" of life:

> [E]ver since the little girl was born, there had been only one desire which filled my life. Where I had failed, she was to succeed. Where I had squandered my energies and opportunities, she was to use them to some purpose. What I might have done but had not done, she was to do. She was to redeem me. I was her natural teacher. Teaching her became henceforth my life-work. When I bought a book, I carefully considered whether it would help her one day or not before I spent the money. Deprived of her, I myself came to a definite and peremptory end. With her to continue my life, there was still some purpose in things, some justification for existence. (130-31)

If his wife's gaze constructs him in this life, his daughter's gaze, itself constructed through the educational function of his text, will continue to construct him – to enable his existence – *after* this life. Home as constructed and constructor, as created and creating.

Melancholy, romantic, and nostalgic, Grove continues his argument, extending its application beyond his personal situation:

> Most serious-minded men at my age, I believe, become profoundly impressed with the futility of "it all." Unless we throw ourselves into something outside of our own personality, life is apt to impress us as a great mockery. I am afraid that at the bottom of it there lies the recognition of the fact that we ourselves were not worth while, that we did not amount to what we had thought we should amount to; that we did not measure

up to the exigencies of eternities to come. Children are among the most effective means devised by Nature to delude us into living on. (131)

Grove imagines a time before "modern civilization" when people's expectations were not so high that they were bound to fall short, regretting that we have now "lost the childlike power of living without conscious aims," and suggesting, "[S]ince we never live in the present, we are always looking forward to what never comes; and so life slips by, unlived" (131).[6] His sketches themselves embody this tension between concern for the present and for the future – celebrating the process of observing nature, yet only while on a journey homeward, revelling in the telling of tales of adventure, yet dedicating these stories to the education of his daughter. Present: future. Process: goal. Horse: house.

But whatever the book's ostensible original purposes, in publishing it Grove sought a wider audience, a hearing, he says, "beyond my own frugal fireside" (12), and the text displays the signs of this duality. For instance, in his descriptions of the land and its weather he makes use of a vast array of similes and analogies that, to function as teaching devices, should compare the unfamiliar to the familiar. Instead, Grove frequently compares things in his family's immediate environment, and that they could thus potentially know, to things that at least his daughter is unlikely to have had any experience or knowledge of – tidal waves, Kentucky, Sweden, Shakespeare, mining camps, World War I, the Black Hills, caves, India, Gibraltar, boa constrictors, gorillas, leopards, and "Southern countries," for example.

These comparisons function as Grove's own homemaking process as much as anything else. In seeking to know the prairie space, and in that sense to make himself at home in it, he draws on his wide range of experiential and textual knowledge, reinscribing it in a new context in order to write his new place, to invent his world. He is obsessed with naming, with finding a language to read and write the landscapes he encounters: a certain culvert "will henceforth be known as the 'twelve-mile bridge'" (22); the sun goes down "two hours from 'town,' as I called it" (23); a certain house "became a much-looked-for landmark to me on my future drives. I learned that it stood on the range line and called it the 'White Range Line House'" (25); a fan-shaped arrangement of clouds he has "for many years been calling 'the tree'" (148). He says, "'Observing' means to me as much finding words to express what I see as it means the seeing itself" (121). Language, in this sense, *enables* perception.

In a footnote early on in his text, Grove tells us, "Anybody at all familiar with the district through which these drives were made will readily

identify every natural landmark. But although I have not consciously introduced any changes in the landscape as God made it, I have in fairness to
the settlers entirely redrawn the superimposed man-made landscape" (22).
An odd comment, this, as if the two could be so easily separated. Much of
Grove's description, it is true, is of objects and phenomena that we would
consider "natural," but his journeys are plotted along and mapped around
the identification of landmarks that are overwhelmingly of human origin –
roads, cattle-paths, fences, farm buildings, telephone posts, bridges, and small
towns, for example. And it is also largely these human signs that make his
trips interesting and mark the passage of time through space: "This north-
south road was in the future invariably to seem endlessly long to me. There
were no very prominent landmarks – a school somewhere – and there was
hardly any change in the monotony of driving" (118). Landmarks function
for him as minor centres of gravity, pulling him along from point to point
in his journeys north and south. With "home" they share the aspect of
being known and familiar.

Learning to successfully read the signs of place is crucial if Grove is to be
at home in the space, and not lost, both literally and figuratively. Where
there are not already signs in and of place he must create them, as he does
through developing his powers of observation and understanding of natural
phenomena, comparing what *to him* is unknown to what is known.
Grove's most extended and lengthy simile compares the snowed-under
prairie to the sea, a comparison that even in his time had a long history,
especially among European immigrant writers, but that, as Kroetsch points
out on behalf of Prairie-raised readers (like Grove's daughter), is "Greek to
us, / Grove" (*SHP* 47). This relationship among knowledge, memory, and
home is crystalized in one of Grove's favourite expressions, "it came home
to me," suggesting the sudden realization of what he has had at least the
capacity to know, if not the actual knowledge of, all along, and mirroring
in interesting ways Freud's theory of the uncanny, *unheimlich* ("unhomely"),
as the re-presentation, the un-repression, of that which was once *heimlich*.[7]

Yet, if several of Grove's references seem to be aimed at a readership
other than the family for whom he claimed primarily to be writing, another set of references seem to be deliberately aimed at a local audience.
He uses first person plural pronouns to indicate himself and other Prairie
inhabitants, as in "Many a snowstorm begins that way with us" (108), and
he works his way out of or around many description and definitional problems by calling on his audience's prior and shared knowledge, as in "Who-
ever has seen the trees like that – and who has not? – will see with his
mind's eye what I am trying to suggest rather than to describe" (65), or

"Doubtless all my readers know how a country road that is covered with from two to three feet of snow will look when the trail is broken" (110). Again, Grove appears to have it both ways in terms of audience.

Is, then, his claim that his family is his central audience something of an alibi in yet another sense, masking his larger aspirations and concealing his anxiety over the possible reception of his first book? And if so, then are his claims about the centrality of home in his thoughts and motivations also something of an alibi, necessitated by his construction of home as audience, and masking a fundamental egotism and obsession with movement and travel?[8] These are, perhaps, ungenerous questions but in any case ones in regard to which the text remains indeterminate. We do not have any of the conventional signs of irony or self-consciousness that would allow us to untangle the various tensions and paradoxes in Grove's text, to assign "truth values" to certain of his statements rather than others.

Perhaps his wife and daughter could tell us more, but since Grove constructs home only as object, a silent centre of gravity around which he can circle, they can never really speak. Despite Grove's obsession with naming as a means of knowing and understanding, his wife and daughter remain unnamed in his text. They remain types, abstract ideas or ideals, perhaps because, as Grove says in his essay "The Happy Ending, . . . an ideal realized would be an ideal destroyed. If God revealed Himself, He would be dead. The aim, the ideal, to be of value as a guide, must be unobtainable. A beacon reached is a beacon put behind; a beacon never to be reached will always beckon" (*Needs* 88).

There may also, however, be a less positive and noble motive for Grove's family silence. For his wife and daughter to speak might be to rupture his writing of them as a peaceful site of comfort and security, for just as Grove observes of the wind, home can have very different meanings and effects *inside* the house from *outside* it: "In the open the howling and whistling of the wind always acts on me like a soporific. Inside of a house it is just the reverse; I know nothing that will keep my nerves as much on edge and prevent me as certainly from sleeping" (111). And so the sketches end always with Grove approaching the house, never quite making it as far as the door, never crossing the threshold.

## Lorna Crozier's *Inventing the Hawk*

Lorna Crozier's poems in *Inventing the Hawk* begin on the other side of the threshold, writing home from within it. As Grove dedicates his book to his wife and daughter, so Crozier dedicates hers to her mother, brother, and recently deceased father, but where Grove turns the indirect objects of his book into its direct objects, grammatically (and metaphorically) speaking, Crozier grants hers a measure of subjectivity within the text. The result, perhaps inevitably, is that where Grove's home is passive, static, silent, and idealized, Crozier's is active, dynamic, noisy, and realistic; where Grove's promises comfort and safety, Crozier's delivers conflict and danger, the unpredictability of "sleeping with snakes" (29). The home she writes is like the "new poem" she imagines: "It will bark and growl / and some days it might bite / but always without fail, / it will let you in" (129).

Home for both writers, then, is centred in family, but Crozier's sense of family is considerably more complex, ambivalent, and paradoxical, as suggested by the epigraph from Alice Derry that opens her text: "This is the walled city, family. Within, / all the love and hate a body needs." Walls can keep things out, protecting against expected or unexpected outside dangers: "Across the yard I see my neighbour / on his front step. He waves, / then points a rifle at my head" (109). Walls can also keep things *in*, creating stability through containment. In the best case, such stability offers a sense of physical and psychic security, the comfort, reassurance, and sense of connection across time that knowledge and repetition can bring. Thus a farmer "walks his combine / in long sure rows all the way / to the horizon and doubles back, / doing what his father did" (89), while the daughter in "Repetitions for My Mother" wishes her mother would "live forever," "out of bed every holiday at six / to stuff the turkey" (77), and she slides down the buffalo stone her mother used for a slide, "loving this rock / (as it was, as it is, / as it will be)" (94), and swims in the lake her mother swam in, "wanting to feel what she felt / as a child" (99).

Through its involvement with repetition, memory thus also becomes a kind of home, and Crozier's personae often see the known past in the unknown present. At a train station: "A man who could be my father / sweeps the steps with an old curling broom, / his name printed on the handle" (86); in the middle of the night a baker pinches names into bread loaves, and "It could be your father's name, your mother's" (3); a paperboy and his sister "could be my brother and me" (78); and her brother on his paper route could have been her mother:

> he'd wait for me
>
> lift me up and put me in his bag
>
> on top of the papers he had left,
>
> carry me home like a kangaroo
>
> nestled in the pouch, warmed
>
> by his body, my eyes barely open,

> as if I'd slipped out of him
>
> seven years after he was born,
>
> he, as much as my mother,
>
> giving me this life. (79)

Memory and home have an uncanny, *unheimlich*, aspect in Crozier's poetry, involving not only people, but also animals, insects, and plants. A white horse enters her house: "He looked at me / and we knew each other" (38), while a dragonfly "looks at you / as if it knows / exactly / who you are" (63), and the triangular eyes carved on a pumpkin "look at you / as if they know your face" (131). Such familiarity is startling because unexpected among "strangers," and experiencing it can be quite "unsettling." Yet in Crozier's poems the uncanny also offers a reassuring sense of continuity and connection, of being at home, grounded, in the world.

If walls can enable such positive continuity through containment, keeping people, things or memories "in place," they can also, in the worst case, be imprisoning. Tradition and ritual can have a negative, damaging effect, as we see in an image of parents sitting at a breakfast table, trapped in their rigid patterns of behaviour:

> They have promised God to live together,
>
> they have promised their children
>
> they'll never part. His hands are shaking.
>
> He is trying to move a spoon full of sugar
>
> from the bowl to his cup without spilling any
>
> on the table. She is tearing a Kleenex to pieces
>
> in her lap. (70)

A father with the DTs, a mother who channels her anxiety and anger into small, mindless acts of destruction, the silence between them, all are endlessly repeated in the mind of the child who watches them, who wishes to "move them to another place, another table, / a different morning in their lives" but finds that "[s]till / they do the same things with their hands" (70). Bound in a social and religious contract that seeks permanence, their lives are reduced to a deathly stasis.

The doubleness and ambiguity of walls is also present in another way in which they can protect by keeping things in, creating privacy by concealing whatever may be going on within them. Viewed from the outside, a walled city can appear very calm, coherent, unified and controlled – the idealized image of home and family that Grove projected. In the acknowledge-ments section of her book, Crozier says, "I want to thank my mother for allowing me to reveal some old family secrets," and, while this should not be read as an invitation to overly simplistic autobiographical readings of her work, it does suggest the way in which her poems crawl through cracks in the walls, open doors, stand naked in windows at night, like the lonely woman in "Dictionary of Symbols" exposing herself to a man on the street below: "This is what it looks like, she says, / this pale celestial body, faceless / as the moon is faceless, coldly luminescent" (6).

The revealing of "family secrets" amounts to the leakage of information that shatters the outside view of the walled city as a stable point of peace and order. The woman who stands in the window and turns on the inside light, for instance, does so "on a summer evening when all her children / are asleep, when her husband kneels on a bed / in another house, entering a woman / from behind, so he can watch himself" (5). Crozier writes of the scars that result from such betrayals and infidelities, sometimes treating the pain with cool, dry wit and a measure of dark humour. A woman who is given recipes at a dinner party by "the woman / who intends to make love to my husband" (24), for instance, consoles herself with the idea that at least she'll "know if he's been with her – / the smell of garlic / where her fingers sweep across his belly" (25). And it is not only women who suffer in these poems – men too can be scarred by such experiences, though in a rather different sense. In the prose poem "Home Care," a woman finds her boyfriend "fishin'" in her friend's bed and kicks him in the face wearing cowboy boots, with the result that "there'll be a scar there three inches long saying howdee-do every time he looks in the mirror and he's the kind of guy who has to shave twice a day for the rest of his life so that's a lot of lookin'" (23).

Other forms of betrayal are too serious to admit any comic treatment or ironic detachment, as those suffered by a woman who the speaker says is no longer friends with her: "I knew what she wanted no one else to know" (33). This woman "covered her mouth, / not wanting anyone to see / the bruised and broken lip / where her husband had punched her with his fists," and all the speaker can do is watch her go back every evening "to her husband's house / where some nights she was loved and others / beaten black and blue" (32).[9] The walls of secrecy that the woman wants to keep in place protect her husband's ability to abuse her in private, to fully con-trol the space so that it is indeed *his* house. To move the knowledge outside the walls into the public sphere, as Crozier's poem does, is to disrupt the order of things.[10]

The blend of love and violence that the woman in this poem experiences as "home" is characteristic of Crozier's refusal, for the most part, to idealize or oversimplify. The suggestion in her poetry that a positive and caring love can exist side-by-side with, or develop out of, at least certain forms of violence can be read as a type of realism: "Everything does not move toward a perfect end," she says. "Not even art / can make it so" (126). Another poem, however, "Living Day By Day," appears to romanticize violence by positioning it in a narrative with a suspiciously "happy ending." The speaker compares her present relationship to its beginning, recalling

> those terrible fights,
>
> he and I struggling to be the first
>
> to pack, the first one out the door.
>
> Once I made it to the car before him,
>
> locked him out. He jumped on the hood,
>
> then kicked the headlights in.
>
> Our friends said we'd kill each other
>
> before the year was through.
>
> Now it's ten years later.
>
> Neither of us wants to leave.
>
> We are at home with one another,
>
> we are each other's home,
>
> the voice in the doorway,
>
> calling *Come in, come in,*
>
> *it's growing dark.* (40)

Here the voice that calls you home *is* your home – home speaks, but the price of subjectivity is complication, a realization and acceptance of the turbulence beneath the constructed calm of surface.

This interest in and acceptance of "imperfection" can also be seen in the elegy "Facts about My Father." The term "facts" indicates the nearly neutral point of view of the speaker, who uses a language of description that is free of terms of judgement or evaluation, even while the majority of the "facts" themselves paint a rather unflattering picture of a greedy, bigoted, self-centred, and irresponsible alcoholic, one who was off betting on horses when his daughter was born, so that the "first time he held me, Mom was mad, he was hungover, his hands shaking" (73), and who was "drunk at my grade twelve graduation, stayed out the night before and arrived home just as Mom and I were leaving for the gym" (75).

Yet the mood of the poem is not anger, but regret and loss, and Crozier undercuts the reader's ability to make any easy judgements. For instance, learning about the father's eviction and displacement from his family farm so that his brother wouldn't get drafted generates a measure of sympathy, and some of the "facts," especially those that deal with him away from the domestic space, speak of wonder and respect: his hands and arms were "huge from working hard" so that "he won all the arm-wrestling matches at the Healey Hotel" (71), younger men admire his pool-playing prowess and his El Camino, and his "brains were in his hands, he could fix anything, his fingers knew exactly what to do" (71). Even his being the "district killer" who "shot dogs and horses for the neighbours without batting an eye" (72), is double, suggesting a hardness or coldness in his character, but also a practical nature and stoicism in fulfilling a needed social role.

Crozier's interest in these less "domesticated" aspects of domestic life is mirrored in her concern for vanishing animal species and her regret that

> . . . Only the animals
>
> man has tamed or broken
>
> remain, less
>
> beautiful than they once had been,
>
> for all that is wild
>
> has gone out of them. (7)

She is like her favourite uncle, Jack, who "knew the homeplace / as the others didn't," seeing and appreciating the energy and spirit in the "wild places and the creatures / who lived there: . . . *This* was the land to him, / not just what was broken, / the acres the other uncles fought over" (91-92). The irony or paradox is that "breaking" land or animals, bringing them into or under a system of order and control, makes them useful or productive within that system, but it also damages them. It is simultaneously a creative and a destructive act.

The same goes, it appears, for human beings and the system of "domestic order." Crozier says that her father's speedboat racing, "the waves / lifting him and banging him down," represents "a violence he could understand, / that same dumb force raging inside him" (80-81).[11] He smokes a pack of cigarettes a day while in the hospital for lung cancer, and sneaks out of the hospital for a beer the day after an operation, suggesting not so much a death wish as a crazy untamed spirit and lust for life. Yet, when he goes out drinking at other "inappropriate" times – during the birth of his child, the night before and day of his daughter's graduation – the actions appear hurtful and inconsiderate. The very characteristic that makes him an attractive figure in one context or manifestation can, in a different one, make him unattractive.

Crozier's deconstruction of idealized home life is allied with her broader "realist" aesthetics. For instance, she parodies the pastoral tradition of poetry and its idealized view of rural life, asking: "Why did the poets lie to us" about

> the silence ("O, sweet silence of the golden field")
>
> beautiful if the crop is full
>
> but enough to drive you mad
>
> as you wait for your child
>
> for the first time in her life
>
> to hear the sound of rain. Of *rain*. (90)

Similarly, watching a Canada Day Parade with its simplistic view of boys and girls growing up to be "Oilman" and "Oilman's wife," she tells her friends, "[I]t was as if I'd stumbled / into a movie set in the fifties, that simple / stupid time when everyone was so unaware" (80). And this anti-nostalgic observation is further complicated in the next stanza when she says that in telling the story of the parade she doesn't mention her father, "sitting beside me in a wheel chair," or the fact that "[i]n the fifties he wouldn't have been / here beside us but somewhere down the street, / alone and cocky, drunk or about to be" (80).

If the fifties weren't so much a time of "unawareness" as of "acceptance," Crozier's poems suggest that such acceptance and compromise were essential aspects of homemaking long before that time, and that they continue to be so. Crozier's grandmother, for instance, "always wanted to be a gypsy," longing "to go somewhere, to be on the road / in a caravan, everything she owned / rolling on wheels" (92) so that "nothing held you to one place":

> Strange desire for a woman
>
> who stayed forever on the land
>
> she and Grandpa broke,
>
> a woman who bore seven children,
>
> all moving no farther than the nearest town. (93)

The poem "Cleaning Fish" ironizes the idea that things will be different and better for later generations, that "awareness" will translate into constructive action, that needs and desires will match reality in some happier way in the future. The speaker remembers, "Dad, a little drunk, every summer Sunday / brought home a pail of perch," while "Mom, who had spent the day alone / with me, sat on the back step, / mad as she could be and gutted them." She also remembers swearing she'd "not do that / for anyone," that she'd "never be as unhappy / or alone as they / believing then / I'd keep every single vow I made" (68-69).

One of the extreme forms of compromise represented in Crozier's book is first suggested in the poem "Getting Pregnant," which details common and uncommon myths about ways that you *can't* get pregnant, such as "if you eat garlic, / if you wear a girdle, / if it's only your second time" (21), and ending with: "You can't get pregnant / if he tells you / you won't" (22). In the context of the poetic list it appears in, this reads first as a "male line" to evade issues of consequence and responsibility, but in the context of a later poem it speaks quite differently of male control over female reproduction. The speaker of "Living Day By Day" says:

> I have no children and he has five,
>
> three of them grown up, two with their mother.
>
> It didn't matter when I was thirty and we met.
>
> *There'll be no children,* he said, the first night
>
> we slept together and I didn't care,
>
> thought we wouldn't last anyway. (40)

"Still," the speaker says, ten years later, "I'm often asked if I have children" (40), suggesting not only the felt pressures of social norms and traditional gender roles, but also a very personal sense of loss and anxiety. To deal with this, the speaker transposes her procreative desire onto the very relationship that has suppressed it, saying, "Sometimes we have so much / we make another person," a daughter who dances at night, "her dream hair flying" (40-41).[12]

The notion of woman as the creative and ordering centre of home is both parodied and reinforced in the heavenly domestic drama "On the Seventh Day":

> On the first day God said
>
> *Let there be light.*
>
> And there was light.

> On the second day
> God said, *Let there be light,*
> and there was more light.
>
> *What are you doing?* asked God's wife,
> knowing he was the dreamy sort.
> *You created light yesterday.* (10)

A bumbling and forgetful God spends the first five days creating and re-creating light, so that his wife eventually has to step in and take over: "Everything he'd forgotten / she had to create / with only a day left to do it" (11), and she thinks, "*Go out and multiply,* yes, / she'd have to say it" (12).

Crozier's poems here and elsewhere tend to work off very traditional gender models; women are represented as the primary home-makers, and it seems to be mainly women who suffer the cruelties of men at home — neglect, betrayal, and physical abuse. Her "home" appears as a tragic hero of sorts, attractive and appealing, yet carrying within itself the seeds of its own destruction. If home is a female construct and men so frequently appear dysfunctional or "out of place" in the homes that women create for them, then perhaps this is because the women created homes to fulfill *their own* needs, and the men's needs are either different enough that they can't co-exist without inherently causing conflict and pain of one sort or another, or they simply need a separate space of articulation. Like Grove out on his cutter or Crozier's father at the Legion, these men may need to construct their own "alternative homes" elsewhere, in places where *they* have creative and ordering power.[13]

Given this rather cynical view of the inherently problematic nature of home, it is perhaps surprising that more people don't just abandon the idea entirely, like the woman who "walked into the river / and didn't come back," who

> made a list of all the men
> she'd ever loved,
> left it for her husband by the coffee pot,
> his name on the bottom,
> underlined twice
> for emphasis. (108)

This is the ultimate form of leaving home, dying for love. Yet, if home can *provoke* such flights, it can also *enable* more positive forms, and Crozier's poems overwhelmingly, again and again, picture people *coming* home, approaching rather than leaving it. Home in Crozier's poetry is equal to primary human relationships that are fraught with anxiety and disappointments – relationships that, no matter how flawed, can be the compasses by which life finds its directions: "*Father,* I say out loud / for I have driven here without a map. / I have lost my bearings. *Father*" (85). Home is like the horses who can console the speaker despite her fear of them, as "the eye is more beautiful / because horses have walked through it" (139), or like the "Angel of Happiness":

> You might see her as a bluebird
>
> and remember the old joke.
>
> Yes, there's that miracle
>
> of colour, that sudden flight,
>
> but there's also birdshit,
>
> meaning everything
>
> has a price. (83)

The price of home may be intense emotional or physical pain, but it is a price that Crozier's poems suggest is generally worth it.

The speaker of "On the Writing of a Love Poem" asks, "Is it vain to want to be a book / for him?:... It would be a simple tale," she says, "but one that would not fail to hold him, / the word hearth repeated several times," some of it written "on her skin and some / in the air around her," and

> on the final page, in the patient telling
>
> of her body is a sign that spells
>
> home for him. The familiar name –
>
> wherever he has gone –
>
> that will take him in. (37)

Accommodation, a taking in and making room for another in one's life – physically, intellectually, and emotionally – is at the centre of Crozier's conception of home. It enables and is generated out of a kind of love that depends on compromise and acceptance, that can come and create home as easily as a man can come to a woman's door, "a man with a brass cornet covered in frost or a bouquet or roses brittle as glass or a need so large it will lift her off her feet and into the future he has planned" (113). Home offers the irresistible pull of "place," in the sense that Ostenso's Caleb Gare used the term, of having a social role to fill, a place, as Berger says, at the heart of the real. The certainty of acceptance that home and love offer enables the freedom to roam and return, and, when home is your love, when your lover is your home, it can even offer release into flight through the part of the body "closest to the sea" with "the oldest brain, prelapsarian, / soft moss and weeping fern":

> . . . you feel it
>
> flex and flutter
>
> beneath your lover's tongue
>
> as feather
>
> after slow inevitable feather
>
> it dreams the world's
>
> first wings. (17)

## Dennis Cooley's *this only home*

While Crozier's characters fly *in place*, without leaving the ground, the characters in Dennis Cooley's *this only home* fly *into space*. And if Grove's wife is in some sense "*his* world," the world that Cooley's protagonists circle is "*the* world," *our* world, the planet earth. The shift from the singular "his" to the collective first-person plural "our" accompanies the radical collapsing and identifying of spaces usually considered discrete; the shift in spatial perspective also involves a revisioning of "private property" as essentially "public," and thus may be read as a stage in the development of the Marxist utopia that John Berger believes will overcome the twentieth-century phenomena of displacement and alienation: "The one hope of recreating a center now is to make it the entire earth. Only worldwide solidarity can transcend modern homelessness" (67).

In sharp contrast to both Crozier's and Grove's association of privacy with *home*, Berger associates *homelessness* with a negative sense of privacy – a sense that Raymond Williams says prevailed before the sixeenth century. Williams argues that is was at this time that the negative associations of "'withdrawal' and 'seclusion' came to be replaced, as senses, by 'independence' and 'intimacy,' [and that] . . . [p]rivate, that is, in its positive senses, is a record of the legitimation of a bourgeois view of life: the ultimate generalized privilege, however abstract in practice, of seclusion and protection from others (the public); of lack of accountability to 'them'; and of related gains in closeness and comfort of these general kinds" (*Keywords* 242, 243).

Grove's "sheltered bluff" and Crozier's "walled city of family" rely on precisely this separation of public and private: in Grove's text it enables the silence and invisibility that are necessary for the construction of his "ideal" home; in Crozier's text it enables various forms of violence *within* the private sphere, yet the distinction between the two spheres, if problematized, remains virtually intact. The move to consider a *single* "sphere," the planet earth, on the other hand, appears to break down the public/private distinction on a very large scale.

Ironically, Cooley's text breaks down this distinction only by using it in a different form. As is perhaps appropriate in a secular universe where there is "no god or goddess" (74), Cooley reveals the public *through* the private, comparing the unknown to the known using the anthropomorphic metaphor of the human body. In one poem the speaker looking at the earth sees "paired lakes / they could be ovaries they flow / into Lake Winnipeg receives them / fish through fallopian tubes" (118), while in "Madagascar" forests are described as "torrents of green the earth / in torment bleeds away" (61) and during the "Thirty Years' War" the earth is "on a rack its whole body / ripped & bleeding" (3). In another poem one of the cosmonauts describes earth as "a giant heart bright heart / we circle and circle round," while "the sharpest mountains are more / like molars than anything," snow is "skin on land," rivers are "dark as blood on the back / my hand in the wrists is an estuary" and the lights of Moscow are "thousands & thousands of veins / something alive and inconsolably beautiful" (19).

The earth-as-body metaphor also has a highly gendered dimension. Like Grove, and to a lesser degree Crozier, "home" is female and the earth frequently takes the form of the female body. One cosmonaut addressing his daughter refers to earth as a kind of cradle "moving you in sleep" (22), but later the earth and daughter attain grammatical equivalence: "that's earth / that's you" (23). Another cosmonaut views the Bahama Islands and says they

<blockquote>
float in blue satin

her slip is

sometimes green

a queen

you love

to touch.  (54)
</blockquote>

In other poems the earth is "belle  of the ball," a "blue  lady" (99), or
"spinning its blue wool . . . earth on the back porch of space . . . rocking
away earth everybodys / gramma rocking away the old lady / going at it
till the end of time" (58). In a more derogatory vein, the American astronauts describe the earth as an aging, battered, and neglected woman:

> she's in bad shape all right this momma
>
> taken a terrible beating
>
> skin peeling away in scabs she's quite a sight
>
> . . . . . . . . . . . . . . . . . . . . . . . . .
>
> all jowls and belly and we pat her
>
> on the bum listen old lady
>
> you sick or just goofing off or what
>
> we been too long in the pub she
>
> gives us the cold shoulder a deadly cold.  (101)

Cooley goes beyond Grove's gendering of home as female, however, in
that he genders the opposite of home – the unknown as source of wonder
and adventure – as female too. Thus the early astronomers are depicted as
"peeping toms," obsessed with "peering up into the flimsy fabric the skirts
stars are sewn to," and turning "their courtly attentions to the sky" (11). To
escape the monotony and horrors of their earthly lives, they leave "their
families sleeping wives dreaming neglect" and

> . . . hold glass to their eye
>
> study a dark lady who wears lights
>
> on her breast the milky way
>
> they squat under muddy lives
>
> want beauty want grace court romance
>
> surcease from war, witches crackling to death. (13)

Similarly, Galileo watches all night "the silk robe slip from a smiling moon,"
and when the moon figuratively turns her face away from him he is a
"disappointed lover / stands watch over the stars / faithful as Gatsby / in
love" (26-27). This gendered anthropomorphizing of both earth and space
is one of Cooley's primary homemaking strategies, and one aspect of what
E.F. Dyck calls the "small / large, near / far *topos*" that permeates Cooley's
text ("Home Places" 33).

Textual deictics, those words and phrases that locate us in space and time, are complicated by the fact that the poems use not a single lyric voice but a variety of voices speaking out of different times and places. The place of articulation of the speaking subject shifts rapidly between various points on earth and various points in space, so that "here" and "there" have no stable reference and become blurred. Poised at the threshold, Cooley's text offers views of the heavens from earth and of the earth from the heavens, and its dominant theme involves those on each side wanting to get at, if not to, the other.

In his Foreword to *The Home Planet*, the collection of photographs and statements by cosmonauts and astronauts that Cooley says was the original source and inspiration for the poems in his book (Acknowledgements), Jacques-Yves Cousteau says that the pictures taken from the moon celebrate "the birth of a global consciousness that will help build a peaceful future for mankind," as they demonstrate that "borderlines are artificial, that humankind is one single community" (Kelley).[14] While it may at first appear odd that Cooley, a self-declared and committed "Prairie poet," would engage in a poetic project calling for such "universal solidarity," the two positions in fact rely on a similar sense of the politics and poetics of place and community – the identification of a "home planet" is simply a larger-scale version of the identification of the various spaces of the Prairies as forming a more-or-less coherent "region."

Such regions, as Williams has noted, "are only fully constituted when they fully declare themselves" (*Writing* 238), and the constitution and declaration – the (re)construction and promotion – of the Prairies as region has arguably been one of Cooley's primary creative and critical tasks in his work to date.[15] The sense of place in *this only home* can be seen as an entirely compatible and logical extension of "regionalist" principles; what is significant about the extension, given the politics of Canadian regionalism, is that in Cooley's expansion of place from Prairie to planet he skips over what might be seen by some as a "natural" intermediary zone: nation. Instead, the expansion argues against the "classroom view" of the "bright globe, . . . our teacher spun & stopped," asking "what is this country / where is this" (*this only home* 144).[16]

Knowing one's "place" is still a key homemaking strategy in Cooley's text, but it takes a cosmic twist here, involving not only finding a new language with which to know and name the earth in its new perspective, but also to know and name that perspective itself – the "place" of humans and the earth within the larger scheme of the universe.[17] The very fact that we use the term "space" to describe the physical universe outside of or other than the earth and its atmosphere indicates the largely "uninscribed" quality of that realm, at least to the popular, or lay, imagination, and to make the self at home in that space consists largely of inscribing it with the significance that will transform it into "place."

Cooley's text conveys the feelings, if not always the factual information, associated with the kind of scientific knowledge described by astronaut Eugene Cernan:

> I know the stars are my home. I learned about them, needed them for survival in terms of navigation. I know where I am when I look up at the sky. I know where I am when I look up at the moon; it's not just some abstract romantic idea, it's something very real to me. See, I've expanded my home. (Kelley)

Just as Grove needed to know the prairie space in order to be literally and figuratively at home in it, so Cooley develops navigational strategies for knowing this larger space. The speaker of the poem "this only world" says, "settlers I have heard on the Canadian prairie / moved into a huge silence wavered / on air there like birds in a desert / & emptiness not to be believed" (130), making explicit the connection between Grove's and Cooley's tasks, and also suggesting one more of Cooley's homemaking strategies: to "fill" both the silence and emptiness, either by attending to what is already there but not readily perceived by eye or ear, or by giving voice and physical form from within the perceived void.

Examples of such "skywriting" techniques are many, beginning with the first poem, which provides the stars with a complex and colourful epic story line, complete with epic hero:

> some bloop out, swim dark seas one line
> red dwarf  red giant  white dwarf  black dwarf
> some nudge into a more gnarled story
> yellow dwarf  yellow giant  red giant  blue giant
> slide into the first line then into white dwarf black dwarf
> another string twists, fuse into spectacular violence
> no one can ignore blue dwarf  blue giant  yellow
> supergiant  red supergiant gathers itself, epic hero,
> the gigantic explosion we call supernova. (1)

The speaker marvels at "the wonderful names they follow, on their way to death" (1). Contrary to the popular view that naming is a controlling and blandly scientific way of knowing and possessing, Cooley here indicates that knowing through naming not only needn't diminish the wonder of the phenomena, but that it can be a source of wonderment in itself, especially perhaps for a poet who loves language.

The skies, for Cooley, are "full / with possibilities with stories" (69), and he remembers "how the Greeks looked / out & saw themselves / written in stories stars / told in constellations" (73). The old stories are no longer adequate for the modern cosmonauts, however, as one observes "strange constellations come out / turn out of time fall out in silence / from stories we always told ourselves / found comfort in, felt at home among" (25). Approached from a modern perspective, "we look out & / the electric stars speak / their hiss & crackles speak / our deaths their deaths" (73). Learning to attend to these figurative voices, to write new stories appropriate to the new reality, means to borrow a language from them, as when in the poem "navigation" one of the cosmonauts says they "learned to be at home / in the stars / the lines we would / take from them" (111). Language as a means of knowing, then, involves a give and take, with humans both imposing and acquiring words and their meanings and syntax.

One descriptive strategy for speaking of earth and space from their new perspectives is the use of simile and metaphor. In addition to Cooley's dominant anthropomorphic metaphor comparing both earth and sky to the human body, a plethora of vernacular similes and metaphors are also used, so, for instance, the mouth of the Mississippi seen from space looks like "a spinach leaf" (55), a thunder storm "runs through easy as a horse farting" (93) and the revolving of galaxies is likened to "revolving / doors at Eaton's in deepest winter" (106). Similarly, stars are "a scatter of dandruff" and earth is "serene as an Easter egg" (123), while space travel "is when you were a kid in an elevator / you were new from the farm / and you left your stomach on the ground" (47). At other times the struggle to find the appropriate language and comparison is made visible, as when one cosmonaut says the world "floated by no not a rattle / or a ball nothing like that / a garden" (5).[18]

Significantly, a great number of these vernacular similes and metaphors are explicitly domestic in nature. Clouds are "sheepskin slippers scattered / sleepy on blue carpets" (19), the blueness of the earth is "bluing in laundry" (33), "creatures falling out of the stars" are "ourselves come back to our / selves spiralled inside selves / homey as shoelaces" (45), stars are "a tablecloth laid on the sky" (74), the orbits of planets are "like a set of mixing bowls" (117), and earth is "mushy in march as oatmeal" (151). Such comparisons function to imaginatively merge earth and space, allowing the reader to have a measure of comfortable familiarity despite the new strangeness of this cosmic "world."

Yet the poems also involve a counter-tendency to defamiliarize and discomfort the reader, for the flip side of wonder at the earth's beauty is fright at its fragility: earth is "inside its thin bubble / ,breathing / so thin you gasp in terror" (29). This inherent fragility is compounded by damaging human activity, and Cooley presents what might be called a "new environmentalism" – one that considers the effects not of the land on humans but of humans on the land.[19] On several occasions the earth is depicted as an ailing body; we are shown, for instance, that "something's wrong / something's died," and "the whole planet / could be haemorrhaging" (78), so that with the cosmonauts "we know earth / is imperilled impelled on / mad dreams we ourselves fuel," realizing that "there is a terrible sickness / that will lead to death / the earth is about to fall" and feeling "a home / sickness a longing / none of us has ever felt" (114). "Homesickness" here carries both its old and a new meaning: the longing for return is accompanied and intensified by a new awareness of the home planet's "sickness."

The poem "east of eden" contributes to this sense of the earth's decline. In it, a Mr. Underwood says that current pictures from space show "the earth so smudged the photos are no longer / so bright or beautiful as they were / 25 or 30 years ago": Lake Chad "had totally dried up the Sahara / sprawls across it" while "across the oceans ships clean / their tanks scrawl ink / behind them it streaks," prompting the conclusion that "we are bad house keepers" (33).[20] The poem's title reference to Eden makes explicit a biblical metanarrative of decline, of a fall from a state of innocence and grace into one of corruption and dis-grace, which runs through several of the other poems as well.

One space traveller says, "we were children there / this huge swimming pool," while earth was "a garden we wondered in wandered at / everything untainted we tended / the way children bend & peer" (5), reversing usual prepositions – to wonder *at* and wander *in* – and perspectives. The association of the archetypal garden with innocence leads to an emphasis in the poems on children and their "untainted" wonder, as when one speaker observes "such starriness / only lovers could imagine or children" (85) and another says, "you would feel like a child" on a space walk (143). This emphasis also shows in the formal use of nursery rhymes to structure poems, as in "holy cow" and "felt," which begins "like that cow / jumped o / ver the / moon" (18). Appropriately, Adam and Eve also make cameo appearances: cosmonauts walking in their garden at the space station are "like the first people" (95) and astronaut James Irwin stands on the moon wondering "how all alone Adam and Eve must have felt" (135).

The prose piece "Apollo II What They Will Leave Behind" demonstrates that the "house keeping" skills of the American astronauts in space are also defective. After a detailed description of the space craft's manoevres, Cooley says, "The papers say that much of the payload will be abandoned. They will leave a variety of equipment and litter," and he provides a list of such debris including an American flag, a "Laser Ranging Retro-Reflector" and "used fecal containers and urine bags" (133-34). Taking the long view that is central to so many of the poems, Cooley observes that their footprints "will remain on the moon for half a million years," and he counters Pope Paul's hailing of the astronauts as "'conquerors of the moon" with the fact that "[o]utside the Manned Space Center auditorium in Houston, as the Eagle lands, black demonstrators carry signs saying '41 cents a day is not enough'" (134-35). Recalling an earlier suggestion that the space travellers "could be gods" (126), Cooley also critiques the polluting, acquisitive, and commercial nature of the American space program by recalling, "A Babylonian legend tells how a god rapes the moon, then replaces her with his son Sin" (135).

Given the double perspective of the poems, which provide us with views from both earth and space, it is fitting that the text also offers multiple centres of gravity. In the early poem "Thomas Digges," we get the scientific view that the sun is the centre around which all the planets revolve:

The Orbe of Satvrne Makinge His Revolvtion in 30 Yeares

The Orbe of Jvpiter Makinge His Periode in 12 Yeares

The Orbe of Mars Makinge His Revolvtion in 2 Yeares

The Great Orbe Carringe This Globe of Mortalitye

His Circvlar Period Determineth Ovr Yeare

The Orbe of Venus Rovleth Rovnd in 9 Monthes

The Orbe of Mercvry in 8 Dayes

The Sonne. (7)

This astronomical centre, however, is replaced by the earth and its human inhabitants as the text's primary centre of gravity. Just as "the seasons wobble sweetly around us" (16), the cosmonauts and astronauts orbit earth. Seen from space, the earth has a "sudden weight" (56), and one traveller, remembering how "Newton said the greater / the mass the stronger the pull / the further the distance the less attraction" comes to

> know only i am in a stone
>
> I am a stone
>
> a child swings round &
>
> round as a moon a child tugs
>
> from far away holds me here
>
> keeps my thoughts
>
> from swarming
>
> from flying  off
>
>
> my daughter on the other end
>
> the cord stronger than gravity
>
> feel the cord how it vibrates,
>
> heart in my hand. (37)

In an earlier poem, Cooley has Galileo saying, "[I hear] the sounds of drunk lovers in the lane / and I turn my face to the sky" (32), symbolically turning his back on human relations and love in his pursuit of scientific knowledge, including the view that the sun is at the centre of the solar system. Cooley the poet, however, returns us to an older earth-centred view, to human wonder, desire and fear, to the body, and to the human heart as the ultimate centre of gravity.

# Displacement and Replacement

*4*

life on the reservation was nowhere
a shrinking circle getting smaller
choking up old ideals and dreams

(Willow Barton, *"Where Have the Warriors Gone?"* 12)

wolf runs as he feels the breath of diesel monsters
and the forest turns to concrete under his feet
and trails turn to back alleys                          .
the sounds of breaking glass and curses

(Duncan Mercredi, "dreams of wolf in the city" 3)

Growing up in a Chinese restaurant is ethnic
When first the word was out it might shut down
I had to ask where will Main Street Indians go?
I still see cleavers chasing, hear strange cursing
My mouth knows what is the Soup of the Day
One time this guy said Poon Tang to us girls
We ran home scared because we didn't know Chinese

(Marie Annharte Baker, "Exchange Café" 34)

Leaving is sometimes survival.
But energies mustered, must make the journey home.

(Bren Kolson, "The Barren Journey Home" 130)

Displacement is central to much of the Prairie experience, as it perhaps is to twentieth-century experience in general. As John Berger says, "Emigration, forced or chosen, across national frontiers or from village to metropolis, is the quintessential experience of our time" (55). Similarly, Andrew Gurr has suggested that the search for a literally or figuratively lost home as a source of identity is a variety of self-analysis especially characteristic of twentieth-century literature in general, even if it is "hardly so much the kind of therapy that leads to a cure as a compulsive scratching at an incurable itch" (10-15). Canadian immigrants, many of whom had prior experiences of displacement within the "old world," began "placing" themselves on the Prairies in large numbers only in the last 120 years. Many indigenous people were forced onto the Prairies by earlier European settlement to the east and south, and then were further displaced from their Prairie settlements to reserves or transient (because landless) Métis communities.[1] Further, rural to urban migration is a phenomenon affecting both Native and non-Native cultures.

Accompanying these forms of physical displacement are associated psychological and cultural displacements, and Prairie writers use a wide variety of literary genres to represent and embody a correspondingly wide variety of strategies for conceiving the interrelationship between these components. Emma Lee Warrior's short story "Compatriots" makes its social criticisms indirectly, relying on irony to convey the absurdity of the present situation in which both culture and people are disconnected from place. Maria Campbell's autobiography *Halfbreed* depicts the devastating effects of colonial displacement on Métis communities more directly and makes a strong case that restoration of culture must be predicated on the restoration or invention of a homeland. Rudy Wiebe's novel *Peace Shall Destroy Many* presents a complex double-edged situation in which a group of Mennonite people searching for an independent homeland on the Prairies contributes to the displacement of the people Campbell's text is concerned with. And, finally, Uma Parameswaran's book of multi-voiced poetry, *Trishanku*, suggests that when a literal "journey home" is impossible, a symbolic social or psychological return through a metonymic merging of landscapes – a symbolic replacing of displacement – may be nearly as effective.

## Emma Lee Warrior's "Compatriots"

The usual connection between home, place, and identity is given an ironic twist in Emma Lee Warrior's story "Compatriots," where a sympathetic description of reservation life is combined with a critique of appropriation of Native spirituality by Europeans.[2] The Blackfoot Reserve in southern Alberta where the story takes place (and which perhaps mirrors the Peigan Reserve where Warrior grew up) is quite empty of what is typically thought of as "Native culture," which is instead centred, rather ludicrously, in Germany. Helmut Walking Eagle, a kind of modern-day Grey Owl,[3] has come to Canada from Germany to learn and then teach the Native culture to Canadian "Natives," and another visitor from Germany, Hilda Afflerbach, draws the main character, Lucy, into her first exposure to Helmut's version of what might be (should be?) "her own" culture.

The problems of cultural preservation and commercialization are alluded to right from the beginning of the story when we hear that Hilda came to the reserve with Lucy's aunt Flora after meeting her at the Calgary Stampede (48), which is a frozen icon of mythologized by-gone "cowboy culture." In retrospect, this early reference ironically foreshadows the static, iconicized version of "Indian culture" that appears at the end of the story: every time Lucy sees Helmut, for instance, she is "reminded of the Plains Indian Museum across the line" (57). In both cases culture is "fixed" in the attempt to preserve it, in both cases culture is taken out of the hands of its original practitioners and controlled by outside forces, and in both cases these outside forces operate for financial gain.

Hilda has come to Alberta seeking information about Native culture, and Flora says she "[m]ight as well get the true picture" (49), meaning she might as well experience the harsher realities of reserve life like the absence of indoor plumbing. Yet the first thing Hilda asks Lucy is if she has heard of Helmut, and it quickly emerges that her primary interest is in meeting *him*, apparently to find out about Native culture indirectly from him, rather than directly from the Native people themselves: "'I hope he can tell me things I can take home,'" she says, adding, "'People in Germany are really interested in Indians. They even have clubs'" (50). There is a referential or "realist" element to this portrayal of German interest in Native Canadian culture, which the German scholar Hartmut Lutz accounts for partially in terms of environmental awareness:

> There are a lot of young people [in Germany], not only young people, old people, who are really concerned about what is happening to our Mother [earth], and fight to protect her. And that's the only way. And we get a lot of help from Native people. There are young people coming over here [Canada] to learn. There are some Native people going over to Europe to teach. There are also some "instant medicine men" trying to make money, but I'm not talking about those. (Campbell, "Interview" 65).

The problem with this is, for one thing, that somebody *should* talk about the "instant medicine men," and, for another, that they might not always be so easily distinguished, if the general idea of cultural appropriation is an accepted social norm.

However honourable Helmut's initial motives might have been, he does seem to be doing well on his book sales: copies of his book *Indian Medicine: A Revival of Ancient Cures and Ceremonies* sell for twenty-seven dollars each in bookstores (58), but ironically, and perhaps somewhat patronizingly, he "sells them cheaper to Indians" (56). Meanwhile, his accommodations for the sun-dance ceremony taking part on the north side of Lucy's reserve include an ostentatious and culturally incongruous Winnebago, as well as a big teepee symbolizing his "ownership" (and hence control) of Native culture: "The inside of the teepee was stunning. It was roomy, and the floor was covered with buffalo hides. Backrests, wall hangings, parfleche bags, and numerous artifacts were magnificently displayed. Helmut Walking Eagle sat resplendent amidst his wealth" (57). Warrior's use of the word "wealth" in this materialistic sense calls into question his supposed "spiritual wealth." In addition, the reference to buffalo hides ironically recalls the history of European slaughter of the animals, and the destruction of the way of life their existence had enabled.

There is a sharp contrast drawn between the recuperation of cultural traditions going on across the river – the river acting as a symbol of division between worlds or realms – and the everyday cultural life of Lucy's side of the reserve. Alcoholism, for instance, one of the legacies of colonialism, is clearly a problem there. A grocery-store sign directs customers, "'Ask for Lysol, vanilla, and shaving lotion at the counter'" (53), and Lucy's husband has not come home the night before, arriving in the morning hungover and late for work. Her gentle and kind uncle, Sonny, is also a victim of this imported disease – as deadly in its own way as the earlier imports, smallpox and tuberculosis: "It was no use to hope he'd stop drinking. Sonny wouldn't quit drinking till he quit living" (52). Already displaced from a more traditional way of life, Sonny now faces even further displacement as a direct result of the first, as he tells Lucy, "'The cops said I have to leave town. I don't want to stay 'cause they might beat me up'" (52).

Ironically, Sonny's own inability to effect permanent positive change in his own life allows him to see, or at least doesn't prevent him from recognizing, the problematic political dimension of Helmut's supposed identity change, his "turning Indian": "'How could anybody turn into something else? Huh? I don't think I could turn into a white man if I tried all my life. They wouldn't let me, so how does that German think he can be an Indian.

White people think they can do anything – turn into Chinese or Indian – they're crazy!'" (53). Another ironic contrast involving Sonny and alcohol comes with the story's closing reference to a ceremonial sweat, which Hilda thinks would be "real Indian" (59), and which recalls an earlier "secular sweat." The story takes place on a very hot day, and Sonny "fashioned a shade behind the house underneath the clothesline in the deep grass, spread a blanket, and filled a gallon jar from the pump. He covered the water with some old coats, lay down, and began to sweat the booze out" (54). Sonny's modern "sweat" may be read symbolically as a parodic ritual purification of white culture, as it represents a temporary return to a "native" or "natural" or "pure" (that is, sober) state.

In yet another ironic contrast, Lucy herself has never been to a sun-dance, a fact that Hilda finds ludicrous:"'But why? Don't you believe in it? It's your culture!'" (50). Lucy says she isn't interested in going and explains that it isn't in fact *her* culture and that her reserve has never had annual sun-dances:"'Over on the Blood Reserve they do and some places in the States, but not here'" (51). She views the ceremony as a recent import based on a problematic generalized or homogeneous sense of "native" culture: "'It's mostly those mixed-up people who are in it. You see, Indian religion just came back here on the reserve a little while ago, and there are different groups who all quarrel over which way to practise it. Some use Sioux ways, and others use Cree. It's just a big mess'" (51). She isn't interested in trying to place herself within the "new" culture, since she believes that it has no connection to any "old" culture of hers, but even as she claims to know what is "right and wrong" regarding such matters, she ironically reveals that many Native people are following a different set of rules:"She herself didn't practise Indian religion, but she knew enough about it to know that one didn't just join an Indian religious group if one was not raised with it. There was a lot of the conflict going on among those people who were involved in it. They used sacred practices from other tribes, Navajo and Sioux, or whatever pleased them" (53-54). The attempt to forge a unified cultural tradition may have the positive motive of unifying people for power and survival, but it also replicates the erasure of difference involved in European stereotypes and totalizing accounts of indigenous people, and also facilitates mastery or control of the culture by outsiders.

Lucy recalls another infamous case of appropriation south of the border, again showing her ironic double-vision of being both aware and unaware: "She'd read in the papers how some white woman in Hollywood became a medicine woman. She was selling her book on her life as a medicine woman. Maybe some white person or other person who wasn't Indian would get fooled by that book, but not an Indian" (53). Similarly, Lucy believes that "most of the Indians wished Helmut would disappear" (50), yet the rest of the community not only tolerates him but in some cases actually accepts his version of Native spirituality. Flora, for instance, has learned what she knows of the sun-dance from books, including Helmut's (56).

Ironies intensify at the literal and figurative "camp site" of this doubly misplaced cultural artifact when Flora asks her half-cousin Delphine if she can camp next to her. Delphine, irritated, tells her, "'You're supposed to camp with your own clan,'" and Flora, lost, can only respond, "'I wonder who's my clan'" (56). The "foreignness" of the culture on what perhaps should have been its "home ground" is patently clear: "Delphine had grown up Mormon and had recently turned to Indian religion, just as Flora had grown up Catholic and was now exploring traditional beliefs. The same could be said about many of the people here" (56). The same European colonization that displaced indigenous cultures and established the reserve system is now associated, through the figure of Helmut, in the displacing of the imposed systems of belief.

Helmut, it emerges near the end of the story, has gained most of his cultural information from his Blackfoot wife, Elsie; Flora says of their partnership and "his" book, "'He's the brains; she's the source'" (58). In a surprising turn of events, when Hilda finally meets Helmut, the question she asks him isn't about Native culture at all, but whether or not he is familiar with her home town in Germany. She is engaged in her own displaced homemaking process, seeking a connection with her home ground even from this distance. Helmut refuses to answer her directly, angrily referring to his wife and saying, "'Why don't you ask *her* questions about Germany,'" adding, "'She's been there'" (58).

The geographical confusions and ironies have come full circle here. Helmut, a visitor to Canada, affiliates himself with the Native culture of the place he visits, completely disavowing any association with his filial culture, identity, and place, while he tries to displace his filiative ties onto his Native Canadian wife, affiliating her with Germany on the basis of her visit(s) there. Their roles have been switched entirely; the absurd reigns. Hilda has come to Canada to learn about Native Canadians and ends up asking about Germany to a man who has "turned Indian." And in one final irony, the story ends with Flora's inviting Hilda to a sun-dance the following weekend: "I have a friend up north who can teach you about Indian religion,'" she says. "'She's a medicine woman. She's been to Germany. Maybe she even went to your home town'" (59).

## Maria Campbell's *Halfbreed*

Maria Campbell's *Halfbreed* also uses irony and humour on occasion to make its point, but for the most part her criticisms are presented bluntly and directly, as befits an autobiographical text with an explicitly didactic purpose: early on, she addresses the white portion of her audience directly, announcing, "I only want to say: this is what it was like; this is what it is still like" (9). The text is written using a personal, first-person storytelling voice in a "plain prose" style, with a minimum of decorative or "literary" devices such as explicitly figurative language. The basic narrative moves along in chronological order, speeding up at times and slowing down at others, but generally consistent in its forward movement and absence of large gaps. This narrative is embedded in an envelope pattern provided by an introduction that places the speaker, Campbell, at the end of the narrative journey that the text describes, at the point when she first decides to write about her life.

Because this text, like much other life writing, appears resistant or unsuited to traditional forms of literary analysis, and because it makes its points so clearly and directly on its own, mainstream literary scholarship has tended to ignore it. However, it represents an important perspective on Prairie homemaking that cannot be ignored here, and in itself performs the "groundbreaking" or "foundational" work that enables more explicitly literary work to follow.

Like Salverson's and many other autobiographies, Campbell's concerns not only her individual personal history but also that of "her people," the Métis, and it is now considered a landmark and a classic in Canadian Native women's writing. The writers Lenore Keeshig-Tobias and Daniel David Moses, for example, have called Campbell "The Mother of Us All" for her example in speaking out against systemic racism and her contribution in clearing a space for Native voices to be heard (Campbell, "Interview" 41). In a related vein, critic Janice Acoose argues that *Halfbreed* is a seminal and crucial text chiefly because it is the first in Canadian literature that "challenges existing stereotypes and images of indigenous women by providing a vivid spiritual, social, political and economic context" (90).[4] Campbell's text itself, then, is an example of literary homemaking, as it accomplishes "in language" many of the liberatory effects it aspires to "in life."

The Introduction opens with the sentence "The house where I grew up is tumbled down and overgrown with brush" (1), and her description of the "home place" she returns to after seventeen years' absence continues to interconnect and associate both human and vegetative landscapes with images of decline and decay. A pine tree beside the house is "dried and withered," the graveyard is "a tangle of wild roses, tiger lilies and thistle," the blacksmith shop and cheese factory "have long since been torn down," and the store is "old and lonely," appearing, "like the people it serves," to "merely exist" (1). The only positive aspects of the description are a family of beavers "busy working and chattering," and gophers scurrying "back and forth over the sunken graves" (1), seemingly oblivious or indifferent to the human tragedy that is so amply in evidence. Finding her childhood environment in such a distressing (vs. comforting) state, Campbell says she realized that she could never again find "home" in this place: "Like me the land had changed, my people were gone, and if I was to know peace I would have to search within myself" (2), and this search appears – in heavily condensed form – in her autobiography.[5]

The defining feature of Métis reality, for Campbell, is the people's tenuous present connection to the land. In chapters 1 and 2 she traces the early history of dislocations that lead to this condition, documenting how the Métis came to Saskatchewan from Ontario and Manitoba "to escape the prejudice and hate that comes with the opening of a new land" (3). According to Campbell's history, fear that the government wouldn't respect their land rights in Manitoba led to the Red River Rebellion of 1869, following which many Métis settled in southern Saskatchewan. There, when settlers and the railway moved in, their status as "squatters" was ignored by the lands–claims acts,[6] leading to the Riel rebellion in 1884 and the migration of many Métis to "the empty pockets of North Saskatchewan" (3-6).

Her clan settled northwest of Prince Albert, in "Spring River,"[7] and, when in the 1920s the land was opened for homesteading, most of her people took homesteads to keep possession of the land. Unable to "break" the land, however, due to lack of money for implements, the fact that the land was largely rock and muskeg, and the people's temperaments being suited to their traditional trapping and hunting economy rather than farming, the homesteads were soon reclaimed by the government Land Improvement District authorities. For a time the Métis became squatters on the land, but when the new owners chased them off they were forced onto the "road allowances," the crown land on either side of road lines. They became known as the "Road Allowance people," and so, Campbell says,

> began a miserable life of poverty which held no hope for the future. That generation of my people was completely beaten. Their fathers had failed during the Rebellion to make a dream come true; they failed as farmers; now there was nothing left. Their way of life was a part of Canada's past

and they saw no place in the world around them, for they believed they
had nothing to offer. They felt shame, and with shame the loss of pride
and the strength to live each day. (7-8)

The name "Road Allowance people" encapsulates the strong causal link
that Campbell establishes between a diminished sense of identity and a
"placeless" sense of place.

Geoffrey York has documented the degenerative cycle that Campbell's
people and many other Natives were, and are, caught in. "Land," he asserts,
"will always be the key to survival for aboriginal people" (140). He demonstrates how the loss of land, and hence of the resource base, means the
loss of the traditional economy and way of life, which often leads to a life of
welfare dependency and a lack of self-determination. This in turn produces
stress, anxiety, fear, and depression, which often manifest themselves in crime
and alcoholism (107-40).

Although Campbell's family lived in almost constant poverty, they never
accepted government assistance out of pride and fear of government inter-
ference: "Dad was afraid that if we received help they would visit our house
all the time" (84). Instead, government regulation and the lack of the Métis'
own land forced Campbell's father to hunt out of season and "in the National Park which was illegal," so, ironically, "the game wardens and the
RCMP were constant visitors at our home" (59) anyway. After her father is
put in jail for six months for poaching what she humorously calls "the
King's game" (71), Campbell comments very sarcastically:

> The Law will do many things to see that justice is done. Your poverty,
> your family, the circumstances, none of it matters. The important thing is
> that a man broke a law. He has a choice, and shouldn't break that law
> again. Instead, he can go on relief and become a living shell, to be scorned
> and ridiculed even more. . . . I used to believe there was no worse sin in
> this country than to be poor. (61)

Campbell's great-grandmother on her father's side, Cheechum, used to
tell her "that when the government gives you something, they take all that
you have in return – your pride, your dignity, all the things that make you
a living soul" (159). But, despite the family's attempts to be self-sufficient,
the lack of land sometimes meant extreme poverty and even prejudice
from their Indian relatives on the neighbouring reserves: "We were always
the poor relatives, the *awp-pee-tow-koosons* ["half people"]. They laughed
and scorned us. They had land and security, we had nothing" (25). Later,
when an attempt is made to bring Métis and status Indians together to

effect political change through the "tactic of strength in numbers," speaking "with one voice," the proposal "was rejected by the Treaty Indians. They felt that the militant stand that would be taken by such an organization would jeopardize their treaty rights. 'The Halfbreeds,' they said, 'have nothing to lose, so they can afford to be militant'" (182).

Other degrading social forces also took their toll on Campbell's family. In Campbell's first residential school, for example, she says: "We weren't allowed to speak Cree, only French and English, and for disobeying this, I was pushed into a small closet with no windows or light, and locked in for what seemed like hours"(47). Even when a school is built closer to home, Campbell's little sister still suffers from linguistic prejudice: "Because we used a mixture of Cree and English at home, her pronunciation was poor. The teacher would shake her and say to the class, 'Look at her! She is so stupid she can't even say 'this', instead of 'dis'" (87-88).

At one point, several Métis men accept some Co-operative Commonwealth Federation (CCF) Party relief work clearing land:

> There was very little money for fancy equipment but plenty of manpower – the Halfbreeds from the MLA's riding. . . . Daddy and I drove over by buggy that day to see them. When we arrived the men were in harness like horses, pulling up stumps and trees. Dad started to laugh when he saw Alex Vandal coming towards us pulling a tree, sweating and panting. He looked at us and said, "Danny did you know the new government felt sorry for us because we're called 'Halfbreeds'? They passed a law changing our name and now we're CCF horses. The Americans are going to pay good money to come and look at us." (70)

Though Alex is speaking ironically here, the tourist industry's interest in identity as commodity recalls two further incidents, one when Campbell is young and a group of American tourists ("Long Knives") ask if they can take the family's picture (40), and the other when she is older, down and out in Calgary, and a friend advises her, "Once summer comes we can make a few dollars here and there. The Calgary Stampede always needs Indians. There's no need to go out and earn a living on the street. We can fix up outfits for ourselves, and go to pow wows, and put on for white people, and get paid" (155).

Campbell is horrified when she thinks of herself "dancing for a place in society" and feels that it is just the same "as putting on a welfare coat to get government money" (156). The cumulative effects of such limited options for her and her family are a loss of identity and self-esteem. When Cheechum recounted the history of her people to Campbell as a young girl, she said that the white man saw that dividing the Métis against themselves was "a more powerful weapon than anything else. . . . They try to make you hate your own people" (51), and Campbell shows she has succumbed to this when she says of her people and culture "I hated all of it as much as I loved it" (117).

As in the pattern that York observed, in Campbell's text, alcoholism and crime – especially violence against women – are indeed the end result of the Métis' history of physical and spiritual dislocation. Among her many positive childhood memories are also bad ones from trips to town to sell roots and berries. The shift from country to town is accompanied by a shift in self-perception: "The townspeople would stand on the sidewalks and hurl insults at us" (36), and the adults "were happy and proud until we drove into town, then everyone became quiet and looked different. The men walked in front, looking straight ahead, their wives behind, and, I can never forget this, they had their heads down and never looked up" (37). After selling their goods, "[t]he men went to the beer parlour, promising to be out in half an hour" and the women and children "waited and waited until finally Mom and some of the braver women drove to the outskirts of town, set up tents and made a meal" (37).

When the men finally returned, the drinking party would continue outside the tents, while the children "would crawl out back of the tent, to hide in the bushes and watch until they all fell asleep" (38). White men would come by to dance and sing, inevitably "bothering" the women, and in response the Métis men "would become angry, but instead of fighting the white men they beat their wives. They ripped clothes off the women, hit them with fists or whips, knocked them down and kicked them until they were senseless. When that was over, they fought each other in the same way" (38). Campbell says that her summers "were spent in this way until [she] was thirteen and those trips to town always became more unbearable, because little by little the women started to drink as well" (38).

Soon, problems with alcohol come even closer to "home," as Campbell's father, her husband, and even Campbell herself all succumb to alcoholism. Her father becomes involved in a political movement to try to replicate in Saskatchewan the success of the Métis in Alberta, who "had organized an association and had gotten colony lands through one united voice" (72), but, when in his eyes the movement fails, he starts to drink and on occasion becomes violent: "Sometimes he'd hit Mom" and "[o]nce he even slapped Cheechum" (75), his own grandmother.

After Campbell's mother's death, the "relief people" continually threaten to take her six younger brothers and sisters away to place in foster homes, and to avoid this she eventually marries, at fifteen, a white man who she thinks can support them all. After the first couple of months, however, he "began to drink. Soon he lost his job and had to find another. I was pushed around the first few times he was drunk, but then he started to beat me whenever the mood hit" (122). As a result, her siblings are soon taken away, a major part of her home is destroyed, and it isn't long before she herself begins drinking and a long struggle with alcoholism and drugs.

Paralleling her earliest experiences with the adults' drinking during visits to town, Campbell's own alcohol problems also involve a rural/urban dichotomy. She recalls, "[A] city meant all sorts of exciting things to a little girl" (39). As a young adolescent she "thought about the big cities [she] had read about with good food and beautiful clothes, where there was no poverty and everyone was happy," deciding that she "would go to these cities someday and lead a gay, rich, exciting life" (87). Soon her "constant ambition was to finish school and take [her] family away to the city" (94), but when her husband tells her he is going to take her and their young baby to Vancouver and she doesn't respond he taunts her: "What's the matter with you? You always wanted to go to the big city" (124).

They stop in Kristen, Alberta, on the way to Vancouver, and, after her husband temporarily abandons her there, her spirits are broken by her husband's sister's racism and she "start[s] drinking and partying a lot. I figured 'What's the use' – people believed I was bad anyway, so I might as well give them real things to talk about" (129). Ironically, when they do finally make it to the "big city," she finds herself living in slum conditions even worse than what she had experienced at home: "I had lived in poverty," she says, "and seen decay but nothing like what surrounded me now" (131). When her husband leaves her a second time she falls into a life of prostitution, heroin addiction, drug-running and depression, and when she finally decides to make a clean break with this part of her life it comes as no surprise that her first thought is of a return to rural life: "I could quit if I made up my mind. I could leave and work on a farm" (144). She gets a job cooking on a ranch outside Calgary, and says that when she got there, "[F]or a minute I felt like I was home" (147).

A more lasting sense of home comes, however, only with sobriety and involvement with Native politics. When she is hospitalized after a suicide attempt, the hospital officials will release her only on the condition that she join Alcoholics Anonymous, and she finally finds a group where she feels at home: "It was a mixture of real down-and-outers, some white, some Native, drunks from skid-row, ex-cons from various institutions and women like myself. It was good: I understood these people, and they understood me. It was here that I met the people that would play an important role in the Native movement in Alberta" (167). Cheechum had always told her that she had "many sisters out there" (170), and it is among the "sisters" and "brothers" of Native activists that she finds that extended sense of family.

Becoming politically active involves revising her childhood dreams, but Campbell presents the process as one destined to happen, tracing it back in her genealogy to her great-grandmother Cheechum, "a niece of Gabriel Dumont" whose "whole family fought beside Riel and Dumont during the Rebellion" and who "never accepted defeat at Batoche," always holding out hope that some day things would be different (11). Campbell says that her people "have always been very political" and as a child she listened to the adults argue politics: "They talked about better education, a better way of life, but mostly about land for our people" (72). When her father had become involved in the new Alberta-based political movement, she says, "Cheechum was excited for the first time and would pace the floor until Daddy got home from his meetings" (72). But the Mounties, wardens, and other authorities weren't pleased – even Campbell's teacher joked that "Saskatchewan has a new Riel. Campbells have quit poaching to take up the new rebellion" (74).

Campbell's mother was also less than supportive of her father's activities, and Campbell says, "[I]n a way she too betrayed Dad by not understanding what he had to do. Her concerns were for her family. She didn't realize that what happened outside was important too" (76), suggesting the strong link between public and private concerns, and that the "inner" home would never be able to be stable and secure until the "outer" one was made that way too. Campbell too has to go through a process of moving from the personal to the public. When Campbell was a child, Cheechum told her, "Go out there and find what you want and take it, but always remember who you are and why you want it" (98), but when she does "go out there," Campbell gradually realizes that her search for "symbols of white ideals of success" (134) is taking her down the wrong path:

> I began to understand what Cheechum had been trying to say to me, and to see how I had misinterpreted what she had taught me. She had never meant that I should go out into the world in search of fortune, but rather that I go out and discover for myself the need for leadership and change: if our way of life were to improve I would have to find other people like myself, and together try to find an alternative. (166-67)

When Campbell does return to her geographical home place, it is as an invited speaker to Alcoholics Anonymous inmates at Prince Albert Penitentiary, and when she goes to see her father at Spring River, she says, "I tried to find something that was familiar in the land around me. The old log houses were gone and in their place grew wild rose bushes; . . . our house – the house I had missed so much – looked lonely and dilapidated" (172). When she visits the local town, St. Michel, she is horrified to find the streets "full of Native people in all stages of intoxication," a man "beating his wife behind a building," and children looking on "as though it was all quite normal" (173). Back on the Métis settlement,

> something had changed. The gentle mothers of my childhood were drunkards now, and neglect was evident everywhere. . . . The country side had changed too. Fires had swept through parts of it, often deliberately set by men out of work and money. Welfare was cut off in the summer months, but the Forestry Department paid wages for fighting fires. There was nothing left to hunt or trap, and only Daddy still trapped in the National Park. (173-74)

Once again, Campbell witnesses the devastating effects of the lack of a homeland on her people, and when she returns to Alberta to resume her political activities it is with a renewed sense of urgency – a feeling that "there was no time to waste" (177) – and also with the security that comes from knowing that even if she can't "go home again" in a literal sense, at least she now has new "brothers and sisters, all over the country" (184).

This final metaphorizing of family serves, in a sense, to shrink or collapse space, so that the "home place," rather than simply being lost, is now redefined to extend over the entire country. It may at first seem that this redefinition negates or diminishes the urgency of Campbell's argument regarding the need for specific land claims, but in fact the two versions of home are complementary. In order to pursue the acquisition of a homeland on the local level, she must first transpose her sense of home and community onto the larger regional or national level where political action can be effected (and effective). Ironically, then, in both the metaphorical and literal senses, Campbell can attempt to go home only by first leaving it.

## Rudy Wiebe's *Peace Shall Destroy Many*

Rudy Wiebe's novel *Peace Shall Destroy Many* is set during World War II, in 1944, in the fictionalized northern Saskatchewan community of Wapiti, where a small group of Russian Mennonites who immigrated to Canada in the 1920s are trying to establish a safe and separate homeland where they can follow their tradition of non-violence and the "ways of their fathers." The community's founder, Peter Block, is resolved that the only way for his people to retain their cultural identity is to segregate themselves completely from the outside world and all it represents – including the Native population that surrounds their community. Ironically, in order to establish a homeland for his pacifist community, he destroys the already precarious homeland of the neighbouring Métis settlements, and in this he mirrors the paradoxical situation of Canada sending troops to fight in the war: like Block, "'[t]he whole land is geared to destruction so that it will not be destroyed'" (13).

Ironically, it was such destructive conditions that the Mennonites were trying to escape when they came to Canada. The father of the novel's central character, Thom Wiens, is described as being "serenely at ease in the Mennonite community life of Central Russia" until the "upheavals of Russian life after 1917" drove him away (21). The Russian famine of 1921-22 looms large in their memories and imaginations (26), and the character Annamarie reminds Thom, "One reason our parents fled to Canada – why our fathers left Holland and Prussia – was to be protected from serving in war" (46).[8]

For Block, the motivation to begin over in a new place "began in the forests of Siberia where he had been sent as a conscientious objector in World War One" (125). While working in one of the "Forstei" bush camps in lieu of military service, he is nearly killed in an initiation prank, and having had an awareness of his own mortality thrust upon him he is seized with an intense "son-necessity" (126) – the desire to have a son to carry on his family line after he is gone. In his patriarchal and patrilineal culture, he feels that his daughter is "not enough; she would help form someone else's family. He, the lone survivor of thirteen children, was a mere vacancy without a son" (126).

After Russia withdrew from the war, he returned home to the "western fringes of the Ural foothills" (127), only to be followed there by civil war and famine, and when at last his wife bears the male child he has sought he ends up viciously killing a man who had threatened his son's food supply and thus, by implication, Block's hopes for the future: "[H]e sprang at the man, seized him away with a strength that knew no source save madness, and smashed the crook-nosed head back and forth, his frozen hide mitten like a club on his hand" (131).

The knowledge that he had killed a man with his own hands drives him to be "in the first group of emigrants to find exit to Canada in 1925" (132), and, though he later tries to forget this ignoble beginning, it continues to shape his construction of the Wapiti community:

> In the unmolested prosperity they had enjoyed at Wapiti, he had almost forgotten the fury that in 1927 drove him to the wilds of Saskatchewan, or why he had begged the first Mennonites to join him there in the desperate hope of perhaps again building a community such as their fathers had known in the golden days of Russia. The need for the community had grown to be a driving imperative to him as his dread increased that if he were left alone to grub at a homestead for the rest of his days, he must sink under the thought of what he despaired to forget. (124)

There is irony in his desire to establish a community that follows "the ways of the fathers," since neither Block nor *his* father can provide an appropriate "example for his son": "He wanted to raise his son as he himself, neglected by a careless father, had not been" (132).

Just as Block cannot escape his own violent past, neither can he escape the violence of the world. World War II, although ostensibly "far away," is in fact central to the novel, and it functions in several ways: it acts as a reminder of the sin and violence of the outside world that the Mennonites are trying to escape, it provides an occasion for theological debate about the practice of non-violence, it creates subplots involving individual characters' responses to being "called up," and it enables an examination of Mennonite affiliation with Germany.[9] The "presence" of the war in Wapiti is both imaginative and real, and it overdetermines the Mennonites' home-making strategies in Canada just as World War I did for them in Russia: "The irony of Peter Block's existence was, though he would rather have suffered death than participate in war, The World Wars of his time had shaped his life" (125).

Chapter 1 opens with an auditory and visual image of practising fighter planes: "The yellow planes passed overhead swiftly and in thunder" (11), and the novel is punctuated throughout by war reports coming in over the radio, the primary means of connection between Wapiti and the rest of the world, so that there is "[a] whole world listening to men killing themselves savagely" (43). The war "disrupted even the inviolability of the mail-order catalogue" (212), but, recalling Gander Stake in *Grain*, the community is also benefiting economically from it: "[W]ar prices had almost cleared them of their debt" (22), and Annamarie notes sardonically, "The whole world is now in it. We can't avoid it. Father raises pigs because the price is high: some men charged up the Normandy beaches last Tuesday with our bacon in their stomachs" (47).

Beyond these concrete reasons for being concerned with the war, however, the community also shares a more abstract interest in it:

> The war intrigued the Mennonites, partly because they saw it as the culmination of world evil from which they had strictly, consciously, severed themselves, partly because Germany was the storm centre. In the 1920's Germany had been their stepping stone from the tyranny they fled in Russia (few considered that Nazi Germany had little in common with the Hindenburg regime), but more than that, their own language told them that some 400 years before their own fathers had been German – and Dutch, which heritage they retained in their Low German dialect. They were honestly horrified at Hitler's ravage of Europe, but beneath often lurked the suspicion: "Only a German could set the whole world on its tail like this" (29-30).

The doubleness of their reaction, of both horror and admiration, is heightened by what the teacher Joseph calls their "'almost nationalistic interest in Germany'": "'After all,'" he says, "'we are displaced Germans, at least ethnically, and because we haven't had a true home for 400 years, we subconsciously long for one'" (30).

The anxiousness of this desire to affiliate with Germany despite present-day realities also affects Thom. When he hears the BBC report of the liberation of Paris on the radio, Thom feels an uneasy form of regret: "[H]e knew his family had been among the few last to escape the Communists in 1930 because of German government pressure. But that had been President Hinderburg [sic], not the Hitler regime. Yet regret persisted, faintly" (103). Block also shows his anxiety when he explains, "Of course, we do not side with Hitler, though we speak German" (121). This uncertainty surrounding German affiliation serves to further complicate the already unstable nature of Mennonite identity. As Thom explains, the question Who is a Mennonite? is difficult to answer: "'Some say only church members are Mennonites, others that we're actually a race of people. Most who are born with Mennonite names but refuse to join the church don't want to be known as Mennonites – guess they feel somehow it commits them'" (178).

Thom's own name is significant not only in how it connects him to his community and its past, but also in that it is an example of the complex language situation of his community. When Joseph writes to Thom, he addresses his letter "Dear Thomas," and comments, "I really did not know how to write your name, since in Wapiti [the community] it's spoken 'Tom' in English and 'Thom' in Low German and 'Thomas' in High German"

(160). Each of these three languages is used at certain times and carries special significance for the community:

> The peculiar Russian Mennonite use of three languages caused no diffi-
> culties for there were inviolable, though unstated, conventions as to when
> each was spoken. High German was always used when speaking of reli-
> gious matters and as a gesture of politeness towards strangers; a Low Ger-
> man dialect was spoken in the mundane matters of everyday living; the
> young people spoke English almost exclusively among themselves. Thought
> and tongue slipped unhesitantly from one language to the other. (20)

Nevertheless, despite such apparently fluid trilingualism, Thom does experience some translation difficulties when trying to explain the pacifist
principle to his younger brother: "Thom explained as he had known it
himself since he was a child, working the religious idea, among Mennonites
always expressed in High German, into the unaccustomed suit of workday
English. Somehow, while he was plowing, he could not suddenly speak to
his small brother in the smooth German of the church" (16). The church's
language seeming out of place in the fields mirrors Thom's difficulty in
fitting theology into everyday practice, and functions as a metaphor for the
problems involved in transplanting the Mennonite culture to a new land.

If the use of German connects the Mennonites to each other and to their
past, it also separates them from those outside their small community. Block
believes that much of the community's isolation from worldly influences
"'[had] been brought about because [they had] held to the German language
in both church and home'" (59), and Pastor Lepp tells Thom, "'There's
nothing Christian about the language itself. God did not use it to speak to
Adam in the Garden! It happens to be the language our parents spoke, and
we speak, but any other would do as well. The fact is, it's a barrier between
us and the worldly English surroundings we have to live in. There is merit
in that, for it makes our separation easier; keeps it before us all the time'"
(88). Ironically, when the Pastor gives Thom a book to help him teach his
Bible classes he comments, "'One of them is even written in English!'"
(89).

The issue of whether church meetings and Bible classes can be conducted
in English is one of the central controversies in the novel. When the older
church members learn that Joseph has used English in conducting a church
meeting for young people, a meeting is convened to discuss the matter.
One member of the Youth Committee explains, "[A]t the lake Brother
Dueck [Joseph] pointed out that there were some people there from both
districts who were not Mennonites and could not understand German.

Also, we noticed some Indians within hearing distance, and so he suggested he speak in English" (55). Block is angry enough that tradition was changed at all in this way, but when he finds out that Joseph's talk had been critical of non-resistance he erupts in fury: "'You criticized the church before *that* group? You took pains to speak a language they could all understand to slander our church?'" (60). It is clear that in Block's mind English poses a threat to the secure isolation that he has worked to establish.

In addition to trying to keep his community isolated through language, Block is also determined to keep it isolated through space, so that there would always be "the bush between them and the world" (48), and he says that "[i]t was at his insistence that they had bought out all the English years before, despite the deeper debt it forced upon them, that they might have a district of Mennonites" (21). Apart from a drunken Scot (29) and some Polish immigrants – the "poor white stuff that clung along the edges of Beaver district" and who would also be bought out soon (32) – Block's expansionist desires are held in check only by the "four breed families left" (22) and a nearby Cree Reservation. Thom comments, "Mennonites, when they passed nearby, stared as they would at any good land that needed clearing" (30).

Thom's expansionist desires are presented as naïvely motivated by romantic notions of continuity with the past and future. When he works, he is "gripped by the consciousness that his family was carrying on their ancestor's great tradition of building homes where only brute nature had couched" (19), and when he thinks of "the good land that was left" he believes, "[A]ll around the Mennonite settlement lay virgin sections, heavily wooded, enough for children's children" (20). It is only reluctantly and in frustration that he is able to admit that his desire to acquire more land for future generations of Mennonites might have negative repercussions: "'Life on earth is not fair – ever,'" he argues. "'Advantage for one is always balanced by disadvantage to another. Canada can only hold so many people. If I – and you – live and eat here, in a sense that fact makes it impossible for someone else to live and eat here'" (176).

Block, on the other hand, is explicit in his desire to buy out the remaining Métis families as much to get them out of his community as to acquire their land. When his hired man, Louis Moosomin, is "caught by the police in a drinking brawl" and sent to "Prince Albert pen for six months," Block concludes, "'[Y]ou can't change a breed: . . . Once a pig, always a pig'" (74). He believes that "the breeds" are "culturally and morally backward. They – the world – has been trained by its fathers to despise the things we hold precious: cleanliness, frugality, hard work, moral decency, peacefulness" (202).

He tells Thom that they must "'maintain a certain distance between themselves and ungodly people'" and that the Métis and Indians are "'basically different from us – qualitatively. No matter what you do for them, on the whole they remain children. . . . Give a breed ten dollars and he becomes as irresponsible as a lunatic!'" (205). For Block, as in traditional colonialist discourse, the Native people represent the worst aspects of the world he despises.

The rest of the community largely shares Block's view, though they do not necessarily pass judgement in the same way as a result. For Thom's younger brother, for instance, "'Half-breed' . . . was merely a species of being that did certain things he himself was not allowed to do because they were 'bad'" (15). The children are comfortable playing and attending school together, and at the school Christmas play, "[s]ide by side, Mennonites and Métis sat or leaned where they could, eyes intent, listening" (225). For the most part, however, the two communities are as divided socially as they are geographically: when the children leave school, "[t]he breeds vanished north and west, the Mennonites east and south" (120).

One day when Thom comes upon a wood-buffalo skull, he is struck with the ironies and horrors of colonization: "Why was Canada called a 'young' country? White men reckoned places young or old as they had had time to re-mould them to their own satisfaction. As often, to ruin" (82), and he laments his ignorance of Native history: "'There are stacks of European history books to read, yet the Indians – a people living in nearly half the world – lived here for thousands of years, and we don't know a single thing that happened to them except some old legend muddled in the memory of an old crone. A whole world lost. Not one remembered word of how generations upon generations lived and died'" (83). Ironically, he rejects "legend" as not being a "remembered word," but he is at least imperfectly aware of the power issues involved in the recording of history and story.[10]

Joseph also has a limited understanding of the difficult situation of the Métis:

> In the cold when all moose moved across the river and rabbits supplied the only meat, existence, not study, became the problem for the Métis children. Their parents had no concept of planned farming: they ate until there was no more. Labrets, Razins, Mackenzies, and Moosomins, the last the worst. Only a few Mennonites ever neared the Moosomin homestead, and they never went inside the four-walled shack or knew the mixture of common-law wives and husbands and children that were crammed there. Breeds lived as they lived: they were part of unchange-

able Canada for the Mennonites. They associated, to a limited extent, only with Louis Moosomin, and that because in the war-shortage Block had hired him. (31)

Block apparently believes that he can allow cultural "mixing" if it serves his purposes, since in his mind this means he is controlling it. As Thom tells us, Block "handled everyone, Mennonite and half-breed, as if they were pieces of farm machinery: each pawn had a particular spot in his scheme, and each was told what to believe and what to denounce" (207).

Ironically, Block's plan of "limited association" becomes his undoing when he discovers that his daughter Elizabeth has got pregnant by Louis. Elizabeth and the baby die in premature labour, and Block is hit with the realization that "he himself had harboured the snake. His own daughter and a half-breed!" (145). In his fury he "could not but see her as eternally damned for her sin" (153), for "[s]exual immorality was for all Mennonites the nadir of sin; it was equivalent to murder" (180), and the incident renews his determination to drive the remaining Métis families away: "The breeds must go. Too many years he had allowed them to remain on the edge of the settlement, where their dark wolfish faces could betray weak women. . . . He would buy them out personally, every one of them, and send them all to wherever their animal natures could destroy themselves without involving others" (153-54). Resolved that he will not have "drunken jail junk around here," he buys out the Moosomin farm first and tells Thom, "They'll all be bought out by spring" (206).

While it might first appear that his daughter's pregnancy and death simply confirm Block's worst fears and thus retroactively justify his fear and hatred of the Métis and his desire to keep "a certain distance" from them, the novel in fact suggests that it was precisely this "distance" and Block's tyrannical need to control that caused the tragedy. Some years before, Block had refused Elizabeth permission to marry Herman, the man of her choice, and Mrs. Block blames Elizabeth's death on this incident:

> Had she but persuaded him on that night years before when Herman had asked for Elizabeth. If she had died in childbirth married to Herman, it would only have been the lot of a world of wives before her, but now – she could not think of it. It was inexpressible even in her thoughts. Had she but been able to move him that night when Elizabeth begged him for Herman and he was as ice that finally, abruptly, blazed facts like fire. She had thought, There will be another man. But never; only at the final brink of her daughter's womanhood, this. (152-53)

While Block's wife partly blames herself for not persuading him, it is clear that he himself is primarily responsible for the final outcome of his manipulative behaviour. Ironically, after his failed attempt to marry Elizabeth, Herman too becomes involved with a member of the Moosomin family, Madeleine, and the couple is largely shunned by the Mennonite community: "[A] Mennonite just did not marry such a person, even if she was a Christian" (110).

When the doctor evasively tells Thom that Elizabeth died of "'an internal disorder that got out of control'" (148), the description functions as an apt metaphor for the Wapiti community as a whole, and Thom feels that "everything is falling in ruins" (218). In her last words to her brother, Elizabeth advises him to leave the ruined community: "'Thom – go away from here!'" she says. "'God in heaven! Can't you see what's happened to me?'" (140–41). Block's attempt to establish a Mennonite community separate from the world has had only disastrous effects, both for the community itself and its neighbouring Métis community. Mrs. Block finds the "moral" of the story in the Christian view that "'[y]ou have no dwelling place here, but through the Grace of God you can triumph over Sin and Death at last'" (153). When the earthly home fails, Pastor Lepp says, "[M]an goeth to his long home" (156), but, ironically, for Block even this heavenly home is now out of reach: "[H]e had, by every standard he ever believed, damned his own soul eternally" (185).

## Uma Parameswaran's *Trishanku*

While Wiebe's characters struggle ineffectually to maintain the secure, isolated home space they have established, Parameswaran's characters in *Trishanku* reject such segregation, as well as its opposite, assimilation, struggling instead to integrate themselves into Canadian society while retaining their cultural identities. Set in Winnipeg, the voices of fifteen Indian characters, as well as that of "The Poet," meditate and converse on their situations within the new place. The Poet announces in her Invocation the intention to "Begin with one, / Anyone, but make him truly him / And thereby you, and your people / And thereby us" (6). The shift from the third person to the second and then to the first accomplishes the drawing together of particulars into the general, of the individual into the community, that the passage describes. *Trishanku* thus manages to be "representative" of Indian immigrant experience while working only through the particulars of individual experience.

While issues of immigration are by no means the entire focus of the poems, they do play a major role. The title of the book itself indicates the uneasy state the characters find themselves in of being caught between cultures – an experience they share with the characters of Parameswaran's short story "The Door I Shut Behind Me," in which, "Like the mythological king, Trishanku, they stood suspended between two worlds, unable to enter either, and making a heaven of their own" (45).[11]

Much of Parameswaran's work is interconnected in this way, as themes, characters and whole passages reoccur, sometimes with slight changes. For instance, in "The Door I Shut Behind Me," Chander meets a character named Kishen Agrawal on his flight to Canada. On the plane, Agrawal can't figure out how the toilet flushes and gazes lewdly at the air hostess (39), and when they've arrived he becomes overwhelmed with homesickness, missing his wife and children and saying, "I would rather have them around me, and me on my ropestrung cot in my dung-polished courtyard than be this . . . here . . ." (41, original ellipses). In *Trishanku*, Chander recounts his experience of meeting a Mister Satish Mundhra (who played a different role in the short story)[12] who shares Agrawal's character and words: he "didn't know how to flush / the toilet in the Boeing 707," he "eyed the stewardesses lewdly," and he says, "'I'd give anything to be back home / on my ropestrung cot under the monsoon sky / in our courtyard plastered / with sweet-smelling cowdung water'" (19).

Whatever the motives for this kind of intertextuality, its effects are to create a sense of continuity and many-tentacled community, and this effect is even more intense in Parameswaran's play *Rootless but Green are the Boulevard Trees.* The play features many of the same characters as *Trishanku*, and in several instances portions of dialogue from the play appear in slightly varied form in the poems. While several of the subplots differ between the play and poems, the overriding concern with cultural conflict and concourse links the two and provides a kind of mutual interpretive context.

The title of the play itself provides a metaphor for Parameswaran's approach to cultural integration. Near the beginning of the play, Sharad asks his son Jayant, "Can we really grow roots here?" and Jayant answers by referring to the horticultural progress of a neighbouring apartment complex: "[T]hey have twenty-foot trees around the patio and there are five-footers inside the quadrangle, all set up overnight and flourishing like crazy" (14). His father answers, "That would be a most reassuring analogy, Jai, if our poplar hadn't died. . . . They are Ontario poplars and not native to Manitoba, and so it is to be expected that they'd dry up one winter. . . . And if an Ontario poplar can't grow and survive in Manitoba soil, what chance do we have?" (14). This sceptical, pessimistic note is countered, or at least qualified, at the end of the play in a conversation between Jayant and his friends Vithal and Sridhar about an evergreen tree standing outside with snow packed around its base:

> VITHAL: If the temp goes up to zero degrees midweek, as they expect, that would be the end of that. (*He waves at the tree.*)
>
> JAYANT: So what? (*Vehemently.*) What does it matter how long it stands? The point is that it is there, beautiful and green for the length of its life. A day, a hundred thousand days, it is a question of what we do and are, during that time. This evergreen doesn't have one Christly use – it isn't even good as firewood – but it is there and it is green, it is beautiful.
>
> SRIDHAR: And rootless.
>
> JAYANT: Yeah, rootless. Let's face it, Jeesus, no one, but no one has roots anywhere because that's the way things are in 1979 A.D. But we can stand tall, man, and live each day for all it's godamned worth and ours. (55)

Though it is not entirely clear within the play, writing elsewhere Parameswaran connects this tree to "the row of evergreen trees that are planted in the boulevard at Christmas time" ("Ganga in the Assiniboine" 126). The "planting" of trees in snow is also a standard Canadian practice for keeping Christmas trees fresh until they are brought indoors for the holidays and then for keeping them fresh until spring thaw is complete. The play takes place at the end of winter, and given this cultural context Jayant's Christian profanities in the conversation are highly ironic. But more important, the tree functions as a metaphor for one approach to integration, since it suggests that a person, like a tree, can be both rootless and green.

This metaphor applies well to *Trishanku*, where to a great extent the characters thrive precisely because they are not too firmly planted in Canadian soil; for the most part their cultural and spiritual roots go back to India. The book also offers its own central metaphor for integration using another "natural" vehicle – rivers – to carry the tenor. Early in the sequence of poems, Chander recalls a letter from his mother in India reminding him, "[T]his is the land where the Ganga flows" (14), but later in the sequence Vithal says,

> We shall build our temple
> Here where the Assiniboine

> Flows into the Red.
>
> And I shall bring Ganga,
>
> As Bhagiratha did of old,
>
> To our land
>
>          our Assiniboine
>
> And the fluteplayer
>
> Dark as *kaya* blossom
>
> Shall dance on the waters of La Salle. (66)

The Red and the Assiniboine, Winnipeg's two main rivers, are here merged with India's famous holy river Ganga, signifying a subtle coalescing of cultures. In Hindu mythology, Ganga, which flows from the toe of Vishnu, was brought to India from heaven by King Bhagiratha (Leach 440-41), and in this passage Vithal diverts the river's flow one more time.[13] The flute player who dances on Winnipeg's small La Salle River is the Hindu god Krishna, whose name means "black" and whose divine flute the *murali* charmed animals and spirits of nature (Walker II 97, I 560-66; Leach 396). This, then, represents a parallel instance of heaven being "brought to earth."

In her essay "Ganga in the Assiniboine: A Reading of Poems from *Trishanku*," Parameswaran comments on her central river metaphor, connecting it to her view of her role as a writer and her larger social concerns. I quote at length:

> The title – Ganga in the Assiniboine – epitomizes my thesis. Every immigrant transplants part of his native land to the new country, and the transplant may be said to have taken root once the immigrant figuratively sees his native river in the river that runs in his adopted place; not Ganga as the Assiniboine or the Assiniboine as the Ganga, both of which imply a simple transference or substitution, but Ganga in the Assiniboine which implies a flowing into, a merger that enriches the river. The confluence of any two rivers is sacred for the Hindu ethos, perhaps because it is symbolic of this enrichment. In the literary context of the immigrant experience this image has an added dimension. At the confluence, the rivers are distinct, and one can see the seam of the two separate streams as they join.
>
> So also with literary streams; in the early stages the superimposition of one landscape on another, one idiom on another, stands out, alien and out of joint, but farther downstream distinctions blur and fade away. An example would be the assimilation of Jewish and Yiddish words and phrases

> into our popular and literary vocabulary to the enrichment of English
> literature. Given the diversity of ethnic streams Canadian Literature will,
> we hope, extend its frontiers and expand its vocabulary in order to ac-
> commodate the diversity of our multicultural reality.
>
> Thus, what I am looking forward to is not only a time when those from
> India see their holy river in the Canadian landscape but when the aver-
> age literate Canadian would recognize as a matter of course the literary
> connotations of the word "Ganga" and thereby the emotional configura-
> tion of his East Indian neighbours. In short, through the development of
> literary symbols and vocabulary, we can accelerate a cultural synthesis
> that would otherwise take a much longer time. Or, to put it in another
> way, literature not only reflects persistence and change in society but can
> lead society into a better appreciation of our multicultural and ethno-
> centred fabric. (120-21)

*Trishanku*, then, not only represents the homemaking process of its characters, but it is also an example of literary homemaking, creating a special
kind of synthesized literary homeland that will accommodate what the
Poet calls "the miscegenation of cultures" (7).

The hybrid nature of this literary landscape is apparent throughout the
poems, through a multiplicity of allusions to places and cultures and systems of belief. Among the predominant references to India and Winnipeg,
there are references to Italy and Mexico, the British queen and Nehru,
American naturalists Thoreau and Audubon, and Michaelangelo. References to astrology and Greek and Roman mythology abound, and Chander
expresses his guilt at abandoning India with an allusion to Homer: "No
Aneas I, I cannot bear thee. / I ought, you ought, we ought love / love
toosoonhatebecoming love / the land where we're born" (18). In addition
to these explicit allusions, there is also a network of unmarked literary
references, as when Chander explains his emigration with the lines "And
therefore I sailed the seas and came / to this land of endless sky and snow"
(10), putting a northern twist on W.B. Yeats's "Sailing to Byzantium." Similarly, the dying Poornima says, "My eternal summer shall not fade / In the
halls of my father's home" (64), echoing William Shakespeare's Sonnet 18.

Far from being signs of displacement, the majority of these references
serve to indicate an expanded sense of being at home in several different
cultural realms, and this positive view of diversity may not be solely related
to the phenomenon of immigration. As Salman Rushdie has said of narrow
nationalisms that yearn for originary cultural "purity": "One of the most
absurd aspects of this quest for national authenticity is that – as far as India
is concerned, anyway – it is completely fallacious to suppose that there is

such a thing as a pure, unalloyed tradition from which to draw. . . . Eclecticism, the ability to take from the world what seems fitting and to leave the rest, has always been a hallmark of the Indian tradition" (67). So, while the boy Dilip learns French songs in school (23), another character, Savitri, daydreams of "the sonorous majesty of Sanskrit" (77), and Chander resents having to socialize with newcomers from India who speak in a "pseudo-Oxford accent mostly about themselves" (52). Meanwhile, back in India, Chander's father reads "The Hindu first to last / on the stone verandah" while his mother writes to him "[i]n Tamil, 'Om' centred top of the page" (14).

Perhaps the most extraordinary example of "cultural miscegenation" is in the poem that contains that phrase. The Poet begins with British renaissance writer Sir Fulke Greville's line "Born under one law, to another bound," rhetorically asking him, "What will you say of me" who was "born under two laws and bound / to a third?" (7). This complicated web of affiliations is then spelled out in a rather irreverent history of the poet, involving an allusion to Moses being adopted by the Egyptian kingdom that was attempting to control or destroy his own people, the Israelites (Exodus 1-2):[14]

> . . . I was
>
> In love begot, with love laid
>
> On alien bulrushes to be picked up,
>
> Cared for, adopted,
>
> By my fairy godmother –
>
> Dei Gratia Regina
>
> Of the gem set in the silver sea
>
> Seat of Mars etcetera etcetera –
>
> Who dropped me when she withdrew
>
> As sedately as she could
>
> Wrapping the Union Jack around
>
> Her dismembered strength.

Having announced the failure of British Empire, the poem then ends with two possibilities for poetic "action," one Hindu, picking up the book's title, and the other from the Old Testament:

> Shall I hang myself in the sky
> As Trishanku did of old?
> What new Elect shall I lead
> To what Sinai to bring down
> What law? (7)

The use of a triple question to close the poem reinforces the complexity of the situation involved, and it suggests that there will be no easy answers to the frequently difficult situations in which the various characters find themselves.

Earlier in the text, in the Invocation, the Poet announces part of her poetic strategy:"Begin with here / Not with there" (6).This echoes Margaret Atwood's classic remark on the Canadian inferiority complex and the colonial mentality that causes it:"A person who is 'here' but would rather be somewhere else is an exile or a prisoner; a person who is 'here' but thinks he is somewhere else is insane" (*Survival* 18). According to this definition, Parameswaran's Poet is immanently sane, and not in a condition of exile; that is, she appears to be "at home."

Moments of nostalgia are also rarer among the different characters than might be expected. Tara's mother-in-law rejects Canadian practices like closing windows and locking doors, and says, "let me go back / to sun and air / and sweat and even flies and all / But not this, not this" (51), and the character Chandrika says, "The land is green but my heart was barren, / Warm are the people but my heart was lonely, / Money flows in rivers but my heart was dry" (41), but when Savitri criticizes the Canadian medical system ("What aunts would give gratis / My medicare taxes dispense / with a jargon 15 years dated / and a two-hour wait") she acknowledges, after a long pause, that "One can be so sarcastic / When reassured" (68). In an even clearer anti-nostalgic vein, the young man Jayant criticizes his father's occasional romanticizing of his old home:"Distance makes the heart grow fonder, / to hand a cliché to you / my sententious dad," he says, describing the old home as "a sprawling shambles" with "A half-mile walk to the shithouse / and pigs slurping" (27).

Winnipeg is also treated with more realism than romanticism, and nowhere is this clearer than in the many references to racism throughout the poems. Parameswaran demonstrates that cultural diversity is not always viewed as enrichment and that even children are not exempt from the effects of intolerance: Chandrika sees Harjit "pinned to locker floor / by four of his schoolmates / while the fifth lopped off his hair" (54), and Dilip says he likes school but asks his mother, "Ma, you think you could change my name / To Jim or David or something?" and

> When the snow comes, Ma,
>
> I'll get less brown won't I?
>
> It would be nice to be white,
>
> more like everyone else
>
> you know? (23)

Savitri also fears for the children's safety and well-being, warning them of the "white ants," which could be a metaphor for white people and white culture: "Termites they call them here. White ants build hills, burrow under house foundations, eat walls. Krish don't open the door, don't talk to strangers, don't die on me, my darling, the white ants are coming" (77).

Racism also affects the adults and young adults, and it ranges in form from subtle linguistic inflexibility, as when Chandrika notes that everyone in her husband's department anglicizes their last name, pronouncing Chander as "Chandler without the l" (39), to Sharad's feeling that the people around him are "glancing, swiftly but completely / through me: / why are you here?" (34), to Vithal's observation that for Indian immigrants the "fact of life / In this true north strong and free" is that "If your house gets stones and eggs / smashed on windows you'd get action / faster from the Defence League / than from any goddam cop" (67). In one doubly ironic incident, a reporter at a science symposium asks Chander, "What made you take the initiative to bring your Indian kids here?" and Chander later realizes that the reporter had confused him with a schoolteacher who arrives with "a troop of natives behind him" and who "has apparently been at Indian reserves for seven years slaving to get the blighters put together something half decent." Chander wryly observes, "Y'bet they can't make out one brown man from another" (37), pointing out the ignorance behind the European naming of North American Aboriginals.

Vithal's angry response to this sort of ignorance, and its accompanying cultural intolerance, is to try to rally people together: "Look, you guys, we've gotta show them, / Yeah, show the bastards we've as much / right as anyone who's come here / in the last three hundred years" (65). He believes if they "stand together" the dominant culture won't be able to "divide and rule / no more" (65), but Jayant counters with his own form of prejudice, which resists group identification, saying, "What do we have in common, Jeesus, / We and those unlettered louts / with their garlic masalas / and unwashed beards?" (66). A more extreme variety of this desire to disaffiliate with one's own roots is noted by Savitri: "[T]here is Pradeep who has dropped out of our crowd after he got married to one of the library clerks. I wonder why they do that? drop us I mean, simply because she is white. To snub us or for fear we'd snub them?" (76).

Examples of such "snubbing" of the new culture are rare, but do occur, especially among the older characters. When Tara follows another woman to an Italian food store she says, "The stink hits my nose, but I keep my face / From showing no?" And when she sees "whole hunks / of animals hanging from hooks / like we hang bananas" her "stomach churns" and she rushes out (44). In a similar vein, Tara's mother-in-law says, "she cannot breathe this stale air / with yesterday's cooking smells / going round and round," and advises her son,

> . . . cooking should smell good
>
> The leaping aromas
>
> of turmeric and green coriander,
>
> and mustard seeds popped in hot oil
>
> that flavour food, not stink up the air. (50)

Such instances help to contextualize Chandrika's insistence, when speaking about "meeting some VIPS at a party," that "If my brothers and I / do not shake hands with you / (though your palms by your lady's grace, are clean.) / Know it is by our will, not yours" (42). Chandrika appears to be aware that attaining a degree of power is a crucial step in the homemaking process, especially if it is integration (the creation of a third place) rather than segregation (retreat to the first place) or assimilation (acquiescence to the second place) that is the goal. Thus she refuses the dominant culture the right to reject, reserving it instead for her people, and the struggle to build a new place, a heaven suspended between the other two worlds, continues.

# Placing the Self in Motion

*5*

House and garden are islands:
home is a wider territory
of the heart.

(Elizabeth Brewster, *Entertaining Angels* 102)

[I]f every American is several people, and one of them is or would like to
be a placed person, another is the opposite, the displaced person. . . . The
American home is often a mobile home. I know about this. I was born
on wheels, among just such a family. I know about the excitement of
newness and possibility, but I also know the dissatisfaction and hunger
that result from placelessness.

(Wallace Stegner, "The Sense of Place" 199, 201)

*RUNNING AWAY*
Everybody does at least once when they're little
except on the prairie   Where do you run
when your mother can stand outside
and look six miles in any direction?

(Yvonne Trainer, *Landscape Turned Sideways* 91)

Men know they are sexual exiles. They wander the earth seeking satisfaction, craving and despising, never content. There is nothing in that
anguished motion for women to envy.

(Camille Paglia, *Sexual Personae* 19)

Home is a movement.

(Aritha van Herk, "Calgary, this growing graveyard" 334)

If the Canadian home is less often a *literal* "mobile home" than the American, perhaps because of the generally harsher northern climate, it is just as often a *figurative* one. The fact that so many selves have placed themselves, or *been placed*, in motion, moving from one place to another, raises the question of whether it is possible to go one step further and "place" the self *in* motion, *while* in motion, rather than merely leaving one home and establishing another. This home is not a centre of gravity that is other and outside the self but something inside of or identical to the self. Or, perhaps, even more radically, something that "resides in" or is constructed by *movement itself.* Such a notion goes beyond home as verb, "to home," for that still implies an object or goal of the movement; it redefines home as a dynamic noun, a process, an experience, the flux and flow of matter turned into energy.

Robert Kroetsch's collection of long poems *Completed Field Notes*, Aritha van Herk's novel *No Fixed Address: An Amorous Journey*, and Fred Wah's *Alley Alley Home Free* all react to some sort of radical displacement, an uprooting – geographical and/or familial – by embracing a process-approach to matters of home. In Kroetsch's text, the lost (sold) home place and the absent mother figure appear in ghost form through his continual dislocation in and among space, language and relationships. In van Herk's text, the protagonist's unhappy childhood family life leads her to reject any traditional sense of home, and to opt instead for continual movement, placing herself in and with a car, hotel rooms, anonymous lovers and the open road. In Wah's text, a referential sense of external space is abandoned entirely, and place is redefined as body, so that the movement of perception itself becomes a dynamic "homing" process.

## Robert Kroetsch's *Completed Field Notes*

Dislocation – both formal and thematic – is a fundamental principle of Kroetsch's long poems. The persona, geographic location, time sense, poetic structure and linguistic and literary codes in the poems are all complex, shifting and unstable. Given that Kroetsch is considered one of our most "literary" writers, it is interesting that Robert Scholes offers a semiotic definition of literature that depends precisely on such dislocations, using the model of communicative acts popularized by Roman Jakobson:[1]

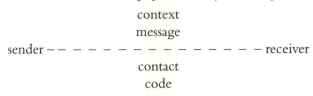

Scholes argues that "we sense literariness in an utterance when any one of the six features of communication loses its simplicity and becomes multiple or duplicitous" (20, 21), and he summarizes these dislocations as follows:

1. Duplicity of sender – role-playing, acting
2. Duplicity of receiver – eavesdropping, voyeurism
3. Duplicity of message – opacity, ambiguity
4. Duplicity of context – allusion, fiction
5. Duplicity of contact – translation [e.g. of oral or visual into verbal], fiction
6. Duplicity of code – involved in all the above   (31)

Further, he argues that "literariness does not equal literature until it dominates any given utterance" (22). In other words, the greater the dislocation of the six elements from their usual (straightforward, non-literary) functions, the more likely we are to define an act of communication as literature.

Kroetsch's long poems utilize all the duplicitous strategies that Scholes outlines, and more. For instance, the personal nature of several of the poems tempts the reader to an autobiographical reading, but the poems also incorporate a great deal of "found material" – dictionary definitions, seed catalogue entries, immigration propaganda documents, and traditional jokes, for example – in which authorship is at least double and thus problematic. Further, it is arguable that one of the poems' primary interests lies in the deliberate and conscious construction of a duplicitous persona, as suggested by the persona's repeated assertions "I've sworn off myself" (64), "I'm hardly the same myself" (69), "I am not myself" (140), "I'm not myself" (226, 265), "I'm beside myself" (230), and "I AM/naught" (267), as well as in the poem "Mile Zero":

> muse
> I figure
>
> . . . . . . . .
>
> self, portraying
> self   (135)

Here, the "I figure," the constructed persona, becomes, in a sense, its own muse, and the act of "portraying" a self that is not itself becomes the primary artistic concern.

Several poems put readers in a position of eavesdropping on the private correspondence and conversations of this persona, and there is an element of voyeurism in following the sexual escapades of the subject who writes, "I know you'd be appalled at the idea of a faithful lover. I'll do my best" (243). The dislocations of opacity, ambiguity, and allusion – literary, classical, self-referential – permeate the text, and the translation of oral, vernacular discourse into literary print discourse is also a key strategy.

All these "literary" dislocations serve to reinforce and heighten the text's profound sense of geographical dislocation, as the setting moves between Kroetsch's place of origin, the Prairies, and several sites both in and outside Canada. Critic Smaro Kamboureli (a version of whom also appears as a character in several poems) has written that, when the desire to locate an origin,

> often in effect a memory of colonialism, privileges absence, it locates origins in a place that has not been directly or recently experienced – Europe, the Old World. In Kroetsch's poems, however, the desire for origins does not privilege the place from which his ancestors came, but rather the place to which they came – the small prairie town, the New World.
>
> Although his early long poems, *The Ledger* and *Seed Catalogue*, deal with the place he was born in, the tension that generates the desire for place occurs when the poet no longer inhabits his place of origins. Locality in his poems derives from a profound sense of dislocation. (105-06)

Further, she argues that Kroetsch "does not undertake a journey of nostalgia" because he is "[e]ntirely at home with language" and "distrusts the absolute certainty that any single place might offer him" (106).

Almost exactly the opposite could also be argued, however, as is appropriate for such a duplicitous text. In my reading, for instance, Kroetsch's poems embody a "memory of colonialism" of a very different sort, their dislocation derives from a profound sense of locality, not vice versa, and the persona *does* undertake a journey of nostalgia, constructing a home not *in* but *through* language, which may be the only means to access or recover a "lost place," and which is not an end in itself, not equivalent to the created psychic connection or condition.[2] Despite the high postmodernism of *Completed Field Notes,* the referential function of language, while questioned, is never entirely eliminated, still maintaining its "pointing" function that sets the mind of both writer and reader along a particular trajectory. In addition, the performative function of language may bring into being a kind of reality outside, or other than, the language itself.

This "homing" process begins, appropriately enough, at the beginning of the text. Structurally, the first three of the twenty collected long poems comprise a kind of biographical and textual place of origin, a "home base" for Kroetsch and the rest of the text, by being about, set in, or associated with the prairie space where he grew up. The text's prologue, "Stone Hammer Poem," introduces the family farm in Alberta, which has been "lost" due to a combination of factors. The first of these is the speaker's "memory of colonialism," as right from the outset the poem presents the history of European colonization of the Prairies as problematizing its status as "home ground." The stone hammer of the title, found by the poet's father "on a rockpile in the / north-west corner of what / he thought of / as his wheatfield" (6), reminds the poet that "the / buffalo's skull / is gone" (1). Used as a paperweight on the poet's desk, as he says, "where I begin / this poem" (2), it is also "located" as the origin of the poet's writing, initiating a meditation on the flawed concept of land ownership.

Aware that the stone must have a prior history, the speaker identifies it as a "pemmican maul" and wonders if it

> fell from the travois or
> a boy playing  lost it in
> the prairie wool or
> a squaw  left it in
> the brain of a buffalo or
>
> it is a million
> years older than
> the hand that
> chipped stone . . . (2)

He imagines a Blackfoot or Cree man losing the maul, and in frustration (and possible later delight) over the unknowability of its past says, "I have to / I want / to know (not know) / ?WHAT HAPPENED" (4).

This interest in the history of the stone is linked with an interest in the history of the land, defined in terms of a problematic sense of ownership, and the speaker lists, in short lines, the long lines of its succession, beginning with the assertion

> Now the field is
> mine because
> I gave it
> (for a price)

> to a young man
> (with a growing son)
> who did not
>
> notice that the land
> did not belong
>
> to the Indian who
> gave it to the Queen
> (for a price) who
> gave it to the CPR
> (for a price) which
> gave it to my grandfather
> (for a price) who
> gave it to my father
> 50 bucks an acre
> (*Gott im Himmel* I cut
> down all the trees I
> picked up all the stones) who
>
> gave it to his son
> (who sold it). (5)

The ironic, contradictory phrase "gave it / (for a price)" is replaced only at the end by the more business-like word "sold" – a shift suggesting that the speaker has at last come to fully and directly acknowledge the economic, capitalist foundations of the place he knew as home.

The mention of the newest buyer's "growing son" also suggests that this process of exchange will continue into the future, and that ideas of ownership are necessarily temporary, transient. As a result, the speaker believes he can own the land only by *not* owning it anymore, that is, that possession through memory alone is in fact more secure and lasting – more "real," in a spiritual or psychological sense, than supposedly real (legal, economic) ownership. This kind of memorial possession and writing work to enhance each other, as through the writing of the loss or absence of the home place it simultaneously becomes present, taking on a concrete existence in the poem and in the writer's (and reader's) mind.

Besides colonialism and its attendant capitalism, family relations also function in the poem as a major problematizing factor, primarily through their

absence. Kroetsch's father after retirement is described as growing raspber-
ries, "lonesome for the / hot wind on his face, the smell / of horses, the
distant / hum of a threshing machine," and

> . . . lonesome for his absent
>
> son and his daughters,
>
> for his wife, for his own
>
> brothers and sisters and
>
> his own mother and father. (6)

With family members either deceased or dispersed, and his entire cultural
relationship to the land dissolved, there is little left of home at home, and
little reason for Kroetsch to undertake a literal, physical return to place,
since, while the geographical space might appear quite the same (and even
that is not guaranteed), the activities and people that inscribed it as home
would no longer exist there. The space would, quite literally, not be the
same place. The stone, however, sitting on the poet's desk, "smelling a little
of cut / grass or maybe even of / ripening wheat or of / buffalo blood hot
/ in the dying sun" (7), offers a more direct (ironically by being indirect)
link to place through writing and remembrance, smell being the sense
most strongly associated with memory.

The second long poem, "The Ledger," is set in Bruce County, Ontario,
and continues the first's concern with history, generations, and colonialism,
taking the concerns with ancestry, colonialism, and economics back two
generations and using a found ledger as a record of settlement activity. The
poem documents the destruction of nature and human culture involved in
the creation of a new home place: "To raise a barn; / cut down a forest. / To
raise oats and hay; / burn the soil" (13), "departures: the trout stream,"
"departures: the birch-bark / canoe" (17). The 1861 census question and
answer, "'Indians if any' / none" (18), throws ironic light on the colonialist
immigration rhetoric of "self-made men who have made Canada what it
is" (16):

> the pioneers, whose self-reliant industry and progressive enterprise have
> conquered the primeval forest, and left in their stead, as a heritage to
> posterity, a country teeming with substantial comforts and material wealth,
> and reflecting in its every feature the indomitable spirit and true manli-
> ness of a noble race, whose lives and deeds will shine while the commu-
> nities they have founded shall continue to exist. (28)

This rhetoric of permanence, of community as a legacy of empire, is also undercut by the poem's repeated emphasis on the double movement of arrivals and departures, which suggests that physically leaving home has a long history in Kroetsch's family. The inhabitants of Bruce County, though "intending to stay" (19, 22, 29), often move on, like those in Kroetsch's family who "go west / to homestead" (31), and the poem suggests that stasis, the failure to move on, is equivalent to death: "A man that lies permanently in some place. / A woman that lies permanently in some place. / A resident. Obsolete. / The book of final entry" (28). However, this insistence on movement is countered by the pull back toward home, as Kroetsch imagines the desire of his great-grandmother, "buried in Spring Lake, Alberta" (24), "to be interred / in the plot of Ontario earth / next to the ledger that / covered her first husband" (27), Kroetsch's great-grandfather. The comment "Tombstones are hard / to kill" (31) suggests this strong connection between memory, death, and place, since tombstones act to (literally) inscribe space into place with the memory of death, and, by extension, of life.

Noting this preoccupation with memory, Kroetsch's current family members become literary critics: "everything you write / my wife, my daughters, said / is a search for the dead" (13). Especially in regard to the maternal, this observation holds true for many of Kroetsch's subsequent long poems as well. For instance, in the later poem "The Frankfurt *Hauptbahnhof*," Kroetsch searches for, or at least expects to find, signs of his great-grandmother again. Even more significantly, the association in "The Ledger" of the great-grandmother with fear and desire begins an encoding of the female that runs throughout the rest of the text: "What did most men feel / in her presence? Terror. / What did they do about it? Proposed" (24). The poem's insistence in its last line, "You Must Marry the Terror" (31), echoes in the rest of the poems through the presentation of women primarily as agents of pain and objects of desire.

This version of the female is brought very "close to home" in the third long poem, "Seed Catalogue." Here the poet's memory of his mother (who died when he was thirteen) and her funeral wake is collocated with his initiation into sexual relations, suggesting a connection between the two. The poet figure rejects the strict Catholicism of the priest, who tells him that "playing dirty is a mortal sin, . . . you'll go to hell / and burn forever" (36), in favour of climbing into a granary and being "like / one" with a girl named Germaine.[3] Similarly, he rejects the male world of his father, who "was puzzled / by any garden that was smaller than a / quarter-section of wheat and summerfallow" (34), and who tells him, "the next time you want to / write a poem / we'll start the haying" (43), by spending time with his mother in her garden and by continuing to write.

Speaking in interview, Kroetsch has commented on this early experience of gendered space and activity:

> I had allergies so that I couldn't do a lot of the male work in buildings – but I could work out of doors. I would do out-of-door work but I couldn't work in the barn or anything like that. But I couldn't work in the house either because that was the sphere of female activity – and I was the only son and the oldest, and all those privileged things. And the one place where I found a kind of open field was the garden because a garden is ambiguous on a farm. It involves women's work but often the men help. (Neuman and Wilson 21)

Later in the same interview, Krotesch comments on his relationship with his mother and its ambiguously erotic nature:

> I kept the mother figures, especially, very silent at the center of the writing, partly because my own relationship with my mother was so painful, that I've only recently even put it into print at all. And I think part of my move to autobiography was daring to say that my mother died when I was so young and I was very close to her. . . . I told you about finding a picture of my mother when she was sixteen years old and about how my erotic relationship to this woman has shocked me – my sense of desiring the woman in that photograph – which I'm going to have to write about.[4] (Neuman and Wilson 22)

Kroetsch goes on to ask, "What is quest really about? It's sexual, it's looking for that fulfillment" (23), and he acknowledges, "[T]here's a kind of obsession in my work with finding a female muse" (23), linking the inspiration or drive for writing with the sexual quest, which is also associated with his absent mother.

Returning to the garden of the poem, though a "hired man" is pictured helping there, the space is overwhelmingly associated with Krotesch's mother, who twice whispers to him, "Bring me the radish seeds" (33, 34). In fact, the garden in "Seed Catalogue" is less a site of gender ambiguity than of sexual ambiguity, with the mother's whispered request taking on erotic undertones. This is perhaps more obvious in light of Kroetsch's interview comments,[5] but it is also suggested in the poem through the recurring image of binder twine, which functions as a kind of figurative umbilical cord, "binding" the poet to the place of the mother. Kroetsch remembers (or imagines) his mother in the garden "marking the first row / with a piece of binder twine, stretched / between two pegs" (33), Germaine and he "were like / one" on spread-out paper from "the gunny sacks / the binder twine was shipped in" (37), and he remembers his mother's sweet peas "climbing the stretched / binder twine by / the front porch" (50).

Further, in "Mile Zero," the next poem that explicitly mentions his mother, the binder twine image recurs in the phrase "The bindertwine of place" (134), indicating that mother-memory and the sexual quest are both tied closely with the Prairie home place. Given all of this, we are invited to a psychoanalytic reading of the poet's lovers as mother figures, not in the usual mundane sense of their coddling or nurturing or doing the laundry for him, but because of their painful absences and sexual desireability.

Kroetsch's "shocking" connection between sex and death and home is mirrored in Freud's theory of the uncanny and of the phantasy, "filled with a certain lustful pleasure," of "intra-uterine existence" (397):

> It often happens that male patients declare that they feel there is some-
> thing uncanny about the female genital organs. This *unheimlich* place,
> however, is the entrance to the former *heim* [home] of all human beings,
> to the place where everyone dwelt once upon a time and in the begin-
> ning. There is a humourous saying: "Love is home-sickness"; and when-
> ever a man dreams of a place or a country and says to himself, still in the
> dream, "this place is familiar to me, I have been there before," we may
> interpret the place as being his mother's genitals or her body. In this case,
> too, the *unheimlich* is what was once *heimisch*, home-like, familiar; the
> prefix "un" is the token of repression. (399)

It is often mentioned by critics that there is a large gap between the attention to Kroetsch's mother in "Seed Catalogue" (1977) and the later poems that are explicitly about her. Kamboureli, for instance, says, "It is not a coincidence that it has taken him a decade since his first long poem (1975) to write about his mother in 'Sounding the Name' and 'The Poet's Mother' (1985). He comments on this himself in 1981 when he says in 'Mile Zero': '[I]s not the mother figure the figure at once most present in and most absent from this poet's work?' (*CFN* 132)" (110). What is less often noted is that Kroetsch here is not only asserting his mother's absence, but also her *presence*. If indeed the figure of the lover can be read as a metonomy for his mother – that is, if the poet's female lovers may be read as mother figures – then the mother has indeed been the figure "most present" in his work, and a narrative line can be traced through *Completed Field Notes* of a quest for mother, and home, that is surprisingly consistent and coherent.

The next set of poems following "Seed Catalogue," the fourth through tenth, with the exception of the eighth, "Sketches of a Lemon," are linked by an overriding concern with the libidinal. In the fourth, "How I Joined the Seal Herd," ostensibly a poem about sex with a seal, the poet continues the association established in "Seed Catalogue" of loneliness, loving, and death:

> my nights are all bloody   I whispered
>
> god, I am lonely   as a lover/my
>
> naked body swims in the leak of light
>
> death has a breath too   it smells
>
> of bedclothes   it smells of locked
>
> windows   my nights are all drenched.  (55)

Shortly after this lament, he is unable to "place" himself: "where, exactly, I asked, is – " (55) – a question he cannot complete nor answer.

Similarly, in the sixth poem, "The Silent Poet Sequence," the poet engages in some unusual pre- or post-coital prayer, his crossed fingers indicating an insincere statement or an ironic hope for luck and also, perhaps, resembling the symbols of connection he claims to despise:

> |     | . . . I look at bridges malignantly |
> | --- | --- |
> | and | pray with the first two fingers of each hand crossed |
> | but | she, in the bathroom, washing between her legs, what |
> |     | are you doing on your knees |
> | and | I leap up |
> | but | I think I'm preparing to die. (77-78) |

Shortly after this we find the persona "reading in bed": "I study maps, this is Alberta" (78), completing the connection between sex and the homing instinct or the desire to place oneself.

Another dimension of the same connection, this time the *failure* of sexuality linked to a *dispersed* sense of place, is developed in the intervening fifth poem, "The Sad Phoenician," which begins

> | and | even if it's true, that all my women all have new lovers, |
> | --- | --- |
> |     | then laugh, go ahead |
> | but | don't expect me to cry |
> | and | believe you me I have a few tricks up my sleeve myself. (57) |

Here the poet constructs the persona of a self-mocking but bitter and resentful jilted lover, who claims that his bodily illnesses, perhaps like his emotional scars, "only hurt when I laugh" (61). Though he suggests at one point, "[L]et's pretend that only women suffer" (63), it is only to mock the idea of their suffering, and he angrily attacks and belittles a woman from Swift Current, a woman in Montreal, a woman from Nanaimo, and a woman in upstate New York, who have all rejected him in one way or another, frustrating the homing drive of sex. With the logic of the exasperated and furious, he concludes, generalizing, that "there's no satisfying women, so why try" (62), and he states, "[W]hen the goat wears a halo, then I too shall be faithful, believe me; a man faithful, a woman satisfied" (62), punningly conceding, "[A] stiff has no conscience" (64).

The persona here equates rejection with betrayal, and this betrayal is especially painful for him (and thus elicits such an extreme reaction) because of his association of sexual relations with home: "I, The Sad Phoenician of Love, dyeing the world red, dyed laughing, ha, lost everything, lost home; I, homing" (67). In effect, when the poet loses opportunities for sex he loses home, which, to him, is "everything." As he says, "Horny contains: a reminding. A regretting. A regressing. A returning" (68).

The seventh poem, "The Winnipeg Zoo," begins with the poet figure "exhausted from / moving" (80), and introduces an unnamed female character who "takes her lovers one by one to the Winnipeg / Zoo" (80), and the poet, apparently one of these lovers, writes on a postcard, "I am here, yes, I want to go home" (82). The double sense of this expression, by now more fully established, is also found in the ninth poem, "The Criminal Intensities of Love as Paradise," in a section titled "*Campsite, Home, Away From,*" where the poet, perhaps meditating on a campfire, observes

> . . . the lost & the
> late home always
> found
> in the small flame
>
> lovers are only
> this and more
> a cracking stick
> a mortal sun. (98)

Passion and home here are equally fleeting, able to be "found" only in the necessarily temporary present of experience and memory. When the other campers ask each other "where / they are / from" (99), then, for the lovers the question has an ironical equivalence to the other possible question of where they are *now*.

The tenth and last poem in this second grouping, "Advice to My Friends," again juxtaposes notions of sex and place, loneliness and travel. It opens with a bold and ironic claim of sexual bravado and discreetness: "I've been to bed with some dandy and also skilled / ladies, sure, but would I a bally-hoo start / for the keen (and gossipy) public?" (105), and closes with the poet, melancholy and alone, "having come to this longing / for the familiar, this / ancient longing, / in a strange world" (124). In between, the poet considers a detour in his travels:

> Early yesterday, driving west alone
>
> across the prairies, I thought of swinging
>
> south off Number One to visit shortgrass
>
> country. Down there, everything is real,
>
> even the emptiness. The buttes are bare.
>
> Trees are only a memory. . . . (116)

He blames his decision not to go on a nosey gas station attendant outside Moose Jaw, but the reasons for this are far from clear, and he seems to regret his decision, since he says, "I find the mountains pretentious today" (116).

If his initial desire for more Prairie space was linked to a kind of homesickness (though admittedly he does not consider turning north), then perhaps one of his later "Questions for George Bowering" provides an answer: "What would happen if, just as you / slid into home plate, / the pitcher threw the catcher / an orange?" (122). Absurd though the question may be, it involves issues of what it means to be at home and safe – an issue also raised when the poet is "Reading the Old Guys" and finds:

> *Fair is my love and cruel as she's fair,*
>
> Sam Daniel said, and promptly sailed himself
>
> into his dear love's deep and dang'rous bed
>
> as I have done, somehow confusing port
>
> and storm. . . . (118)

This sometimes alternating, sometimes simultaneous, fear and desire contained in the longing for love and home is horrifically mirrored in a subsequent nightmare vision: "In my dream I'm running / toward the bear. I have no choice" (120).

The eleventh poem, "Mile Zero," is the site of the poet's self-reflexive comment about the presence and absence of the mother figure in the poems between it and "Seed Catalogue." The section entitled "Driving, Accidental, West" begins with the statement of purpose "the shaped infinity / to hammer home" (129), recalling the connection of place and home with the stone hammer of the first long poem, and the poem puns on the idea of the west-quest by using the French for "west" (ouest), suggesting also "where is" (où est), in the phrase "ouest / or quest or" (131). The ties of place as the source of personal and sexual identity are again connected through the sense of smell:

> The bindertwine of place −
>
> The mansource of the man −
>
> The natural odour of the stinkweed −
>
> The ache at the root of
>
> > the spinal thrust − (134)

At this point, Kroetsch, in another self-reflexive manoeuvre, adds in a critical observation by "Ron Smith of Oolichan Books on Vancouver Island" to the effect that "[t]he westward (and return) journey that fascinates Kroetsch is here turned entirely into implication without adequate substance (i.e., ground)" (134).[6] However, the journey toward place has already been interiorized, transformed into a journey undertaken through time rather than space, and "grounded" in the body.

It is when this bodily grounding is denied the poet that he experiences the most pain of unhoming, and the twelfth poem, "Letters to Salonika," presents the ironic situation of Kroetsch being very much not "at home" at home in his apartment in Winnipeg while his wife visits her prior home in Greece, which, significantly, is not in the "same time zone" (151). Here the usual gendering of Kroetsch's horse/house binary is reversed,[7] and Kroetsch writes "the despair of the poet on meeting / reality" (157), experiencing "a dislocation that is real" (155). The reversal of the male adventurer's fantasy of always having a secure home (woman) to return to, which brings release to his wife, brings the poet-figure nothing but suffering: "You on your quest, me here at home. I've burned up half our woodpile. Loneliness and a fire. Loneliness is a fire" (157). Though the poet asserts, "I am home"

(148), he is unable to truly make or become his own home, failing at even trivial domestic tasks: "What am I supposed to do with the eggplant in the fridge?" (142). The poet's odd injunction to "never bite a hollow radish" (156), and his even odder claim that he is "so much the farmer" (159), link the absence of his wife in this poem with that of his mother in "Seed Catalogue."

The poet's initial response to his wife's abandonment, which he calls "unkind" and "unnatural" (140), is to want to re-place his wife in what at the beginning of the poem he insists is "[o]ur home" (139), and on census day he says, "I put you down as a citizen living forever right here in Canada" (145). His second response is to "think about women" in general (158): going to the pool, he says, "I watched a woman, desirable in her bikini, and I thought of you," but on this occasion, at least, one woman is not substitutable for another, and he insists on "[m]y needing you tonight, not a mere stranger in a bikini. My needing the larger and genuine mystery of us, not the complete known of a stranger" (146). Having been hurt "beyond all repair" (140) by his solitude, by having been forced into the usual female "house" role, Kroetsch here adopts the dynamic "inside" view of home, versus the static "outside" view of home.

Kroetsch's third response, toward the close of the poem, is to try to re-assert the usual order of gender relations, by asking his wife to create or become home in the place where she now is, and suggesting that he will then move there, replicating once again the male quest toward the female home. Unable to cope with her absence, he writes, "Find us a house to rent on Sifnos. This is too much" (161) and, later, "When you get to Sifnos, take another look at the house you mentioned. The one by the chapel. The one that you said we might be able to rent a year from now" (165). The poem ends with what may appear to be a compromise, with a Greek translation of the lines from Pound's "The River Merchant's Wife: A Letter" about coming out to meet the lover half-way. Ironically, though, the next three long poems are travel poems in which Kroetsch himself is off, away from home, questing. The male/female horse/house binary is reasserted, and the poet's suffering appears to diminish substantially.

Given the apparent failure of the home given Kroetsch by his now-travelling wife, it is also appropriate that in the three subsequent travel poems Kroetsch directs his attention to other family members, these with "ties" of blood. The thirteenth poem, "Postcards from China," is addressed "To my daughters, Margaret and Laura" (167), and in the fourteenth, "Delphi: Commentary," the poet is in Greece, not with his wife as we might expect, but with his two daughters. He also encounters the ghost of his father there, asking in "his farmer's patient / voice, . . . Did I teach you nothing?" (195). The fifteenth poem, "The Frankfurt *Hauptbahnhof*," finds the poet in Germany, advising himself to "keep an eye peeled / for an ancestor" (198), and he says, "I expected to see the birthplace of one of my ancestors. . . . I expected to find a *Kirche* where my *Urgrossmutter* went to pray" (200). This search for signs of his great-grandmother fails – "not a trace of the old girl" (204) – and the poet is left mourning "the immense sadness of travel" (203).

Significantly, it is at this juncture that the two poems dealing directly with Kroetsch's mother occur, as if, weary with questing and the absence of relationships that can take her place, he turns once again to the original source of his dislocation, trying once again to place himself there. In the sixteenth poem, "Sounding the Name," this re-placing takes a very physical form, as the poet looks at a picture of his mother and then inserts himself into it:

> In the snapshot my mother is seventeen.
>
> She is standing beside an empty chair.
>
> Today is my birthday, I am fifty-six.
>
> I seat myself in the empty chair
>
> in the snapshot. . . . (210)

Not wanting to violate the historical sequence of time, yet wanting to exist with her in the present of the past that the snapshot captures, Kroetsch says, "I am in the house, out of sight, hiding, / so that she won't remember I am not yet / born" (210). Referring both to his future birth and to his present erotic gaze, and thus connecting the two, he announces, "I become her approaching lover" (210).

The erotic connection to his mother is also announced in the seventeenth poem, "The Poet's Mother," when Kroetsch says:

> I have sought my mother
> on the shores of a dozen islands.
>
> I have sought my mother
> inside the covers
> of ten thousand books.
>
> I have sought my mother
> in the bars of a hundred cities.

I have sought my mother
on the head of a pin.

I have sought my mother
in the arms of younger women.

I have sought my mother
in the spaces between
the clouds.

I have sought my mother
under the typewriter keys. (216)

Here travel, writing, sexual relations, and Kroetsch's mother-memory are all explicitly connected, and the heavy repetition of the opening phrase "I have sought" emphasizes both the continual nature of his quest for home and the merely temporary, fleeting satisfactions it has offered. Thick with pain, Kroetsch's poignant appeal "Mother, where are you?" (218) is equivalent to the question of where home is, or can be, for him. The literal home place, his childhood farm, offers no consolation, since it is marked only by her continued absence, and he has no choice but to continue his journey, "placing" himself in and through the movement of the sexual quest.

The next and nineteenth poem, "Excerpts from the Real World," begins with an epigraph suggesting this need to continue searching despite disappointment: "'Perhaps if I call you forever you'll hear me toward the end'" (223). This disjointed poem of disconnected fragments, in most of which the poet is travelling around various sites in Europe and Iraq, recalls "The Sad Phoenician" in its presentation of the anger and bitterness of the jilted and abandoned "jealous lover" (224, 228), whose absent partner is frequently, and significantly, pictured as being away with or preoccupied with *her* mother. He calls his absent lover "a cheatin lyin woman," and, sarcastically punning on "role" and "roll," tells her, "That role of barbed wire you put in my bed. Don't you realize I could have hurt myself, mistaking it for you?" (228). While he appears to have other grievances as well, he tells her, "[T]he quality I dislike most about you is your absence" (228).

Rather melodramatically, the poet states, "I have spent the entire store of my pain. My life is a portrait of the woman who deceived me into hunting the unicorn" (224). While it is not entirely clear in the context of the poem, this could be a veiled reference to the mother figure who, through her early death, initiated Kroetsch's quest for what he sees, quite literally, as a mythical beast: the present, faithful, satisfied woman. He tells his current lover, "Yours are the unicorn's buttocks" and wonders, "[H]ow do I capture you" (229), which is a problematic possessiveness given that he states later that she has a "new lover" (233). "Nothing pleases a perfect wife," he insists, "nothing. I told that to the blizzard. The blizzard shrieked with laughter. Since then I've travelled often to strange places, rain forests and tropical islands" (130), drawing, once again, a connection between the failure of love and Kroetsch's urge to continual movement.

Ignoring his own urge to travel (through space and relationships), he places the blame for the bad state of affairs (pun intended) squarely on the woman's shoulders: "If it is true, as you sometimes insist, that I cannot bear to be loved, why, then, do you, so often, transform yourself into a distant city?" (231). The location of the lover is of crucial importance to him since it is the means by which he locates himself, and he tells her, "Like the ashtray I bought in Edinburgh (the castle, the castle), you remind me of where I once was" (234). This is a very reductionist, objectifying view of woman as souvenir, but it also suggests the very profound way in which women are of key importance to his sense of place and home.

Feeling abandoned by his lover, even as he himself is "absent," Kroetsch tries to bypass the female and connect to place directly: "here, now, today, this afternoon in the Yorkshire Dales, I locate my pain in the descending lines of a prairie coulee" (235). The attempt to replace himself to overcome his homesickness is, however, unlikely to succeed: "I watch for magpies (dancing) in the tulip fields. I try to snare gophers with a fishing line, here, below sea level" (236), and ultimately he can only connect to place by reconnecting with his lover: "Let place do the signing for us. Close the door and let me in" (237). Home, however, is like the horizon, which "is, apparently, a linguistic illusion calculated to make us feel at once secure and heroic" (242) – the poet knows that faithlessness is mutual and continuing, and he says, "My loathing for the human species is exceeded only by my need for human companionship" (243), acknowledging once again the paradoxical force that will keep him in motion.

Near the end of this poem this double pull-push of love is again connected back through time with the poet's first love:

> What I remember tonight is my mother at the kitchen table, cleaning eggs. The crate was not quite full. She sent me out to the barn to find one more egg. It was there, that afternoon, climbing the steps to the hayloft, I fell into the chasm between disbelief and longing. (249)

Here the poet rises, rather than falls, into love, and the egg imagery suggests that the process of doing so is a supremely creative act. But the poem ends with the observation, "Even the two ends of an egg have difficulty understanding each other" (253), and we are left with the knowledge that home, like the unicorn and love, can be had only in the present moment of memory and experience: "I remember clearly now," Kroetsch says, "I went down onto my knees. You put your hand to the back of my neck. The water buffalo, grazing at the edge of the river, lifting its head to your long moan, looked vaguely like a unicorn" (253).

The nineteenth and penultimate poem, "Spending the Morning on the Beach," presents Kroetsch in motion again, this time travelling to various tropical destinations, but in the last poem, "After Paradise," he is soon back home again, in Winnipeg with his lover. He tells this lover, "In my reaching to find you I find I am not yet born" (267), and switching to the third person, perhaps for emotional distance, he tells us, "Even good things have to end, his mother said. This was at his birth" (268). The ultimate good thing here is the ultimate home: his mother's womb. Without birth there is no separation, no pain, no death, no quest, and no necessity to relive the separation and pain and death over and over again during the quest to return. Finding home again in the arms of his lover, the poet attains a temporary measure of security and comfort, but the process of rebirth is followed by another death, and the cycle continues, endless in its torments and ecstasies, its unhomings and homings.

## Aritha van Herk's *No Fixed Address: An Amorous Journey*

Arachne Manteia, the protagonist of Aritha van Herk's picaresque novel *No Fixed Address: An Amorous Journey*, is caught up in a similarly continuous quest to that of Kroetsch's persona, though hers differs in two key respects. First, the family home that she leaves as a young adult is highly dysfunctional, and the memories that she associates with it are primarily negative. Second, and as a result, the journey she undertakes is more an attempt to escape the past than to recapture it. Though she does ironically end up replicating certain aspects of her family history, she firmly rejects the version of home represented by her parents. Rather than using movement as a way to place the self in a past that is no longer accessible except through the present of memory, as Kroetsch does, Arachne uses movement to distance memory and to place herself firmly – and only – within a present self that seeks, it appears, independence above all else. Solitude contains, for her, a "deep-breathing freedom" (213) to be herself and in control of her own life.

However, there is a great deal of ambiguity involved in Arachne's character that complicates any simple, straightforward interpretation of her relationship to the idea of home, and the novel presents a very problematic and complicated version of this concept. Though van Herk spends considerable time developing the circumstances of Arachne's childhood as clues to her psychology, we are given very little authorial commentary or introspection regarding her present psychological state. Arachne's emotional response to events is frequently undeveloped, and sudden shifts and apparent contradictions in character are often left unexplained. For example, she both despises and enjoys the attention that her car, a vintage Mercedes hearse, draws: "She curses the way people stare after her," but at the same time "[t]heir longing makes her smile" (28). Similarly, her family experiences have instilled in her a deep insecurity and distrust of the world, but in her sexual escapades she often appears supremely confident and self-assured.

This unevenness in character development is in part accounted for by the novel's frame, which suggests that the novel has been constructed by the reader, who has been researching Arachne's life, gathering information from various sources and piecing it together into a reasonably coherent narrative. Given this, gaps and inconsistencies in our knowledge are to be expected, since we may never get the whole "real story" (238), but it also seems as if resisting interpretation and understanding is characteristic of Arachne herself. She uses constant movement not only to escape the past but to avoid the self-reflection that would inevitably bring up that past, and she is obsessed with the strategies of disguise, camouflage, and "passing": "She is not so much an actress as a double agent, an escaped criminal who has survived by relying on what slender veneers are available" (141). Faced with a world that for the most part will not accept her as she is, she spends a great deal of time and energy trying to conform to people's expectations of her, and an equal amount of time and energy radically resisting and breaking those expectations.

The main part of the novel takes place in Alberta, where Arachne lives in Calgary with one lover, Thomas, whom she met in Vancouver and moved to Calgary with, while she works as a travelling salesperson, peddling women's underwear in small Alberta towns and having affairs with the anonymous men she refers to as "road jockeys." This narrative is interspersed with retrospective sections describing Arachne's history in Vancouver, from before her birth (in the story of her mother) until she moved to Calgary at age twenty-three. The two geographical locations and the worlds they represent are kept quite distinct but are juxtaposed in ways that show connections between Arachne's past and present, and they also come into physical contact on two occasions: the first when Arachne's mother visits her from Vancouver, and the second at the end of the novel when Arachne makes her "great escape" from the RCMP and kidnapping charges by driving west to Vancouver and then beyond, to Vancouver Island and then into the far north.

Before this final (and anticlimactic) homecoming and departure, however, Arachne's desire to escape the past is mirrored by her refusal to look homeward: "Arachne has not seen Banff since she passed through it with Thomas. She refuses to drive west, circles north and east and south from Calgary but never west, hardly even looks in the direction she came. She would not be able to tell why" (47). Here, as elsewhere, the reader is left to determine the character motivation that Arachne herself is said to be unaware of. Thinking about or understanding her own desire not to drive west would in itself be a form of "looking west" that she avoids, so complete is her desire to refuse the past any hold over her. She would like her life to be compartmentalized like the display cases at the Banff museum: "That is why glass was invented, to cover the displays of the past, prevent the present from touching" (51).

But the past has, of course, constructed her character, and continues to overdetermine her present in certain ways, despite Arachne's illusions of or demands for freedom. This past is centred around a home that, despite its physical trappings, is not really a home at all, at least in any of the usual associations of that word with comfort, security, protection, or being loved and accepted. Though she grew up with her two parents, "she does not think of them as hers. They are Toto and Lanie, two people she lived with as a child, people who occasionally insisted on oatmeal and bed at nine, but never often enough to make a difference" (41). She feels that she "'was either adopted or stolen'" (114), and she tells Thomas, "'When I was little and growing up the way I did, I figured out that I was adopted. I knew I was adopted. It was the only possible answer. I knew I couldn't belong where I was, Lanie and Toto weren't really my parents, I was a baby who ended up there by accident, and someday somebody was going to find out about the mistake and fix it'" (135).

This feeling of Arachne's that she did not belong to or with her parents has at least two identifiable sources, the foremost of which is the abusive nature of her home life. Before Arachne's birth, her mother "ignored the child inside her" (81), and she continued to after she was born, leaving her alone in her crib to go to work when she is only three months old (84). When Arachne is old enough to understand, her mother makes it clear to her that she was not wanted in the first place and often "locked her in the high-fenced backyard while she went off to a Bingo or a shoe sale" (41), giving her "a swat, a smack, a quick box on her ear" (42) if she climbed the fence, as she often did. The narrator tries to modify our reactions to these events, placing them in a more positive light by saying that Arachne grew up "without the choking love of most children" (42) and that "Lanie did not neglect Arachne, she just ignored her" (85), but the "facts" have already spoken for themselves. In fact, these comments make little sense unless we interpret them as the self-rationalizing voice of Lanie speaking through the apparently naïve narrator/reader who is constructing the story.

At any rate, Arachne runs away from home at an early age, and at age nineteen when she taunts her mother about whether Toto is really her father he "broke her arm, a crunch Arachne did not even feel. He threw her onto the sidewalk, slammed the door and locked it," and we are told, "When she hit the sidewalk, Arachne knew she had left home" (42, 159). The claim that Arachne didn't feel the break and the switch in agency, from Arachne being *thrown out* of her home to her *leaving it*, could again be interpreted as another case of the narrator's source trying to put a more positive spin on things; or the lack of feeling could be attributed to shock, and the double agency could be a sign of physically enforced but internally accepted action.

In addition to their emotional and physical abuse, Arachne rejects her parents because of their working-class identity, though here again her response is complex and difficult to sort through. On the one hand we are told, "Arachne knows she is working-class. She has never thought of her narrow life as disabled. She is concerned with survival, self-protection. . . . All the other urges in her life have come from hunger: to be fed, clothed, loved, to possess this thing or that" (76). On the other hand, when she first sees Thomas, although he supposedly represents all the middle-class "respectable trappings she knows she does not want" (77), she feels "a choking lust. Not for him, oh no, but for an indefinable quality that he represents, conveyed in his walk and the angle of his head and the surety of his hands," and she experiences "a sharp gnaw of discontent, a sense of something graspable brushing past" (76-77).

One of Arachne's key associations with upper-class status is the ability to travel. She believes that "Thomas is a civilized snob; he cannot conceive of a woman who has never been away from the city where she was born" (91), and since she has never been outside of Vancouver it is significant that one of her first thoughts upon seeing Thomas is that "[s]he should take a holiday, drive somewhere" (77). The means of her escape into movement, the Mercedes, is also associated with a higher-class status, as it was left to her

by Gabriel, a well-off, elderly gentleman who visited her mother for fortune readings and who becomes, for Arachne, a kind of surrogate father:
"She knew he loved her, loved her the way that no one had ever loved her"
(157); "his silent presence protected her" (158).

Arachne views the car as a "relic of Gabriel's wealth" (78), suggesting,
then, not only his material well-being but also his spiritual love for her. In
a more general sense, the car is also associated with a positive sense of home
since it was with an earlier car that Gabriel took her, as a child, temporarily
away from Lanie to comfort and calm her, "the rhythm of the car wheeling
her into a long cry and then sleep" (80). The statement that he "drove her
home" (80) has the literal sense of her return to Lanie, but in a metaphorical sense it was the drive itself that gave her a feeling of home. In a parallel
later incident, it is in the Mercedes that Arachne first has sex with Thomas,
whom she later comes to identify, temporarily, as her home.

Though they define it differently, the desire for upward class mobility is
something that Arachne and her mother share. Lanie was orphaned at seventeen, when her parents were both killed in the "London blitz" of 1945.
Dissatisfied with her life with foster parents who "neither wanted nor liked
her," she "left it all behind" to move to Vancouver with Toto, a Canadian
serviceman (54). When he finds work in a sawmill and they move into a
two-room apartment, Lanie is "somewhat disappointed" since she "expected
that a Canadian soldier would be better off," but having "nowhere and no
one to go to" she has to try to rely on herself to try to better her situation
(54). She becomes obsessed with the idea of buying a home: "Whatever the
war had done to Lanie, it had taught her the value of security" (56). She
begins work as a fortune teller in a local café and is determined not to get
pregnant, as that would interfere with her work, since "[n]obody wants a
pregnant teacup reader" (57), and hence with her larger goal of stability.

Though she wants to be different from her mother and is "disgusted by
women who need men to rescue them" (141), when Arachne moves to
Calgary with Thomas she finds herself involved in a Pygmalion narrative of
attempted transformation. In a typical contradiction, Thomas is credited
with "saving Arachne, with preventing her from becoming an escapee"
(62), but we are also told that "Arachne is not wrong to credit Thomas with
saving her. Only she knows how narrowly she has escaped, how closely the
past treads on her heels" (103). She considers Thomas "her one solid connection with what she calls 'the real world,' certainly the respectable world,
in which she is an imposter" (103). He offers her "stability, calm, and un-
troubled life" (119), and she "agrees to let Thomas turn her into a respectable woman, or at least the appearance of one" (137). He teaches her table

etiquette and buys her clothing as "camouflage, a disguise" (139) so that she "can pass" (141).

Arachne never feels that these alterations are to anything more than surface appearance, believing that "underneath it all she is still herself" (193), and she never completely escapes the feeling that "[s]he is temporary" and that "he will eventually replace her" (134): "Arachne wants for nothing but does not dare believe that this will last" (180). Thomas believes that she acts out of a "fear of love" (211), and this seems likely since she early on decided that "the only reliable things in the world are tangible" (166). However, she also deeply distrusts the external trappings of security and home that her mother sought, perhaps because she distrusts her mother herself.

Keeping her options open and not wanting to be "unable to get away when the need arises" (68), she wants "to keep Thomas," but at the same time "she will always return to a string of men, bar pickups, road jockeys" (99). Although we *"know that Arachne felt she had found a home with Thomas"* (239), she is well aware of its limits: even while the situation lasts, it can offer her only a very incomplete sense of safety and acceptance. She realizes that "the only way to get anything was to go after it herself" (177) and, ultimately able to depend only on herself, she leaves home several times in her travels and affairs, and when she leaves for the final time it is to escape the police – a force Thomas and respectability certainly cannot protect her from.

In movement she is able to rely on the only two things she herself owns – her body and her car – and the two are brought into association in the statement that she is "faithful to only her body, her reliable, well-tuned body" (220). When she looks at her legs she thinks, "They are hers, they belong to her, she can take them anywhere she pleases" (58), and the car "consolidated her command" (157), giving her a sense of power and agency she otherwise would lack. To her, "driving seems the only sensible way to deal with the world. . . . She is infatuated not with machines but with motion, the illusion that she is going somewhere, getting away" (68). In fact, the Mercedes almost takes the role of her most faithful and protective lover: "[T]he car's life vibrates through her feet and up her spine in palpable massage," and, just as she carries her own past within her body, "she is certain that the car's past resides somewhere in its bones" (48). She is content with the "sensual luxury" of "its fat black body" (78), and she "takes the wheel into her hands like a lover" (303). The security and comfort it offers her is clear when it is described as "an oak and leather incubator" (97). Like a womb, it offers her escape from the world and her life.

We are told that "Arachne travels to travel. Her only paradox is arriving somewhere, her only solution is to leave for somewhere else" (164), yet this insistence on the autotelic nature of movement is countered by the sense that travel involves a quest for some inarticulate desire: "How can she explain her inordinate lust to drive, to cover road miles, to use up gas? There is no map for longing" (171). On her final escape trip she "drives relentlessly, driving into and out of herself, a fierce evasion that can bring her nowhere but is itself enough" (270), but she later finds that "[s]he is desirous of peace; the past three months of oblivion have left her longing to return, not to be out here in the world again, driving, endlessly impelled by motion" (294).

Arachne's motives for sexual relations are also paradoxical and ambiguous. For the most part she denies that they have any emotional or psychological effect. She insists that her road affairs are "'a game, something to do'" (174), and when pushed by her friend Thena offers the rationalization, "'I'm happy with Thomas but I'm not used to things coming to me so easily. If I gamble a little, maybe I'll deserve him more'" (174–75). When she has a fling with an egotistical poet, he is described as "a curiosity, an added exponent" (205), and, just as her mother told her of men – "'You have to learn to work around them'" (61) – "Arachne has learned to get her pleasure fast, catch what she can, has trained her body to pleasure itself" (70).

Arachne also likes the lack of consequences and implications associated with anonymous sex: "There is something square and direct about fucking for its own sake, no other considerations: wifely or husbandly duty, buying, selling, payoff, gratitude" (220). Yet on one occasion she sleeps with a police officer to try to get out of a speeding ticket, and on another the consequences go to the core of her being: "[S]he has to find out if she's alive, if she inhabits the same body as she always has" (198). On yet another occasion, sex is a means to access her "true self": "Arachne is lifted beyond herself. They have not shed their clothes but they are searingly naked, shorn of all costume, all disguise" (188). She is comfortable and secure in her own body, for the most part has creative control over it, and, as a result, is quite "at home" with her sexuality. Like movement, sex contains an element of evasion and escape for her, but the two offer her a means to assert her own identity in a world that she believes judges and rejects her.

When Arachne flees Calgary and the police, she seems to instinctively head west toward the mountains, but she is depicted as lacking agency and control in the path of her journey: we are told that "[s]he had not planned to run away" (242), and that "[s]he tries to drive on, through to Lake Louise, but she can't get out of the traffic circle until the third exit and then she's driving into Banff" (241). When she finally gets out of Banff, "she hits the circle and damn if she doesn't get stuck again. She goes all the way around twice before she manages to escape. But then she is going east, back the way she came" (254). She is aware that the "car is her worst liability," being so easily recognizable, "but she cannot abandon it. Where is she going? If she stopped to answer that, she would stop moving" (270). The need to keep moving becomes her only direction, her only hope of safety.

Following a con artist she meets who tries to sell her a mine, she visits the shack of a miner, "dark and musky, like an animal's cave," and discovers, "This burrow is enticing. She thinks that she too would like to live like this, live herself into a profound and breathing darkness, . . . she is escaping again. No, running toward anonymity, absorption, relief from expectation" (260). As her car did previously, the shack here takes on a womb function, with its protective, reassuring sense of lack of social obligation and its attendant pain. She idealizes the miners' solitary, dark, underground existence, and believes that "[t]hey have what she has always wanted" (261). And in the end she does get a version of this, or at least so we are led to believe.

When she hits the suburbs of Vancouver, she feels she is "driving into her own escaped history, . . . returning to her gasping, squalid childhood," and she thinks that "[s]he should not have come west, should have driven toward the open expanse of prairie and shield. This is a dead end: she'll hit the Pacific and have to stop, retract" (278). The past is indeed a dead end for her; the future may be uncertain, but it is the only escape hatch. She "knows that Vancouver will put her back. She needs to get through it, beyond it, as fast as possible" (280), and figures that she will "get the hell out of this city, go to the island, that's what she'll do, go as far west as the road and the ocean allow, farther than anyone will think of following" (281).

Reaching the western limit of the continent, she thinks, "This is the edge of the world. If only it were easier to fall off" (293). She meets an air force man whose friends were drowned swimming in the ocean at night and who still swims there, feeling that "[t]he water is soothing" (297). He is caught in the past, apparently believing that the war is still on, and his swimming can be seen as a kind of death wish, a desire to rejoin his friends in their underground home. This incident offers one possibility for how to "fall off" the earth, but it is one that Arachne apparently cannot indulge in, since it would imply that she too is bound by the past, shackled to it so tightly that only death could release her.

Instead, she heads back to the mainland and then north, beyond the point where maps can direct her: "She is steeling herself to enter the blank, the dislocated world of the North. Afraid, she is, afraid. After this there is nothing" (302). Fear of captivity overcomes her fear of the unknown, however, as it has so many times before, and to escape detection by the police she continues north, further into *"the ultimate frontier, a place where the civilized melt away and the meaning of mutiny is unknown, where manners never existed and family backgrounds are erased. It is exactly the kind of place for Arachne"* (316). Does Arachne finally arrive at a place she can call home, where she can stop moving and find peace in stasis? Appropriately, we never find out, and the reader/researcher is left in a state of perpetual motion that mirrors Arachne's, on a road that has "no end" (319). What we do know is that Arachne placed herself in motion as the only available means to "place" herself; if the sense of home she achieved appears incomplete or inadequate, it is perhaps only because we are judging it against an impossible and elusive ideal. As Arachne tells Thena, "Try growing up the way I did and you'd be thankful just to survive" (174).

## Fred Wah's *Alley Alley Home Free*

If the need for movement in van Herk's text can be read as a response to a pervasive sexism that genders home female, rooting women in an idealized domestic space and imposing a series of repressive strictures constructing the woman-home as a rigid moral centre, Fred Wah's *Alley Alley Home Free* may be read as a response to a pervasive racism and ethnocentrism that would colour the Prairies "white" and try to prevent other people from homing themselves, or rooting themselves in place. Wah's book makes an interesting ending point for this study, being in many ways the most "radical" of the texts I have discussed. Virtually "unreadable" in the usual senses of that term, it seems more suited to an aural hearing, which requires the hearer's mind to remain fluid and open, than a critical analysis, which tends to fix meaning and create stasis.

In its demand to be "heard," the text creates the effect of a continuous present time-sense that suspends or "unsettles" traditional readerly expectations and desires to know, name, and control, and it is precisely through this "unhoming" of readers and language through their "displacement" into continual motion that the text's voice locates, places, settles, and homes itself. Alluding to the book's title, the back cover blurb tells us: "The intention is to outmanoeuvre the text, get home without being tagged, disrupt the ambitions of meaning as they fall blurred into a blind alley," and the text is constructed so Wah (and the reader who "plays along") is able to "win the game" against "a kind of person who might extend racism or even keep [him] off the block" (33).

Wah's sophisticated poetics and "post-ethnic" politics[8] offer an opportunity to study an aluvial connection between language theory, conceptions of the body, nostalgia for home, and a hyphenated racial existence on the Canadian Prairies. Together these sediments form a complex and layered topography of self and identity. His recent works fall into two general (and not mutually exclusive) categories. In one group, *Alley Alley Home Free* (1992) and the earlier *Music at the Heart of Thinking* (1987) test the limits of syntax and semantics as the writing subject becomes a body at home in its own musicality, playing the body as musical instrument. Because of the non-representational and disjunctive nature of these texts, no conventional sense of place is present. Instead, body memory and histology, the musical press of tissue on tissue, take landscape's place as sites of identification, and Wah's version of Charles Olson's "proprioception" turns writing into a precise visceral and physical act of self-perception.

In the second group, Wah's earlier *Waiting for Saskatchewan* (1985) and his later *Diamond Grill* (1996) take up this specific method of self-awareness to explore the lives of his extended family as they arrived and negotiated the Canadian imaginative, social, and geographic landscape. In these books a traditional sense of place does exist, but it exists in a dialectical relationship with the displacing effects of language and body. Taken together, these two texts provide a kind of referential "frame" (of a more social, externalized sense of place) for the texts published between them, suggesting both the "grounds" for "departure" and an eventual "return."

As one "pre-text" of *Alley Alley Home Free*, *Waiting for Saskatchewan* represents a frustrated search for origins in place, as the book opens with the speaker, Beckett-like, "Waiting for saskatchewan / and the origins grandparents countries places converged / europe asia railroads" (3). Wah's father was a Canadian-born Chinese-Scots-Irishman raised in China, and his mother is a Swedish-born Canadian from Swift Current. This Prairie city, as the site of the confluence of his parents' histories, is "at the centre" (59), a place where, he says, "I knew exactly where I was" (59), and also "the most political place I know" (3), perhaps because it is so restrictively racialized. I quote at length:

> The ethnicity here feels so direct. I mean the Chinese are still connected to China, the Ukrainians so Ukrainian, in the bar the Icelanders tell stories about Iceland, the Swede still has an accent, the French speak French. Here you're either a Wiebe or a Friesen, or not. What is a Métis, anyway? I know when you [Wah's father] came back from China you must have felt more Chinese than anything else. But I remember you saying later

that the Chinese didn't trust you and the English didn't trust you. You were a half-breed, Eurasian. I remember feeling the possibility of that word "Eurasian" for myself when I first read it in my own troubled adolescence. I don't think you ever felt the relief of that exotic identity though. In North America white is still the standard and you were never white enough. But you weren't pure enough for the Chinese either. You never knew the full comradeship of an ethnic community. So you felt single, outside, though you played the game as we all must. To be a mix here on the prairies is still noticed. (62)

Wah says of ("to") his father, "I try to 'place' you," but "I can't imagine what your image of the world was, where you were in it," and he wonders, "[W]ere you always going home to Swift Current, were you ever at home, anywhere" (68). Several prose poems record his own anger at those who ignore "indications about ourselves / such as the relative colour inside of me or inside of you" (42), and what seems to be hurt resignation (perhaps masked by bravado or humour) at the response of people in his Chinese tour group when he tells them his father was raised in China by relatives:

> You were part Chinese I tell them.
>
> They look at me. I'm pulling their leg.
>
> So I'm Chinese too and that's why my name is Wah.
>
> They don't really believe me. That's o.k.
>
> When you're not "pure" you just make it up. (43)

Wah wonders, "[W]hy on earth would they [his grandparents] land in such a place" as the Prairies, but says, "I want it back, . . . my body to get complete" (3). Here landscape is "internalized" to the degree that place literally becomes body: he says "as origin town flatness appears later in my stomach" (3), and a later poem refers to "the stomach's map" (23). Generational narrative becomes geological: "said-again things / left over after / sedimentary hard / embedded rock to tell" (14), as family lineage is written on the body become globe:

> lineal
>
> face, body's
>
> things
>
> a hemi-
>
> sphere. (12)

As a second pre-text of *Alley Alley Home Free*, Wah sets up *Music at the Heart of Thinking* as "writing as a notation for thinking as feeling," which "shapes the voice of the body so that some of the text can be seen as felt" (Notes), and he says he is following the method ("*sans* booze of course") of a monk who would "practice his tai chi while drunk so he could learn how to be imbalanced in the execution of his moves without falling over" (Preface). As the series of prose poems begins, it is clear that a different language economy is at work: "Don't think thinking without heart no such separation within the acting body takes a step" (1). Reading these poems is an act of getting in step, moving into the rhythm, so you cannot help but "notice the body as a drummer preacts [acts before] the hands to do to do insistent so it can come out tah dah" (2).

But this is more than just a musical construction of language; it is also the construction of home in language that has its source in "the body as a place that is as a container has suddenness so the politics of dancing is a dead giveaway to the poet's 'nothing will have taken place but the place'" (22). Place, home, and family, like other phenomena, are "histology filtered sememes" (24) – 'histology' being the study of tissue structure and 'sememes' being the meaning embedded in morphological units. Wah defines an "eme" as an "irreducible (chemical?) constituent in language" ("Notes"), once again emphasizing the organic biological nature of language function. It is the body's recollection, the "memory behind the fingers" (9) that allows an unearthing of the estranged rhythms and improvisational potential within language. This is Olson's proprioceptive body at work – the tell-tale signs of the fingers' dance, the breath's rhythm, the gut's orchestration. As Olson develops his theory, a man's body is "the house he is, this house that moves, breathes, acts, this house where his life is, where he dwells" ("The Resistance" 175), "so that movement or action is 'home'" ("Proprioception" 184).[9]

The nexus of creative momentum is, then, for Wah, a dynamic conception of home in motion. Language opens itself to finding home within its traces and impulses. As movement, "home" crosses the bridge of language to access the diverse accumulations that make up the immigrant self at home: "I write this to you in the Shanghai dialect Mori-san your eyes answer me with the word for sunlight please" (*Music* 15). Rather than reify this connection and presence in a Canadian Prairie landscape, Wah transforms home into a transitory question of "meaning."

The title of *Alley Alley Home Free* signals Wah's voice-over of home as he "unsettles" composition, the sentence, and the word. Home is doubled and fragmented into om

h        e

om       (25)

Here contemplation and a breathing mantra complicate "home" as sign, and its signification becomes fraught with divisions. The thinking, breathing "he" brackets home as a projection outward – of a voice chanting – and a projection inward – of introspection and self-discovery. The essence of meditative practice (and what concentration on a mantra is designed to assist) is suspension of the usual constant barrage of judgement, analysis, fear, anxiety, regret, worry, and desire that keeps human consciousness focussed on the past and the future. Living in the present moment, on the other hand, means allowing experience, stimuli, thoughts, language, to flow through the self, registering their presence but not attempting to control or "know" their meaning, in the usual sense.

This transplanted hermeneutics of deferral seems (s/emes) to be Wah's sense of "home free":

> No single meaning is the right one because no "right ones" stand still long enough to get caught. But because we do not know does not mean we are lost. Something that is strangely familiar, not quite what we expect, but familiar, is present. That quick little gasp at the daydream, a sudden sigh of recognition, a little sock of baby breath. Writing into meaning starts at the white page, nothing but intention. This initial blinding clarity needs to be disrupted before we're tricked into settling for a staged and diluted paradigm of the "real," the good old familiar, inherited, understandable, unmistakable lucidity of phrase that feels safe and sure, a simple sentence, just-like-the-last-time-sentence. (5-6)

Being "home free" is an act of evasion as in the game of hide-and-seek, and Wah is deliberately dis/locating himself in terms of a home in language by using words like "lost," "familiar," "settling," and "inherited." In using this language of place to describe meaning and writing, Wah is binding a conception of home to hermeneutics: what signs lead toward home and how do we read signs in order to follow them there?

Wahs' philosophy of language, then, functions as a "freebasing" subversion of traditional perceptions of place: home free, home base, and home as an altered state ("State") of reality. It is no accident that the model for Wah's poetics, the Shao Lin monk practising his martial arts drunk, is battling "opponents" bent on doing him harm. Canadian society, in its subtle, pervasive racism and rhetoric of ethnicity, is that opponent: "I want one ethnic thing here, / right from the start. Dis- / orientation" (26). The Greek "ethikos" (ethos) rhymes with "ethnikos" (ethnic) meaning "heathen nations" – the "placed self" (ethics) entangled with and resisting the State and its artificial institutions of ethnicity.

Ethos for Wah is not the self in place but the place in self – not the static old self known in the past tense (as in the simplistic "racist" or "ethnic" conception), but a dynamic new self that exists in flux, continually reinvented in the continuous present movement of perception. Ethics, he says, "is probably something that surrounds you like your house it's where you live" (34), and it is the elusiveness of disjunctive poetic language that, while it may seem "unsafe," permits Wah the speed and "drunken" agility to make it home.

# Epilogue: Reading Region

A whole history remains to be written of spaces – which would at the same time be the history of powers (both of these terms in the plural) – from the great strategies of geopolitics to the little tactics of the habitat.

(Michel Foucault, Power/Knowledge 149)

Philosophy is really homesickness, it is the urge to be at home everywhere.

(Novalis, quoted in Berger 54)

Prairie homemaking, as represented in the literature written in and about the region, is overwhelmingly implicated in what Foucault calls the "history of powers," from the geopolitical structures of empire and immigration to gender relations and the "little tactics" of using cloth napkins. The old environmentalist emphasis on the effect of the land on the human psyche and social relations ultimately offers less insight into the problem of home than the new environmentalist insistence on the effect of human culture on the land.

Possible relationships to the land are many and varied. You can attempt to possess and control it for personal gain, as in Ostenso, or you can utilize it for the cause of some "greater good," as in Stead, Ross, and Wiebe. You can politicize it, as in Rebar, or personalize it as in Gunnars, or mythologize it as in Arnason and Parameswaran. You can reinscribe it with a lost cultural significance, as in Warrior, or mourn its loss and try to physically reclaim it, as in Campbell, or abandon it entirely, as in Wah. You can stay put, as in Crozier, or you can depart and return, as in Salverson and Grove, or you can travel far away to gain a different perspective on it, as in Cooley. You can figuratively remain rooted in the past it represents, as in Kroetsch, or you can literally move through it to an uncertain future, as in van Herk. Each strategy has benefits and limitations; each has the potential to place home.

It is a cliché of Canadian literary criticism that Canadian literature is predominantly regional rather than national in character, yet exactly what this means merits further examination. Raymond Williams estimates that the distinction between "regional" literary works and their ostensibly "non-literary" counterparts "began to be significant only in the late nineteenth century, and to be confident only in the twentieth century" (*Writing* 229), and indeed the distinction appears more an ideological than a "natural" one. Undoubtedly Canadian book publishing and distribution often follow regional patterns, and many writers affiliate themselves with particular areas of the country; however, the wide variety of relationships to space mapped by this study challenges many usual conceptions of regionality.

I began this study with the idea that I was going to (re)discover the Prairie home ethos. I had digested the now classic major works of Prairie literature criticism, along with their environmentalist assumptions and the select group of texts used to support them, and I wondered how, in the face of such impossible geometries (the vertical/horizontal dilemma) and cultural confusions (if not outright insanities) these poor Prairie writers and their characters were ever able to make themselves at home at all.

My own perception, based on many years of living and reading on the Prairies, was that in spite of whatever difficulties life there may have produced for them (as life anywhere is wont to do), many Prairie dwellers (both literary and otherwise) are in fact quite firmly "settled" and at home in their places. And the tacit agreement I had with myself was that as I discovered how these others homed themselves, my intellectual home-making project would in turn make the Prairies home for me as well, as I came to know, understand, and "place" myself in relationship to the literary space. Nothing, however, prepared me for the stunning and irreducible variety of approaches to the "home place" that I encountered, complicating both my agenda to identify a regional ethos and the means by which I sought to home myself.

There are, of course, both individual desires to abstract or generalize and institutional pressures to do so. The production of sweeping theories and "grand narratives" continues to be professionally rewarded, even at a time when the only reasonable, tenable "big idea" left is that we should *abandon* the search for big ideas as being inevitably reductive and exclusionary. Ironically, the all-encompassing, totalizing theories so characteristic of today's post-colonial studies (which often over-generalize across regional, national, international, and other borders) run the risk of replicating colonial patterns of domination and control. I have an image in my mind of the successful literary critic as a kind of Caleb Gare figure, out surveying his fields, caressing his flax, and eagerly contemplating the ecomonic rewards and social esteem it will bring him. Substitute "thesis" for "flax" and you get what I mean.

Micro-analysis, then, may offer a point of resistance to the dominant movement to generalize: theory tries to "contain" fiction but fails, as literature maintains its specificity and resists formulaic politicization. In their incessant pluralism, Prairie homemaking and regionality (and my theorizing about them) function as paradigms for the large "post-identity" problem of our time. On the one hand we have the desire to name, know, affiliate, congregate, and identify on the basis of perceived shared experience, interests, or concerns, in order to accrue the personal, social, economic and political benefits of that "group identity" and the action it enables. On the other hand we have ample knowledge of the ways such identifications exclude, silence, marginalize, objectify, over-simplify, stereotype, and oppress. So we balance precariously between the two positions (Linda Hutcheon labels them "complicity" and "critique"): post-modern, post-structural, post-colonial, post-feminist, post-ethnic, post-regional.

According to the classic environmentalist argument, a region is identified on the basis of shared landscape, which in turn produces a shared culture or community ethos. However, as I've shown, the Prairies have neither a single shared landscape nor a single shared culture, and all attempts to define such are necessarily exclusionary or reductive. The environmentalist view also tends to essentialize land and/or culture, resulting in the restrictive assumption that there is a single appropriate culture in each place, or a single appropriate way to place home,[1] and thus misjudging the broad, eclectic, resourceful, and pragmatic range of strategies used by Prairie writers. In fact, the Prairie region's "coherence," if there is such a thing, may lie precisely (and paradoxically) in its variety, its difference from itself, rather than its sameness.[2]

Another conception of "regional" writing, one of the most unflattering, characterizes it in terms of what Williams (speaking of British literature) calls a nostalgic and static "fly-in-amber" quality (*Writing* 230-31):

> Its essential strategy is one of showing a warm and charming, or natural and even passionate, life, internally directed by its own rhythms, as if rural Britain, even in its most remote and "unspoiled" parts, had not been shot through and through by a dominant urban industrial economy. Or, as a variant of this, the "region" is so established, in autonomous ways, that pressures on it can be seen as wholly external: that other life against this region. (*Writing* 231)

Obviously none of the texts I have considered in this study would qualify as "regional" according to this narrow definition.[3] Even classic rural Prairie texts such as Ostenso's and Stead's, while they work in a predominantly "realist" rather than a "romantic" mode, demonstrate a keen awareness of both the region's internal conflicts and the pressures on it from the "outside world."

Moving away from these "naturalized" versions of the regional that attempt to define it on the basis of "intrinsic" qualities, we have more overtly political, "extrinsic" definitions of regionality – versions that, as W.H. New says, are "not simply a descriptive posture but a political gesture" (152). One of these is oppositional, in which region is to nation as nation is to empire, paralleling the situation Seamus Deane describes in the last 100 years of British/Irish history. I quote at length:

> [I]t was quite suddenly revealed that the English national character was defective and in need of the Irish, or Celtic, character in order to supplement it and enable it to survive. All the theorists of racial degeneration ... shared with literary critics and poets and novelists the conviction that the decline of the West must be halted by some infusion or transfusion of energy from an "unspoiled" source. The Irish seemed to qualify for English purposes. .... At this point, faced with this precipitous revision of white European history, the Irish, who had shown a marked inclination toward this view of themselves, finally took possession of the stereotype ... and began that new interpretation of themselves known as the Irish literary revival. .... This is a classic case of how nationalism can be produced by the forces that suppress it and can, at that juncture, mobilize itself into a form of liberation. (12-13)

Taking possession of and revaluing stereotypes has long been a productive means of generating Prairie identity, as can be seen, for example, in the critical privileging of "Prairie realism," and in Dennis Cooley's arguments about the centrality of the "vernacular muse" in Prairie literature.

Just as nationalism can be read as a response to empire, then, a liberatory regionalism can also be produced by the nationalist forces that attempt to suppress it, with the further irony that, in so constructing itself, the region actually *produces* the nation, thus reversing the usual flow of influence and power. In this way regional literatures may be seen as centres of vitality, and the energy sources driving national and global cultures.

Lastly, we have a conception of regionality based on what might be called Canada's internal "politicartography," relying on the kind of ideologically loaded, hierarchical ordering of place in Britain that Williams describes:

"The life and people of certain favoured regions are seen as essentially general, even perhaps normal, while the life and people of certain other regions, however interesting and affectionately presented, are, well, regional" (*Writing* 230). In the Canadian case, it is generally accepted that national identity has been narrowly defined around southern Ontario's cultural production and reception. Southern Ontario, also known as "central Canada," is thus not itself a region, but the centre of the nation, and a text produced there is automatically considered "Canadian literature."

Following this, texts produced elsewhere in Canada, in what are seen as the regions, are automatically considered "regional literature." Under certain conditions these texts, if well-received in central Canada, the United States, or overseas, may be granted "national" or even "international" status, but in many cases the identity of a text is fixed by the political status of its birthplace. If Canadian literature is predominantly regional, then, it may only be because central Canada defines itself so narrowly that the rest of the country – the vast majority – must then be considered regional.

Yet what begins as a political act of naming often ends as an attempt to define on other grounds, as in the desire to identify Prairie literature on the basis of a shared physical landscape, which in turn is presumed to create a shared psychological, social, or cultural landscape, and we are back to the old environmentalist argument. In other words, a rather arbitrary method of categorization begins to shape the reception and interpretation of the texts grouped within it, and eventually to actually *construct* the difference it pretends to merely *label*.

The concept of a regional identity, then, like other forms of imagined communities, is both problematic and productive. Neither the land nor the human cultures operating on it are identical, monolithic totalities. Beginning to understand the ethos of place, the ways we place ourselves in relationship to geographical spaces, requires demystifying and particularizing our accounts of it. To inscribe enabling rather than limiting patterns on experience, we must alter the paradigms that structure our vision. The motive of the ideal must be balanced against the practice of the real. This way lies home.

# Notes

Unless otherwise noted, within extracts all ellipses are mine and all italics are the original author's.

## Prologue

1 Needless to say, this is a highly elliptical and oversimplified, possibly even fraudulent, narrative account of a very complex series of events. The point is not to achieve autobiographical accuracy (all autobiographies are fictions anyway), but merely to outline the general context in which my writing took place.

## Introduction

1 Compare Dick Harrison's comment that, for the settlers, the Prairies "lacked the fictions which make a place entirely real" (ix), and Frederick Philip Grove's comment in a nationalist context that "[l]iterature makes the individual as well as the nation articulate" (*Needs* 28).

2 I use the term "performative" as roughly equivalent to J.L. Austin's "illocutionary" speech act, those cases where saying=doing, as opposed to the "locutionary" act, or communicative act. Because the illocutionary act may not coincide with the "perlocutionary," or the effect of the utterance on the listener, it is clear that the performative is potential rather than necessary and depends on audience agreement (or the fulfillment of "felicity conditions") to carry out its force (Crystal 121).

3 For instance, Bill Ashcroft, Gareth Griffiths, and Helen Tiffin in *The Empire Writes Back: Theory and Practice in Post-Colonial Literatures* (1989) have argued that one of the key features of postcolonial literatures is "the concern with the development or recovery of an effective identifying relationship between self and place" (9), while both *The Cultural Studies Reader* (1993, ed. Simon During) and *The Post-colonial Studies Reader* (1995, eds. Ashcroft, Griffiths, and Tiffin) have sections on space and place. An earlier work in cultural studies is Raymond Williams's *The Country and the City* (1973). More recent studies include Andrew Gurr's *Writers in Exile: The Identity of Home in Modern Literature* (1981), Benedict Anderson's *Imagined Communities: Reflections on the Origin and Spread of Nationalism* (1991), and collections of essays mapping the new "socio-cultural geographies" such as Peggy Nightingale (ed.), *A Sense of Place in the New Literatures in English* (1986), Homi K. Bhabha (ed.), *Nation and Narration* (1990), and Patricia Yaeger (ed.), *The Geography of Identity* (1996).

4 Lamar outlines Turner's hypothesis (36).

5   Three very recent books (all published after my study was substantially complete) have challenged and begun to reverse this environmentalist trend: W.H. New's *Land Sliding: Imagining Space, Presence, and Power in Canadian Writing* (1997) views land and landscape as political and cultural constructions: "'Land,' in consequence, has to be seen as a verbal trope in Canadian writing, not simply as a neutral referent" (5); George Melnyk's *The Literary History of Alberta*, Vol. 1 (1998), opens with the premise that "[w]riters and their books were an integral part of defining the geophysical and social space that is now Alberta" (xv); and the essay collection *A Sense of Place: Re-Evaluating Regionalism in Canadian and American Writing* (eds. Christian Riegel et al., 1998), views region less in terms of "land" than of social, cultural, and political relationships: the essay "Reassessing Prairie Realism" by Alison Calder is harshly (and rightly) critical of the current environmentalist emphasis of Prairie literature criticism and pedagogy, but it stops short of offering any productive alternative.

6   For instance, McCourt insists that regional writers must be able "to understand and describe the influences of the region upon the people who live within its confines," and that if a piece of literature "does not illustrate the influence of a limited and peculiar environment it is not true regional literature" (56). Thus, he criticizes early Prairie writers who in his view did not "comprehend the dramatic impact on character and ordinary human relationships of an environment whose most obvious characteristic was – and perhaps still is – monotony" (19).

    Similarly, Ricou establishes as the "norm" the Prairie writer "presenting a vision of man's encounter with a pervasive emptiness, of which the prairies is only the mirror" (19). Following this standard, his major criticism of Robert Stead's work is that it does not show "that certain values and human characteristics are created or fostered by a particular physical environment" (29), which is apparently linked to his presentation of a "benign and bountiful prairie," and his corresponding failure to explore "man's vulnerability and insignificance in the world" (21). Such restrictive definitions and expectations have led to what Wayne Tefs calls the "hayseed factor," whereby Prairie writers are well-received in central Canada only if their writing conforms to the stereotype of "simple folk learning to suffer on the barren prairie" (46).

    Harrison moves away from a narrow focus on land alone to also consider the crucial concept of culture; however, Harrison's view of land remains, for the most part, a static and originary one. Maintaining that "Canadian prairie fiction is about a basically European society spreading itself across a very un-European landscape" (ix), he focusses on apparent "incongruities between the old culture [brought by settlers] and the new land" (x), and he idealizes the possibility of an "authentic" or "indigenous" Prairie fiction that will "draw the cultural and mythical world of prairie man into line with the physical and historical realities of the plains" (xii). This insistence on an unconstructed reality that exists outside language leads Harrison, like Ricou, to privilege a version of "prairie realism" in which English-speaking settlers are "spiritually alienated from the land" by their cultural relationships to it (101).

7   Kroetsch, in typical gnomic and paradoxical fashion, calls Stegner's *Wolf Willow* "a quintessentially Canadian text" written by "a quintessentially American writer" ("The Cow" 133). Both Kroetsch and Stegner in their own ways create, occupy, and move easily between nationalist and regionalist positions and viewpoints.

8   The "freezing" of culture, for example, often results from an anxiety to recover or
    retain origins or traditions, as can be seen in Winnipeg's Folklorama and the Calgary
    Stampede. After reading an early version of this manuscript, Richard Bailey coined
    the apt metaphor that these examples represent not just frozen but "Dairy Queen"
    culture, alluding to their extremely commercial nature (personal communication, 16
    November 1993). In Uma Parameswaran's *Rootless but Green are the Boulevard Trees,* one
    character describes Folklorama as "a three-ring circus, a zoo ... where everyone visits
    everyone else's cage" (28).

9   Compare McCourt: "The Prairie Provinces constitute the most homogeneous of the
    great natural geographic divisions within this country. . . . [A]ll three, in their settled
    areas, are primarily flat and agricultural; they are hot in summer and cold in winter.
    . . . There are, of course, differences between provinces. Saskatchewan is flatter than
    Alberta and less wooded than Manitoba, and the wind seems to blow harder there
    than anywhere else in Canada" (Preface, n.p.).

10  For example, among Calgary-based writers, Darlene Barry Quaife's *Bone Bird,* Joan
    Cornelia Hoogland's *The Wire-Thin Bride,* and part of Aritha van Herk's *No Fixed
    Address: An Amorous Journey* are set in B.C.

11  It may not be a coincidence that Alberta, the youngest of the three Prairie provinces
    in terms of European settlement, is also "home" to the three texts that I discuss in
    terms of movement and transience in the final chapter of this volume.

12  Needless to say, I am greatly indebted to and wish to build on this tradition, even as I
    question some of its current theoretical bases. In this I exemplify, I suppose, Linda
    Hutcheon's assertion that the postmodern condition symptomatic of late twentieth-
    century Canadian life largely resides in an uneasy balance between complicity and
    critique. Wishing in some way to challenge our inherited structures, we find it
    necessary to use them to do so, and hence end up, in a sense, both deconstructing and
    reifying them simultaneously.

13  One major category that I considered treating but did not is the writing of fictional
    histories, or historical fictions, which function to construct place through providing a
    kind of communal, or public, past or set of myths. This strategy is used, for instance, in
    Andrew Suknaski's writing of Wood Mountain, Saskatchewan, Margaret Sweatman's
    of Winnipeg, Birk Sproxton's of Flin Flon, Thelma Poirier's of the southern Saskatch-
    ewan grasslands, and Roberta Rees's of the Crowsnest Pass, to mention only a few
    examples. Although I excluded this category of "public homemaking" as involving a
    substantially different sense of home from what I am using elsewhere, it would be
    fascinating to also examine these texts for their dialectic of public and private home
    creation.

14  McCourt on Grove: "The tragedy of his artistic life is that so much of his work was
    done in a medium for which he had little talent. His best bits of writing are descrip-
    tive and philosophical rather than narrative" (68); Malcolm Ross on *Over Prairie Trails:*
    "No one, surely, will deny to this first book its permanent place in our literature"
    (100); Cooley, personal communication, spring 1993.

15  For discussions of this contemporary shift in definitions of literature and literary value,
    see Helen Buss's study of autobiography and Marlene Kadar's anthology of "life
    writing."

## Chapter 1

1 The term "imagined community" is Benedict Anderson's.

2 Phillips also points out, correctly, that "hinterland" and "heartland" distinctions may be more important than provincial boundaries in some cases. "Have-not regions," he says, are areas "reduced to an economic hinterland, supplying the resources and buying the products of the industrially developed heartland of Central Canada." So, for instance, northern Ontario may be described as a "crown colony" (*Regional Disparities* 9, 37).

3 A clear example of Ostenso's obsession with the "identity" of her minor characters is Malcolm, "Scotch, with Cree blood two generations back" (163), "the Scotch halfbreed, as he was incorrectly called" (169).

4 Muskeg is a kind of mud composed of rounded grains of sand that will give way under weight. It is sometimes concealed under a layer of dried, stable ground, and railway tracks were sometimes mistakenly laid over it, with the result that when the first train came to cross it whole rail cars were lost. When Caleb debates whether or not he must go around the muskeg, he thinks, "Damn the muskeg! And yet – the autumn had been extremely dry. Perhaps it would hold the weight of a man. No – no, this was madness. The muskeg had not been dry for years. All summer it had been full of water holes" (297).

5 Ontario, of course, considers itself "central Canada."

6 The latter option was unfeasible, given the large numbers of people needed to "settle" the large space of the Prairies on behalf of the empire.

7 Chinese restaurants or cafés are staples of small Prairie towns. See, for example, Robert Kroetsch's "Elegy for Wong Toy" (*SHP* 44-45), Andrew Suknaski's "Jimmy Hoy's Place" (28-30), Fred Wah's Elite Café poems in *Waiting for Saskatchewan*, and Lorna Crozier's "Home Town": "a town / with a Pool grain elevator, a Chinese café, / and one main street no one bothered to name" (*Angels* 109).

8 Stead uses both spellings: granary and grainery.

9 This shows how, as Grove said in 1929, "Canada has already become the granary of the British Isles," but also how what might give the country control or power – its material resources – will never make it the "centre" of the empire, nor give Canadians "a right to be proud of ourselves" (*Needs* 137-39).

10 McCourt, for instance, argues that Gander leaving for the city is "not consistent with the character which Stead has so honestly and convincingly created. If the reader is sure of anything it is that Gander will never leave the farm which has first claim on his heart" (99).

11 According to the back-cover blurb, the play "has played to packed houses in theatres across Canada," and a movie version has now been developed as well. At a performance of the play at Winnipeg's Prairie Theatre Exchange, the strongest audience reactions occurred at moments when the stereotypes were being evoked.

12 See Traugout and Pratt's analysis (338 ff.).

13 Compare the recent phenomenon of GST-inspired cross-border shopping, in which Canadians get the best of both worlds. Ostensibly in protest against high Canadian taxes, they take advantage of lower American prices while at the same time maintain-

ing bragging rights on the Canadian health-care system, which needs that higher tax base to continue to function.

14 To some degree the play also draws on notions of the imagined community in its references to "transnational" First Nations' politics; however, the major focus is on the single Reserve community.

15 The name "Nigger," for most hearers heavy with racist history, is apparently a common Reserve nickname for very dark-skinned Natives (Ian Ross, personal communication, spring 1996). Because it seems that Ross has characters use Nigger's formal name, Sheldon, when they are speaking to him with respect, I have used the name Sheldon throughout my discussion.

16 In his Playwright's Note, Ross credits his mother with helping write the Saulteaux (perhaps representing another layer of homemaking function in the play) and says that the dialect is Manitoban while the spelling is (as also with many of the English words) "as it sounds" (9).

17 Winnipeg is coded as a site of failed economic promise. Rachel was a prostitute there, and Teddy asks Melvin, "Didn't you used to borrow [steal] cars before in Winnipeg?" (78). If the reserve is a poor option for people, the city is worse, although Rachel says at least in the city she has no more expectations: "[I]n the city you know how it is. No one gives a shit, but here . . . I know how it's supposed to be. And it isn't" (55-56, original ellipsis).

## Chapter 2

1 Winnipeg is commonly called the "Gateway to the West," an expression that assumes it is being looked at or approached from the east. See p. 49 herein, where I explore the irony that Gunnars is travelling there from the west.

2 The expression "Regina city" is not, like "the Queen city," local Saskatchewan usage. Like Gunnars's use of "American" spellings for such words as "colors" and "center," the terms "sneakers" for "runners" (27), and "flat" for "apartment" (58, 98), it marks her language as being not quite fully "at home" in Prairie English.

3 The indicative is not really "amodal," of course, but merely the mood we have chosen to label standard or unmarked, and there is no real equivalence between such an unmarked sign and what we think of as "colourless" language. Further, oral styles are as "signful" and convention-laden as literate ones, and even silences can be heavily coded, accruing conventional meanings from their contexts.

4 In his edition of the text, Daniel Lenoski inserted numbered section headings at the points where photographs appeared in the original Turnstone text; the two versions of the text are, arguably, dissimilar enough to warrant separate or comparative study. Because the original edition is out of print and thus not widely available, I am using the anthologized version in my study.

5 Arnason did his Ph.D. in English at the University of New Brunswick, writing his dissertation on the development of realism in Prairie fiction. This can be seen as an academic version of "writing home," as I discussed in the Prologue.

6 Arnason's description of this book as "not a history" but "a journey into memory and myth, a collage of photos, remembrances, poems, statements and fragments" (7) would

apply equally well to *Marsh Burning*, and indeed some portions of text are included in both books.

7 Such, at least, is the view emerging from Prigogine and Stegners's theoretical work on reconciling dynamics and thermodynamics.

8 Personal communication with Arnason, spring 1993.

9 This itinerary represents what Gérard Genette calls "story time" (the order of the events contained in the story being told) rather than "narrative time" (the order in which things are told by the narrator). For instance, Salverson's parents' immigration from Iceland to Winnipeg is narrated, in flashback form, from Winnipeg before the move to Selkirk. Similarly, the story of the family's first move to the United States is narrated later, just as the family leaves for Selkirk. The whole story is presumably narrated (that is, the whole book is written) from the final dwelling place, Calgary. The dates included here are those provided by the text and K.P. Stich's introduction to it.

10 The Saskatchewan Writer's Guild was established in 1948, apparently being the first in North America (see Heinemann 4).

## Chapter 3

1 By my count there are nine of these references using quotation marks and nine not using quotation marks. The use of quotation marks does not appear to depend, as we might expect, on where Grove is located in relation to the place when he names it.

2 Grove was born Felix Paul Greve in West Prussia in 1879 and lived most of his years in Germany until 1909 when he immigrated to the United States, and later, in 1912, to Canada.

3 Kroetsch says, "The basic grammatical pair in the story-line (the energy-line) of prairie fiction is house:horse. To be on a horse is to move: motion into distance. To be in a house is to be fixed: a centring unto stasis. Horse is masculine. House is feminine. Horse: house. Masculine: feminine. On: in. Motion: stasis" ("The Fear of Women in Prairie Fiction: An Erotics of Space," in *Lovely Treachery*, 76).

4 Patrick Lane, in his Afterword to the NCL edition of Grove's text, makes explicit the Odyssean allusion that Grove's invocation of the sea suggests: "Like Odysseus, Grove is a figure of the outward, the man who must endlessly quest and test himself against the elemental world. The challenges he faces on his journeys are always greater than the arrival at his goal, the remembered hearth and home, the wife and child who wait for him" (160).

5 By "makes him real" I mean the text makes real, in the sense of concrete and multiply witnessable, the particular version of "Grove" that he is presenting in the text. Given what is known about the slippery nature of Grove's identity and his presentation of himself, this version cannot be privileged over any other.

6 Compare his "Ask any great man who has achieved greatly whether his achievement is of his aim; he will tell you that in the innermost depth of his heart he knows he has failed" (*Needs* 88). Grove sees the positive side of this failure as its creation of the necessity to continue striving toward something better.

7 Freud observes that "*heimlich* is a word the meaning of which develops towards an ambivalence, until it finally coincides with its opposite, *unheimlich*" (377), and con-

cludes that "this uncanny is in reality nothing new or foreign, but something familiar and old-established in the mind that has been estranged only by the process of repression, . . . something which ought to have been kept concealed but which nevertheless has come to light" (394). Grove uses the term "uncanny" twice (29, 46) to describe his experiences, and on one occasion he attributes what appears to be uncanny knowledge to his horse Dan, who stops and neighs when they pass a certain farm: "He knew where we were. I lowered my whip and patted his rump. How did he know? And why did he do it? Was there a horse on this farmstead which he had known in former life?" (48).

8   This tension is manifest, for example, in two ways during Grove's emergency trip home to attend to his ill daughter: first in his "confession" – "I thought but little of the little girl's side of it; more of my wife's; most of all of my own. That seems selfish" (130) – and second in his guilt over succumbing to the "merriment" of his surroundings en route (132). A generalized audience anxiety is indicated on several occasions, as when he describes the effects of wind on snow and says "it always has a strange fascination for me; but maybe I need to apologize for setting it down in writing" (112).

9   Just what the term "love" means in this poem is indeterminate. Crozier often uses the term in complicated, ambivalent senses, as in "We call this fear love, this tearing, / this fist, this sharpened tongue / love. I could kill you, I say, / many times. . . . You spit words at me / like broken teeth and I, stupid / woman, string them into poems, / call them love" (*Humans* 56).

10  See also Crozier's treatment of incest scars and family sexual abuse in the poem "Fathers, Uncles, Old Friends of the Family," where a child who is asked "Where did he touch you?" answers "Here  and here, / those places no one ever named" (*Angels* 30). Again, here, silence enables abuse; language and naming confer power, are prerequisites to action.

11  "Dumb" here may suggest an inability to translate feelings into words – a kind of repressive silence that can erupt in violence. Crozier says her father "doesn't have a favorite book. The only thing he reads is *The Swift Current Sun*. He follows the lines with the one good finger on his right hand, the nail bitten to the quick, and reads everything three times. I don't know how much he understands" (76).

12  Compare the poem "There Will Be No Children," published over ten years earlier, where the idea of a child, "Small / as a fallen bird, . . . dies / in the far corner of your mind," but "will be born again / until you bury it in my bones" (*Humans* 12).

13  Witold Rybczyski traces the feminization of the home in western European culture to seventeenth-century Holland. Contributing factors to the emergence of women's control over domestic space were the movement of men's work and social activities to separate places outside the house, and the decrease in the use of servants for household work (70 ff.).

14  Kelley's text is unpaginated, so citations will not include page numbers.

15  See, for instance, the construction of local history and legend in *Bloody Jack*, individual poems such as "prairie romance" and "prairie vernacular," which name and give character to the region (*Perishable Light* 7-9), the politico-critical manifesto in "The Vernacular Muse in Prairie Poetry" (*The Vernacular Muse* 167-222), and his work editing two collections of prairie poetry (*Draft* and *Inscriptions*).

16 This argument is complicated by a subtle form of nationalism that portrays the American astronauts as generally cruder, less "poetic" and more materialistic and technologically oriented than the Russian cosmonauts. (Part of this may be seen in the examples above of the "earth-as-woman.") Cooley asserts that this bias is a direct reflection of the Americans' and Russians' own words in *The Home Planet* (personal communication, spring 1993), but, if so, he does appear to have exaggerated it.

17 "Place" here is used in the sense that Caleb Gare used the term, referring not only to a social order but a "natural" one as well.

18 David Creelman attributes such hesitations and indeterminacies to Cooley's concern with "linguistic uncertainty" in "a post-Saussurian age of displacement" (20, 21). While this is certainly an important influence on Cooley's work in general, *this only home* provides its own motivation for language difficulties through its setting and theme.

19 Further examples of this "new environmentalism" in contemporary Prairie poetry may be found in Elizabeth Philips's *Time in a Green Country* and Thelma Poirier's *Grasslands: The Private Hearings*.

20 David Creelman views this conclusion as "reductive and overly didactic" (23), failing to see both its inherent wittiness and its appropriateness in the context of the book's overriding concern with the environment.

## Chapter 4

1 On this east-west migration, see the history outlined by Robert Hunter and Robert Calihoo in *Occupied Canada: A Young White Man Discovers His Unsuspected Past* as well as Chapter 1 of Maria Campbell's *Halfbreed* (see p. 102 ff. herein).

2 See Jeannette C. Armstrong and Barbara Goddard (separate works) on Darlene Barry Quaife's *Bone Bird* and Lenore Keeshig-Tobias on Margaret Atwood's *Surfacing* for a representative sample of current attitudes toward this issue in literary contexts, involving the appropriation (or misappropriation) of voice, story, and culture in writing.

3 Grey Owl, otherwise known as Englishman Archibald Stansfeld Belaney (1888-1938), acquired fame and a living writing and promoting books written out of an assumed Native identity.

4 For Julia V. Emberley, this challenge is largely effected through Campbell's use of parody: "By overtly wearing the mask of the stereotypical image, the Native no longer resembles the stereotypical image of the 'Native'; thus, the image is shown to be different from itself" (160). To be effective, obviously, the seams of the performance must be visible, and it is Campbell's contextualization that establishes the ironic distance necessary for the parody to be recognized.

5 The handwritten manuscript of *Halfbreed* was "over 2,000 pages long" ("Interview" 42), while the published version runs to only 184 pages.

6 Campbell says: "Our people believed the lands acts discriminated against them, stating that they had to live on the land and wait three years before filing a claim. They had lived on the lands for years before the lands acts had ever been thought of, and didn't believe they should be treated like newcomers" (4).

7   A footnote to the text advises that some names of people and places have been changed (7).

8   The experiences of Russian Mennonites in their journey out of Russia to the Canadian prairies is explored further in Wiebe's later epic historical novel *The Blue Mountains of China.*

9   Compare the narratological functions of World War I in Stead's *Grain*, discussed herein, p. 22.

10   This interest in Native history finds fuller development in Wiebe's later historical novel *The Temptations of Big Bear*, which takes place around the time of the second Riel rebellion. Unsurprisingly, this novel has come under some criticism for its appropriation of Native story and voice.

11   Compare Salman Rushdie's comments on Indian emigrants: "I suspect that there are times when the move seems wrong to us all, when we seem, to ourselves, post-lapsarian men and women. We are Hindus who have crossed the black water; we are Muslims who eat pork. And as a result – as my use of the Christian notion of the Fall indicates – we are now partly of the West. Our identity is at once plural and partial. Sometimes we feel that we straddle two cultures; at other times, that we fall between two stools" (15).

12   The name change appears inexplicable, except perhaps as a comment on Chander's faulty memory.

13   In *Rootless but Green are the Boulevard Trees*, Savitri offers a further gloss on Vithal's desire to build a temple at the confluence of the Red and the Assiniboine when she says, "Some day, I hope, Vithal and all of you will realize that we have already built that temple because we carry our gods within us wherever we go" (35).

14   In an episode similar to this one involving Moses, and also that of Jesus and the massacre of innocents, Krishna escaped a killing of male children ordered by the tyrant Kamsa because of his fear that Krishna would destroy him (Walker II 560-61).

## Chapter 5

1   Jakobson's essay uses the terms "addresser" and "addressee" rather than "sender" and "receiver" (see *Language in Literature* 66).

2   An example of the inadequacy of language as a home can be found in the poem "Letters to Salonika," where the poet tells his absent wife, "You hurt me into this novel [*Alibi*], by going away" (139), and, "[I am] trying to fill my emptiness with words" (140). The word "trying" here indicates the ultimate futility of the enterprise, and he later says, "I want / no words" (163), indicating that he will be satisfied with nothing less that a real body, his wife/home.

3   Ironically, the priest's warning does play out in future poems: as Kroetsch "falls" into carnal knowledge, he will indeed "burn forever," but with passion and the pain of absent or lost love.

4   The interview was published in 1982. A photograph of Kroetsch's mother, and the connection of the erotic to her, occur in two later "mother poems" published in 1985.

5   David Arnason, who does not cite the interview but who is no doubt aware of it, calls the mother's whisper "the unspeakable, incestuous, erotic invitation": "It is an

equivocal invitation into sexuality and art, because it is also an invitation to death" ("Robert Kroetsch's *Seed Catalogue*: The Deconstruction of the Meta-narrative of the Cowboy" 82).

6 The comment was made on "the original version of the poem (1969)" (134). "Mile Zero" as it appears in *CFN* consists of this poem overlaid with numerous footnotes and inserted later poems.

7 See my discussion of the binary in the section on Grove's *Over Prairie Trails* on p. 70.

8 R. Radhakrishnan describes the position of the "post-ethnic" as follows: "The constituency of 'the ethnic' occupies quite literally a 'pre-post'-erous space where it has to actualize, enfranchize, and empower its own 'identity' and coextensively engage in the deconstruction of the very logic of 'identity' and its binary and exclusionary politics. Failure to achieve this doubleness can only result in the formation of ethnicity as yet another 'identical' and hegemonic structure. The difficult task is to achieve an axial connection between the historico-semantic specificity of 'ethnicity' and the 'post-historical' politics of radical indeterminacy" (199).

9 In Wah's 1996 "biotext" *Diamond Grill*, the narrator remembers and collects family history through a "heterocellular recovery" (1) in which the father is identified "decanting through [the narrator's] body" as a process of "[s]ynapse and syntax" (12) and "[b]iology recapitulates geography; place becomes an island in the blood" (23). Essays by Ed Dyck, Jeff Derksen, and Manina Jones in *Beyond Tish* (ed. Douglas Barbour) all deal with language and the body as place.

## Epilogue

1 Much current postcolonial theory labours under this assumption. As the authors of *The Empire Writes Back: Theory and Practice in Post-Colonial Literatures* say, "The gap which opens between the experience of place and the language available to describe it forms a classic and all-pervasive feature of post-colonial texts" (Ashcroft, Griffiths, and Tiffin 9).

2 The desire to locate a cohesive regional ethos is not unique to Prairie literature criticism. Janice Kulyk Keefer, for instance, writing on Maritime literature, says, "What I wish to emphasize is the fundamental coherence of the Maritime ethos and vision, and also its significant points of difference from other regional cultures and from what we have been taught to think of as 'the distinctively Canadian'" (xii). The editors of the more recent *A Sense of Place: Re-Evaluating Regionalism in Canadian and American Writing* (ed. Riegel et al.) argue instead, as I do, for "the need to define the writing of particular regions in more pluralistic terms": "regionalism as a political and literary discourse is underpinned by assumptions that warrant interrogation; region, like race, gender, class and sexuality, is not an unproblematic category and must be theorized not in isolation but in relation to other elements central to the construction of subjectivity and of literature" (xiii, xii).

3 David M. Jordan accepts the view that "regional" authors are "preoccupied with the effect of a specific place on individual identity" (127), but he argues against the view (similar to the one Williams outlines here) that this concentration "can produce only sentimental autobiography" (127-28).

# Works Cited

Acoose, Janice/Misko-Kìsikàwihkwè (Red Sky Woman). *Iskwewak–Kah' Ki Yaw Ni Wahkomakanak: Neither Indian Princesses Nor Easy Squaws.* Toronto: Women's Press, 1995.

Anderson, Benedict. *Imagined Communities: Reflections on the Origin and Spread of Nationalism.* Rev. ed. New York: Verso (1983) 1991.

Armstrong, Jeannette C. "Writing from a Native Woman's Perspective." *in the feminine: women and words / les femmes et les mots.* Conference Proceedings 1983. Eds. Ann Dybikowski, Victoria Freeman, Daphne Marlatt, Barbara Pulling, and Betsy Warland, 55-57. Edmonton: Longspoon Press, 1985.

Arnason, David. "The Sunfish." *50 Stories and a Piece of Advice,* 61-75. Winnipeg: Turnstone Press, 1982.

_____. *Marsh Burning.* Winnipeg: Turnstone Press, 1980. Rpt. in *a/long prairie lines: An Anthology of Long Prairie Poems.* Ed. Daniel S. Lenoski, 257-317. Winnipeg: Turnstone Press, 1989.

_____. "Robert Kroetsch's *Seed Catalogue*: The Deconstruction of the Meta-narrative of the Cowboy." *Contemporary Manitoba Writers.* Ed. Kenneth James Hughes, 79-92. Winnipeg: Turnstone Press, 1990.

Arnason, David, and Michael Olito. *The Icelanders.* Winnipeg: Turnstone Press, 1981.

Ashcroft, Bill, Gareth Griffiths, and Helen Tiffin. *The Empire Writes Back: Theory and Practice in Post-Colonial Literatures.* New York: Routledge, 1989.

_____, eds. *The Post-colonial Studies Reader.* New York: Routledge, 1995.

Asimov, Isaac. *Asimov's New Guide to Science.* New York: Basic Books, 1984.

Atwood, Margaret. *Surfacing.* Toronto: McClelland and Stewart, 1972.

_____. *Survival: A Thematic Guide to Canadian Literature.* Toronto: Anansi, 1972.

Bailey, Richard W. "The English Language in Canada." *English as a World Language.* Eds. Richard W. Bailey and Manfred Görlach, 134-76. Ann Arbor: University of Michigan Press, 1982.

_____. "Dialects of Canadian English." *English Today* 27 (July 1991): 20-25.

Baker, Marie Annharte. *Being on the Moon.* Winlaw, B.C.: Polestar Press, 1990.

Barbour, Douglas, ed. *Beyond Tish.* Edmonton: NeWest Press, 1991.

Barthes, Roland. *Writing Degree Zero.* Trans. Annette Lavers and Colin Smith. New York: Hill and Wang (1953), 1968.

Barton, Willow. "Where Have the Warriors Gone?" *Writing the Circle: Native Women of Western Canada.* Eds. Jeanne Perreault and Sylvia Vance, 8-18. Edmonton: NeWest Publishers, 1990.

Berger, John. *And Our Faces, My Heart, Brief as Photos.* New York: Vintage International (1984), 1991.

Bhabha, Homi K., ed. *Nation and Narration.* New York: Routledge, 1990.

Brewster, Elizabeth. *Entertaining Angels.* Canada: Oberon Press, 1988.

Buss, Helen M. *Mapping Our Selves: Canadian Women's Autobiography.* Montreal and Kingston: McGill-Queen's University Press, 1993.

Calder, Alison. "Reassessing Prairie Realism." *A Sense of Place: Re-Evaluating Regionalism in Canadian and American Writing.* Eds. Christian Riegel, Herb Wylie, Karen Overbye, and Don Perkins, 51-60. Edmonton: University of Alberta Press, 1998.

Campbell, Maria. *Halfbreed.* Halifax: Goodread Biographies/Formac Publishing Co. (1973), 1983.

_____. "Interview with Hartmut Lutz." *Contemporary Challenges: Conversations with Canadian Native Authors.* Ed. Hartmut Lutz, 41-65. Saskatoon: Fifth House Publishers, 1991.

Cooley, Dennis, ed. *Draft: An Anthology of Prairie Poetry.* Winnipeg: Turnstone Press, 1981.

_____. *Bloody Jack.* Winnipeg: Turnstone Press, 1984.

_____. *The Vernacular Muse: The Eye and Ear in Contemporary Literature.* Winnipeg: Turnstone Press, 1987.

_____. *Perishable Light.* Regina: Coteau Books, 1988.

_____. *this only home.* Winnipeg: Turnstone Press, 1992.

_____, ed. *Inscriptions: A Prairie Poetry Anthology.* Winnipeg: Turnstone Press, 1992.

Creelman, David. Rev. of Dennis Cooley's *this only home. Journal of Canadian Poetry* 9 (1994): 19-24.

Crossley-Holland, Kevin. *The Norse Myths.* Markham, ON: Penguin, 1980.

Crozier, Lorna. *Humans and Other Beasts.* Winnipeg: Turnstone Press, 1980.

_____. *Inventing the Hawk.* Toronto: McClelland and Stewart, 1992.

_____. *Angels of Flesh, Angels of Silence.* Toronto: McClelland and Stewart (1988), 1993.

Crystal, David. *The Cambridge Encyclopedia of Language.* New York: Cambridge University Press, 1987.

Deane, Seamus. Introduction to *Nationalism, Colonialism and Literature: Essays by Terry Eagleton, Fredric Jameson and Edward W. Said.* Minneapolis: University of Minnesota Press, 1990.

Derrida, Jacques. "Structure, Sign and Play in the Discourse of the Human Sciences." *Writing and Difference.* Trans. Alan Bass, 278-93. Chicago: University of Chicago Press, 1978.

During, Simon, ed. *The Cultural Studies Reader.* New York: Routledge, 1993.

Dyck, E.F. Introduction to *Essays on Saskatchewa Writing.* Ed. E.F. Dyck, ix-xxi. Regina: Saskatchewan Writers Guild, 1986.

_____. "Home Places." Rev. of Dennis Cooley's *this only home* and Don Kerr's *In the City of Our Fathers.* NeWest Review (February/March 1993): 33-34.

Emberley, Julia V. *Thresholds of Difference: Feminist Critique, Native Women's Writings, Postcolonial Theory.* Toronto: University of Toronto Press, 1993.

Foucault, Michel. *Power/Knowledge: Selected Interviews and Other Writings 1972-1977.* New York: Pantheon, 1980.

Freud, Sigmund. "The Uncanny." In *Sigmund Freud: Collected Papers.* Vol. 4. Trans. Joan Rivière, 368-407. New York: Basic Books (1919), 1959.

Genette, Gérard. *Narrative Discourse: An Essay in Method.* Trans. Jane E. Lewin. Ithaca, NY: Cornell University Press, 1980.

Goddard, Barbara. "The Politics of Representation: Some Native Canadian Women Writers." *Native Writers and Canadian Writing*, 183-225. Canadian Literature Special Issue. Ed. W.H. New. Vancouver: University of British Columbia Press, 1990.

Grove, Frederick Philip. *It Needs to Be Said . . .* Toronto: Macmillan, 1929.

_____. *Over Prairie Trails.* Toronto: McClelland and Stewart (1922), 1991.

Gunnars, Kristjana. *Settlement Poems 1.* Winnipeg: Turnstone Press, 1980. (Cited as *SP1*.)

_____. *Settlement Poems 2.* Winnipeg: Turnstone Press, 1980.

_____. *Zero Hour.* Red Deer: Red Deer College Press, 1991.

Gurr, Andrew. *Writers in Exile: The Identity of Home in Modern Literature.* New Jersey: Humanities Press, 1981.

Hall, Donald. *Kicking the Leaves.* New York: Harper and Row, 1978.

Harrison, Dick. *Unnamed Country: The Struggle for a Canadian Prairie Fiction.* Edmonton: University of Alberta Press, 1977.

Hawking, Stephen W. *A Brief History of Time: From the Big Bang to Black Holes.* Toronto: Bantam, 1988.

Heinemann, Michelle. "Saskatchewan Writers Guild: Its History and Impact on Writing in Saskatchewan." *Essays on Saskatchewan Writing.* Ed. E.F. Dyck, 3-21. Regina: Saskatchewan Writers Guild, 1986.

Hoogland, Joan Cornelia. *The Wire-Thin Bride.* Winnipeg: Turnstone Press, 1990.

Hunter, Robert, and Robert Calihoo. *Occupied Canada: A Young White Man Discovers His Unsuspected Past.* Toronto: McClelland and Stewart, 1991.

Hutcheon, Linda. *The Canadian Postmodern: A Study of Contemporary English-Canadian Fiction.* Toronto: Oxford University Press, 1988.

Jakobson, Roman. *Language in Literature.* Eds. Krystyna Pomorska and Stephen Rudy. Cambridge, MA: Harvard University Press, 1987.

Jameson, Fredric. *The Political Unconscious: Narrative as a Socially Symbolic Act.* Ithaca, NY: Cornell University Press, 1981.

Jordan, David M. *New World Regionalism: Literature in the Americas.* Toronto: University of Toronto Press, 1994.

Kadar, Marlene, ed. *Reading Life Writing: An Anthology.* Toronto: Oxford University Press, 1993.

Kamboureli, Smaro. *On the Edge of Genre: The Contemporary Canadian Long Poem.* Toronto: University of Toronto Press, 1991.

Keahey, Debbie. *the d word.* Winnipeg: Staccato Chapbooks, 1995.

Keefer, Janice Kulyk. *Under Eastern Eyes: A Critical Reading of Maritime Fiction.* Toronto: University of Toronto Press, 1987.

Keeshig-Tobias, Lenore. "Interview with Hartmut Lutz." *Contemporary Challenges: Conversations with Canadian Native Authors.* Ed. Hartmut Lutz, 79-88. Saskatoon: Fifth House Publishers, 1991.

Kelley, Kevin W., ed. *The Home Planet.* New York: Addison-Wesley, 1988. Foreword by Jacque-Yves Cousteau.

Kolson, Bren. "The Barren Journey Home." In *Writing the Circle: Native Women of Western Canada.* Eds. Jeanne Perreault and Sylvia Vance, 130-31. Edmonton: NeWest Publishers, 1990.

Kreisel, Henry. "The Prairie: A State of Mind." Rpt. in *Trace: Prairie Writers on Writing.* Ed. Birk Sproxton, 3-17. Winnipeg: Turnstone Press (1968) 1986.

Kroetsch, Robert. *The Stone Hammer Poems.* Lantzville, BC: Oolichan Books, 1976. (Cited as *SHP.*)

_____. *Completed Field Notes: The Long Poems of Robert Kroetsch.* Toronto: McClelland and Stewart, 1989. (Cited as *CFN.*)

_____. *The Lovely Treachery of Words: Essays Selected and New.* Toronto: Oxford University Press, 1989.

_____. "The Cow in the Quicksand and How I(t) Got Out: Responding to Stegner's *Wolf Willow.*" In *Beyond Borders: An Anthology of New Writing from Manitoba, Minnesota, Saskatchewan, and the Dakotas.* Eds. Mark Vinz and David Williamson. Minneapolis/Winnipeg: New Rivers/Turnstone, 1992.

Lamar, Howard R. "The Unsettling of the American West: The Mobility of Defeat." *Crossing Frontiers: Papers in American and Canadian Western Literature.* 1978 Conference Proceedings. Ed. Dick Harrison, 35-54. Edmonton: University of Alberta Press, 1979.

Leach, Maria, ed., and Jerome Fried, assoc. ed. *Funk and Wagnalls Standard Dictionary of Folklore, Mythology, and Legend.* New York: Harper and Row, Pubs. (1949), 1984.

Limerick, Patricia Nelson. *The Legacy of Conquest: The Unbroken Past of the American West.* New York: W.W. Norton, 1987.

Mandel, Eli. "Writing West: On the Road to Wood Mountain." Rpt. in *Essays on Saskatchewan Writing*. Ed. E.F. Dyck, 145-61. Regina: Saskatchewan (1977), 1986.

McCourt, Edward. *The Canadian West in Fiction*. Rev. ed. Toronto: Ryerson (1949), 1970.

Melnyk, George. "On the Roots of Identity." Interview with Walter Hildebrandt. *NeWest Review* (June/July 1993): 10-18.

_____. *The Literary History of Alberta*. Vol. 1. Edmonton: University of Alberta Press, 1998.

Mercredi, Duncan. *Dreams of the Wolf in the City*. Winnipeg: Pemmican Publications, 1992.

Neuman, Shirley, and Robert Wilson. *Labyrinths of Voice: Conversations with Robert Kroetsch*. Edmonton: NeWest Press, 1982.

New, W.H. *Land Sliding: Imagining Space, Presence, and Power in Canadian Writing*. Toronto: University of Toronto Press, 1997.

Nightingale, Peggy, ed. *A Sense of Place in the New Literatures in English*. New York: University of Queensland Press, 1986.

Olson, Charles. "Proprioception." In *Poetics of the New American Poetry*. Eds. Donald Allen and Warren Tallman, 181-84. New York: Grove, 1973.

_____. "The Resistance." In *Poetics of the New American Poetry*. Eds. Donald Allen and Warren Tallman, 174-75. New York: Grove, 1973.

Ostenso, Martha. *Wild Geese*. Toronto: McClelland and Stewart (1925), 1991.

Paglia, Camille. *Sexual Personae: Art and Decadence from Nefertiti to Emily Dickinson*. New York: Vintage Books, 1990.

Parameswaran, Uma. "Ganga in the Assiniboine: A Reading of Poems from Trishanku." *Canadian Ethnic Studies* 17, no. 3 (1985): 120-26.

_____. *Rootless but Green are the Boulevard Trees*. Toronto: TSAR, 1987.

_____. *Trishanku*. Toronto: TSAR, 1988.

_____. "The Door I Shut Behind Me." *The Whistling Thorn*. Ed. S. Sugunasiri. Oakville: Mosaic Press (1967), 1994.

Philips, Elizabeth. *Time in a Green Country*. Regina: Coteau Books, 1990.

Phillips, Paul. *Regional Disparities*. Toronto: James Lorimer and Co., 1982.

Poirier, Thelma. *Grasslands: The Private Hearings*. Regina: Coteau Books, 1990.

Pratt, T.K. "A Response to G.M. Story." In *Search of the Standard in Canadian English*. Ed. W.C. Lougheed, 54-64. Kingston, ON: Strathy Language Unit Occasional Papers No. 1, 1986.

Prigogine, Ilya, and Isabelle Stengers. *Order Out of Chaos: Man's New Dialogue with Nature*. Toronto: Bantam, 1984.

Quaife, Darlene Barry. *Bone Bird*. Winnipeg: Turnstone Press, 1989.

Radhakrishnan, R. "Ethnic Identity and Post-Structuralist Differance." *Cultural Critique* 6 (Spring 1987): 199-220.

Rebar, Kelly. *Bordertown Café.* Winnipeg: Blizzard Pub., 1987.

Rees, Roberta. *Beneath the Faceless Mountain.* Red Deer: Red Deer College Press, 1994.

Ricou, Laurence. *Vertical Man / Horizontal World: Man and Landscape in Canadian Prairie Fiction.* Vancouver: University of British Columbia Press, 1973.

Riegel, Christian, Herb Wyile, Karen Overbye, and Don Perkins, eds. *A Sense of Place: Re-Evaluating Regionalism in Canadian and American Writing.* Edmonton: University of Alberta Press, 1998.

Ross, Ian. *fareWel.* Winnipeg: Scirocco Drama, 1996.

Ross, Malcolm. *The Impossible Sum of Our Traditions: Reflections on Canadian Literature.* Toronto: McClelland and Stewart, 1986.

Ross, Sinclair. *The Lamp at Noon and Other Stories.* Toronto: McClelland and Stewart (1968), 1983.

Rushdie, Salman. *Imaginary Homelands: Essays and Criticism 1981-1991.* New York: Granta Books/Penguin Books, 1991.

Rybczynski, Witold. *Home: A Short History of an Idea.* Toronto: Penguin, 1986.

Said, Edward. *The World, the Text, and the Critic.* Cambridge: Harvard University Press, 1983.

Salverson, Laura Goodman. *Confessions of an Immigrant's Daughter.* Toronto: University of Toronto Press (1939), 1981.

Scholes, Robert. *Semiotics and Interpretation.* New Haven: Yale University Press, 1982.

Shields, Carol. *The Republic of Love.* Toronto: Fawcett Crest, 1992.

Sproxton, Birk. *Headframe:.* Winnipeg: Turnstone Press, 1985.

_____. *The Red-Headed Woman with the Black Black Heart.* Winnipeg: Turnstone Press, 1997.

Stead, Robert J.C. *Grain.* Toronto: McClelland and Stewart (1926), 1990.

Stegner, Wallace. *Wolf Willow: A History, a Story, and a Memory of the Last Plains Frontier.* Markham, ON: Penguin (1955), 1990.

_____. "The Sense of Place." *Where the Bluebird Sings to the Lemonade Springs: Living and Writing in the West,* 199-206. New York: Random House, 1992.

Stephansson, Stephen G. *Selected Prose and Poetry.* Trans. Kristjana Gunnars. Red Deer: Red Deer College Press, 1988.

Suknaski, Andrew. *Wood Mountain Poems.* Toronto: Macmillan, 1976.

Sweatman, Margaret. *Fox.* Winnipeg: Turnstone Press, 1991.

Tefs, Wayne. "The Hayseed Factor in Prairie Fiction." *Border Crossings* 9, no.1 (January 1990): 45-46.

Trainer, Yvonne. *Landscape Turned Sideways: Poems 1977-87.* Fredericton, NB: Goose Lane Editions, 1988.

Traugott, Elizabeth Closs, and Mary Louise Pratt. *Linguistics for Students of Literature.* New York: Harcourt Brace Jovanovich, 1980.

van Herk, Aritha. *No Fixed Address: An Amorous Journey.* Toronto: Bantam-Seal, 1986.

_____. "Calgary, this growing graveyard." Rpt. in *a/long prairie lines: An Anthology of Long Prairie Poems.* Ed. Daniel S. Lenoski, 319-43. Winnipeg: Turnstone Press (1987), 1989.

Wah, Fred. "Contemporary Saskatchewan Poetry." *Essays on Saskatchewan Writing.* Ed. E.F. Dyck. Regina: Saskatchewan Writers Guild, 1986.

_____. *Music at the Heart of Thinking.* Red Deer: Red Deer College Press, 1987.

_____. *Waiting for Saskatchewan.* Winnipeg: Turnstone Press, 1985.

_____. *Alley Alley Home Free.* Red Deer: Red Deer College Press, 1992.

_____. *Diamond Grill.* Edmonton: NeWest Press, 1996.

Walker, Benjamin. *Hindu World: An Encyclopedic Survey of Hinduism.* Vols. 1 and 2. London: George Allen and Unwin Ltd., 1968.

Wardhaugh, Ronald. *Language and Nationhood: The Canadian Experience.* Vancouver: New Star Books, 1983.

Warrior, Emma Lee. "Compatriots." Rpt. in *All My Relations: An Anthology of Contemporary Canadian Native Fiction.* Ed. Thomas King, 48-59. Toronto: McClelland and Stewart (1987), 1990.

Wiebe, Rudy. *Peace Shall Destroy Many.* Toronto: McClelland and Stewart (1962), 1990.

_____. *The Temptations of Big Bear.* Toronto: McClelland and Stewart (1973), 1991.

_____. *The Blue Mountains of China.* Toronto: McClelland and Stewart (1970), 1992.

Williams, Raymond. *The Country and the City.* New York: Oxford University Press, 1973.

_____. *Keywords: A Vocabulary of Culture and Society.* Rev. ed. New York: Oxford University Press (1976), 1983.

_____. *Writing in Society.* New York: Verso (1983), 1991.

Yaeger, Patricia, ed. *The Geography of Identity.* Ann Arbor: University of Michigan Press, 1996.

York, Geoffrey. *The Dispossessed: Life and Death in Native Canada.* London: Vintage U.K., 1990.